Contents

Preface   vii
Acknowledgments   xv
Introduction   xix

CHAPTER 1.
The Politics of Nonvoting   3

CHAPTER 2.
Nineteenth-Century Electoral Mobilization
and Demobilization   26

CHAPTER 3.
How Demobilization Was Accomplished   64

CHAPTER 4.
Explanations of Nonvoting   96

CHAPTER 5.
The New Deal Party System:
Continuities and Breakdown   122

CHAPTER 6.
The Reagan Era: Competition for New Voters   *181*

CHAPTER 7.
Prospects for Voter Registration Reform   *209*

EPILOGUE
New Constituencies, New Politics   *248*

APPENDIX A.
How Many People Are Registered to Vote?   *256*

APPENDIX B.
Do Registrants Vote?   *260*

APPENDIX C.
*Misleading the Public: The Abuse of
Registration and Voting Statistics*   *264*

APPENDIX D.
*Current Litigation Challenging Voter Registration
Procedures, by Cynthia A. Williams*   *272*

Cited References   *291*
Index   *313*

Why Americans Don't Vote

Why Americans Don't Vote

Frances Fox Piven
and
Richard A. Cloward

*With a new preface
by the authors*

PANTHEON BOOKS
NEW YORK

Library of Congress Cataloging-in-Publication Data
Piven, Frances Fox.
Why Americans don't vote
Bibliography: p.
Includes index.
1. Voting—United States—Abstention.   2. Poor—
United States—Political activity.   3. Voter registration—
United States.   I. Cloward, Richard A.   II. Title.
JK1987.P58   1988   324.973   87-43012
ISBN 0-679-72318-8

Book design by Tasha Hall

Manufactured in the United States of America

9 8 7 6 5 4 3

Preface

The 1988 election provoked a good deal of debate on the subject of why Americans don't vote. Turnout was down again, to 51 percent of the eligible electorate, sliding toward the twentieth-century low of 49 percent in 1924. The reason, most political pundits concluded, was that people were put off by a campaign both nasty and uninspiring, during the course of which important issues scarcely emerged.

Still, this explanation answers one question only to raise another. Why did the candidates ignore the issues? After all, this has not always been so. During the New Deal and for several decades thereafter, the Democratic party developed quite distinctive appeals and programs. Americans understood those distinctions, and responded to them one way or the other. Something has happened since to limit the alternatives in American electoral politics.

Of course, much has happened: campaign spending at an all-time high; advertising onslaught tactics; and electioneering through covert operations. All of this is true, and important. But it is also true that the active electorate has become increasingly constricted and distorted and that, too, affects campaigns. In other words, the relationship between campaigns and turnout runs both ways. On the one hand, as most analysts emphasize, campaigns without issues depress turnout. On the other hand, low turnout among the less well off sustains campaigns without issues, especially without class issues. The two major parties have become more like Tweedledee and Tweedledum because both compete for votes from a narrow electorate in which a higher percentage of whites and affluent voters participate.

Consider how low voter turnout affects the calculations of presidential candidates. Years in advance of elections, consultants map campaign strategies based on opinion polls and "focus groups" drawn from the limited universe of "probable" voters. As a result, the interests and aspirations of the nonvoting half of the electorate are ignored. Instead, the campaigns target swing voters, which is why southern whites and northern blue-collar Catholics—the so-called Reagan Democrats—have been central to the strategies of both parties in recent campaigns, and why race and racist innuendo have figured so prominently. Low turnout, in short, helps explain how, in an increasingly polarized society, recent presidential campaigns have been able to avoid the issues one might expect elections to raise and why instead we are offered innuendo and a medley of symbols invented by advertising men.

As we explain in this book, our unrepresentative electorate and the resulting low voting rates have their historical roots in the exclusionary voter registration systems established at the end of the nineteenth century. Southern planters pushed through poll taxes, literacy tests, and obstructive voter registration policies to slash voting among blacks and poor whites. Northern businessmen reformers, claiming a "quality" electorate as their goal, introduced similar practices (including poll taxes in a number of New England states). As the new procedures took effect between 1888 and 1924, voting rates fell: from 64 percent to 19 percent in the South; from 86 percent to 55 percent in the North and West; and from 81 percent to 49 percent nationally. And as the electorate shrank, party appeals and strategies also narrowed.

By contrast, during this same era of tumultuous industrial growth in the early twentieth century, working men and poor farmers in Europe were winning the franchise. Their votes, in turn, spurred the growth of socialist or labor parties. In Germany, the Social Democratic party actually won the largest share of the vote once the anti-socialist laws, which had disenfranchised many workers, were allowed to lapse. The Austrian Social Democrats won 21 percent of the vote in 1907, the Finnish Social Democrats 37 percent, and the Belgian Workers' party 13.2 percent—all in the first elections after universal male suffrage had been won. As parties on the left emerged, they in turn helped activate newly enfranchised workers, resulting in the continued rise of voting totals in these parties.[1]

Voting levels did rise in the United States during the Great Depression. Popular discontent, the growth of industrial unions, and big-city political organizations revitalized by Roosevelt's New Deal programs all helped working people hurdle registration barriers, producing a twentieth-century turnout high of 73 percent in the North and West by 1940. The effects of rising participation were immediate and dramatic as the Democratic party's appeals and programs shifted toward these new working-class voters.

Still, this transformation was incomplete. National Democratic leaders continued to be constrained by the racist politics of the southern wing of the party, whose barriers to the franchise kept voting down among poor whites and blacks alike. Southern turnout finally rose in the 1960s and 1970s (although it remains marginally lower than the national average) following the civil rights movement's success in overturning the more extreme barriers to registration, such as poll taxes and literacy tests. Once again, the rise in voting levels had an immediate impact on the two parties as Democratic politicians grew more liberal in response to a stronger black turnout (illustrated more recently by

[1] These data are taken from Przeworski and Sprague (1988: 26–27).

the role southern Democratic senators played in defeating Robert Bork's Supreme Court Justice nomination), while many newly enfranchised whites helped revive the southern wing of the Republican party.

Even as voter turnout rose after 1960 in the South, it fell in the North and West, and the system of personal voter registration must figure as part of the explanation. The overall national turnout slide from the 20th-century high of 65 percent in 1960 to about 50 percent in 1988 was not mainly due to fewer registered voters voting. Based on studies spanning two decades, the Census Bureau concluded that people "overwhelmingly go to the polls" once they are registered.[2]

In 1984, fully 88 percent of registered voters went to the polls, and there is no reason to think the figure fell appreciably in 1988. (Voting was down by several percentage points, but so was the level of registration.)[3] The drop in voting since 1960 resulted mainly from a decrease of roughly 10 percentage points in the registration levels themselves—to 61 percent in 1988 by our estimate[4]—and much of the decline occurred among the less educated and the unemployed, and among residents of major

[2] See appendix B of this book for an analysis of voting by registrants.

[3] But the media continue to disseminate the claim that it is lower voting by registrants, not falling registration levels, which explains the decline in voting. The press relies at election time on data released by Curtis Gans of the Committee for the Study of the American Electorate, as we point out in appendix C of this book. Gans in turn relies on inflated registration numbers from local elections officials who maintain lists bloated with the names of 20 million "deadwood registrants"—people who have died but whose names have not been purged from the lists, and people who have moved and reregistered elsewhere but whose names remain on the lists where they previously lived, so that they are counted *twice* in national totals. Not only does Gans report an artificially high registration level, he treats "deadwood registrants" as if they could vote, and issues reports to the press that millions of registered voters don't go to the polls. For example, a *New York Times* editorial (November 6, 1988) explained low turnout in the 1988 election this way: "Apathy increasingly afflicts registered and *unregistered* alike. The percentage of registered voters who do not vote has steadily declined—from 85.3 percent in 1960 to 72.6 percent in 1984" (emphasis in original). Finally, the reason fewer and fewer registrants appear to vote is that the volume of "deadwood registrants" is growing, mainly because many states no longer purge the rolls as often as they once did.

[4] See appendix A of this book for a discussion of registration-level estimates.

cities where registration levels often account for less than half of the eligible electorate.

A good many commentators claim that registration procedures today are more liberal than ever before. True, poll taxes and literacy tests are gone, but outside the South, the major reform in registration procedures consists of allowing people to register by mail. This reform is more appearance than fact, since provision is rarely made for the wide distribution of the postcard forms. States with mail-in systems do not have higher registration levels, because people may still have to travel to a county seat or to a downtown office in a central city simply to register.

Not only has the voter registration system not been liberalized to the extent claimed by many commentators, but the political parties are also less likely now than in the past to provide "hands on" assistance with registration procedures. National political campaigns run as media events do not put voter registration cards in people's hands. Furthermore, the local party infrastructure created during the New Deal to help overcome registration barriers has decayed. Many of the traditional big-city party machines persist more to organize graft than to organize voters, or they refuse to mobilize potential black and Hispanic voters for fear of fueling racial challenges. The shrinking industrial unions are no longer capable of reaching many unregistered workers, especially the low-wage nonunionized workers in the vast and growing service sector. Without local organizations to help people sign up, registration barriers become more restrictive, gradually driving turnout down.

At first glance, the turnout slide is puzzling; it flies in the face of the logic of competitive elections. The Democrats have lost five of the past six presidential elections. Why doesn't the party therefore exert itself somehow to expand its political base among minorities and the less well off? Of the nearly 70 million Americans who are not registered to vote, two out of three have family incomes that fall below the median, and the opinion polls show that their preferences lean toward the Democrats.

One answer is that the Democrats are more a confederation of individual entrepreneurs than an organized party. Moreover, most of these entrepreneurs are doing quite well; a substantial majority of elected positions below the presidential level are controlled by Democrats who are regularly reelected and so see no need to expand the electorate; indeed, they have good reason to want to keep things as they are. The presidency doesn't matter nearly as much to this establishment of incumbents that reign over the Congress and state and local governments.

Democratic presidential candidates, however, clearly do have reason to try to rebuild majorities by recruiting from below. Still, those motives are offset by others. For one, the incorporation of new groups can be politically disruptive and risky. New voters can precipitate defections among existing constituencies, as illustrated by the Democrats who left the party in response to the incorporation of blacks in the 1960s. Then, too, Democratic presidential aspirants run two campaigns, one for money, the other for voters, and the two can conflict. If vigorous recruitment campaigns were undertaken among the less well off, business contributors might balk, particularly at a time when business wants domestic spending cut. There are, in other words, high costs to be paid for the strategy of recruiting from below, and that is doubtless why Mondale, and later Dukakis, decided not to invest much in voter registration efforts.

But had they decided otherwise, they would still have confronted major logistical problems. Timing is one. Presidential nominees are not selected until midsummer, only two months before registration closes in most states. But mounting a national voter registration campaign is a big job, not least because procedures vary from state to state and locality to locality. Second, even were a Democratic presidential candidate to set out to recruit new voters, there is little by way of a political infrastructure through which to do it. As we said earlier, the local party apparatus has atrophied; money allocated to the state and local parties for voter registration usually ends up in the pockets of party stalwarts who have no interest in expanding the electorate.

The pundits who deplore the fall in turnout call for more enlightened campaigns that will reach and attract more voters. But these exhortations are not likely to carry much weight. The only practical way to produce more differentiated parties is to expand the electorate, and that in turn requires a system of universal registration.

FRANCES FOX PIVEN
RICHARD A. CLOWARD
DECEMBER 1988

Acknowledgments

If our explanation of nonvoting in the United States has merit, there are others who share credit for it. In their careful and critical reading of this manuscript, John Mollenkopf and Joel Rogers confronted us with inadequacies at every page. We benefited as well from comments by Robert Alford, Fred Block, Martin Shefter, James Shoch, and James Peck at Pantheon Books.

In the pages that follow, we present an analysis of the causes of nonvoting in the United States. Our argument is influenced both by the social science literature and by our extensive field experience with organizers and attorneys who are promoting voter registration reform. We are closely associated with the Human Service Employees' Registration and Voter Education Campaign (Human SERVE), an organization working to make it possible for people to register to vote in state, county, and municipal agencies, as well as in private health and welfare agencies. Through these efforts, we have learned in very concrete ways how voter registration arrangements help to depress voting among minorities and lower-stratum groups in the United States.

It would be difficult to overstate our indebtedness to the extraordinary group of organizers who came to be associated with

Human SERVE. Hulbert James, a veteran of the civil rights and welfare rights struggles of the 1960s, served as executive director during the formation and expansion of Human SERVE in the 1982–84 period, and continues as president of the board of directors. Linda Davidoff now directs the program after long experience in electoral politics. Until her recent departure for law school, Cynthia A. Williams managed the national office, eventually as associate national director, and many consider her name synonymous with Human SERVE. Jo-Anne Chasnow, the current associate national director, first joined Human SERVE as field organizer for New Jersey, where she laid the groundwork for registration services in the municipal agencies of Jersey City, Trenton, and Newark. In Texas, Lafe Larson, a former ACORN organizer, created a statewide coalition which led in 1984 to the first gubernatorial order requiring that registration services be established in state agencies. In New York, Kenneth Grossinger successfully mobilized private health and welfare agencies—from settlement houses to community health centers —to offer voter registration services. At the same time, Janice Kidd, together with volunteer organizers Louise and George Altman, recruited hundreds of people to devote time to canvassing for new registrants in New York's welfare and unemployment offices.

As Michigan state organizer, Roseanne Handler collaborated with the Michigan Civil Liberties Union to prepare the first major legal challenge to elections officials who refuse to deputize volunteer voter registrars, including the personnel of government and private agencies. Similar challenges have since been mounted against elections officials in a dozen states by a coalition of voting rights organizations. Another important lawsuit was prepared by Human SERVE's California organizer, Barbara Facher, in collaboration with Mark Rosenbaum of the southern California chapter of ACLU. At both the trial and appellate levels, California courts handed down precedent-setting decisions requiring all Los Angeles County employees to offer to register citizens using the services of their agencies. Other staff and volunteers who contributed during the 1984 campaign period include: Penny Von Eschen, who directed the Freedom Summer '84 Campaign, sponsored jointly with the Youth Section of the Democratic Socialists of America and the United States Student Association; Janice Kydd who organized volunteer registrars in New York City; headquarters staff members Jack Clark, Susan Davidoff, and Connie Taylor; Margot Beutler, Oregon organizer; Robin Leeds, Massachusetts organizer; Bill Jones, Florida organizer; Professor Tommie Brown, Tennessee organizer; Darryl Jordan, Ohio organizer; Taunya Jenkins, West Virginia organizer; Guy Costello, Illinois organizer; Professor Paul Wellstone, Minnesota activist; Professor David Wineman, Detroit activist; and John McGettrick in New York City. As a result of staff changes since 1984, Catherine Willis has assumed responsibility for work in New York and New Jersey, Susan Phillips in California, Wayne Thompson in the South, and Jeri Rasmussen as Washington representative.

The Human SERVE reform effort would not have been possible without the help of many others, only a few of whom can be noted here: George A. Brager, former dean of the Columbia University School of Social Work; New York City Council member Ruth Messinger; Victor Gotbaum, District Council 37-AFSCME; Don Hazen, formerly with the foundation committee on voter registration and now publisher of *Mother Jones*; Blair Clark, a member of Human SERVE's board of directors; Sherrod Brown, Ohio secretary of state; Farley M. Peters, Center for Policy Alternatives; Richard Gilbert, American Public Health Association; Steve Kest of ACORN; Richard Boone of the Field Foundation and Joan Davidson of the J. M. Kaplan Fund; Lani Guinier of the NAACP Legal Defense and Educational Fund; Frank R. Parker, Lawyers' Committee for Civil Rights Under Law; Ira Glasser of the American Civil Liberties

Union; and Arthur Eisenberg of the New York chapter of ACLU.

Finally, as so often in the past, David Hunter's counsel and support have been critical. And when we need organizing advice, we always turn to Timothy Sampson. Frances Goldin, our literary agent, is also special to us.

Introduction

This book is about the institutional arrangements that produce massive nonvoting by lower-class and working-class people in the United States. We focus on nonvoting because the distinctively harsh development of industrial capitalism in the United States during the twentieth century can be attributed partly to it. And unless voting by lower-stratum people can be expanded, they will be the ones to bear the costs of the economic transformation that the United States is now undergoing.

An emphasis on electoral politics may surprise some readers. A good deal of our work in the past has concentrated on the role of protest movements in advancing the interests of groups at the bottom of American society. In *Poor People's Movements*, we argued that it was when political discontent among the lower classes "breaks out of the confines of electoral procedures that the poor may have some influence."[1] Our view in brief was that poor and working-class people sometimes exercised power when they mobilized in mass defiance, breaking the rules that governed their participation in the institutions of a densely interdependent society. And we summoned our studies of the role of

[1] Piven and Cloward (1977:15).

protest movements of the 1930s and 1960s in winning major reforms as evidence for this thesis. Consistently, the virtual absence of large-scale protest during the 1980s facilitated the spate of domestic policies that has dramatically worsened the bias of public policy against working- and lower-class groups.

Although movements and voting are sometimes treated simply as conflicting alternatives, the bearing of each on the other is in fact multifaceted; each form of political action both undermines and supports the other, as we tried to show in our earlier work. There are, for example, ways in which electoral politics suppresses the possibilities for collective protest. The elaboration of electoral arrangements entails a system of powerful meanings and rituals that define and limit the appropriate forms of political action. The very availability of the vote, and of the social ritual of the periodic election, is like a magnet attracting and channeling popular political impulses. Other forms of collective action, and especially defiant collective action, are discredited precisely because voting and electioneering presumably are available as the normative ways to act on political discontents. In addition to constraining the forms of popular political action, the electoral system tends to limit the goals of popular politics, and even the orientations of popular political culture, to the political alternatives generated by the dominant parties. Further, involvement in electoral politics exposes people to the fragmenting influences associated with electioneering, and can thus weaken the solidarities that undergird political movements, a development that takes its most extreme form under clientelist or machine modes of appealing to voters. And, finally, electoral political institutions generate seductions that distract people from any kind of oppositional politics. People are hypnotized by the circuses of election campaigns, while their leaders are enticed by the multiple opportunities to gain (often trivial) positions in the electoral representative system. In short, involvement in electoral politics channels people away from movement politics.

Despite the zeal and overstatement with which this sort of

view is sometimes expressed, it is supported by a long and serious intellectual tradition. Reinhard Bendix, for example, argued that the class consciousness of European workers was enhanced precisely because they were barred from electoral participation during most of the nineteenth century;[2] Ted Robert Gurr and some other movement analysts explicitly posited that electoral institutions channel people away from protest;[3] and Murray Edelman stressed the symbolic manipulation associated with electoral participation.[4] And there is clearly some broad historical "fit" between the idea that electoral arrangements constrain protest movements and the actual course of movements in American history. For instance, as electoral participation expanded in the first third of the nineteenth century, and particularly with the emergence of machine-style political organization, early workingmen's insurgencies did, in fact, tend to become absorbed in regular party politics. And, at the end of the nineteenth century, the Populist movement was fragmented, diminished, and ultimately destroyed by its venture into national electoral politics. Much of the momentum of the labor movement of the 1930s was lost as it became absorbed in Democratic party politics. Similarly, the black movement dissipated as it turned "from protest to politics" in the 1970s.

The bearing of electoral politics on movement politics is more complicated, however. Some aspects of the electoral environment nurture rather than suppress movements. True electoral politics usually absorbs political activism so that people do not turn to protest. Nevertheless, the idea of popular rights associated with democratic electoral arrangements encourages the belief that change is possible, and by the efforts of ordinary people. This is the implication of the core democratic idea, the idea that ordinary people have the right to participate in governance by choosing their rulers. Furthermore, movements also may be

[2] Bendix (1964).
[3] Gurr (1968).
[4] Edelman (1971).

nurtured by the protection that electoral politics provides. The anticipation of adverse voter reactions often restrains state leaders from the use of repression as a way of dealing with political defiance.

Some electoral conditions are more conducive to movements than others. Movements tend to arise when electoral alignments become unstable, usually as a result of changes in the larger society that generate new discontents or stimulate new aspirations, and thus undermine established party allegiances. In the United States, electoral volatility is associated particularly with large-scale economic change, and especially with economic collapse. When the allegiance of key voter blocs can no longer be taken for granted, contenders are likely to raise the stakes in electoral contests by employing campaign rhetoric that acknowledges grievances and gives voice to demands as a way of building majorities. In other words, movements are more likely to emerge when a climate of political possibility has been created and communicated through the electoral system.

Movements also win what they win largely as a result of their impact on electoral politics. The issues raised when masses of people become defiant sometimes break the grip of ruling groups on political interpretations so that new definitions of social reality, and new definitions of the possible and just, can be advanced. In turn, the issues raised and communicated by masses of defiant people activate and politicize voters, and sometimes attract new voters to the polls who alter electoral calculations. It is by their ability to galvanize and polarize voters, with the result that electoral coalitions fragment or threaten to fragment, that protest movements score gains in electoral-representative systems. When political leaders make policy concessions, it is to cope with threats of electoral cleavage, or to rebuild coalitions in the aftermath of electoral defections. In this way, the electoral system not only nourishes and protects movements, but in addition gives them some leverage with state leaders. The influence of voters is also enhanced, for movements activate electoral constituencies and make their allegiance conditional on policy responses. The life course of movements can only be understood, in short, in relation to the electoral environment in which they emerge, and on which they also have an impact.

There is also broad historical confirmation for this aspect of the relationship between movements and electoral politics. In the 1930s, striking industrial workers were able to force a wavering New Deal administration to support government protection for collective bargaining. The strike movement had so antagonized business groups as to eliminate any possibility that the New Deal could recover their support, and it also threatened to put at risk the votes of working-class voters on whom the New Deal depended. Similarly, in the 1950s and 1960s, the southern civil rights movement forced national Democratic leaders to throw their weight behind legislation that would dismantle the southern caste system and strike down some of the procedures by which blacks and most poor whites had been disenfranchised. The reason is that the civil rights movement had both precipitated defections among southern whites to the Republican party, and jeopardized the votes of growing numbers of blacks in the cities of the Border States and the North.

The relationship between movement politics and electoral politics is thus complex. When we wrote *Poor People's Movements*, it was in part to specify some of these complexities, if only because earlier analyses of protest movements tended to ignore their electoral environment. But there was one major feature of the American electoral system with which we did not deal. We did not call attention to the distinctive pattern of lower-stratum nonvoting in the United States, nor explore its implications for the emergence and evolution of protest movements.

How, then, does the twentieth-century history of massive nonvoting by poorer and minority people bear on the fate of movements in American politics? At first glance, one might expect large-scale nonvoting to reduce the effectiveness of the electoral system in suppressing movements. However, the methods by which people are made into nonvoters matter. When whole categories of people are denied the vote as a matter of state policy, their exclusion may well strenghten their collective identity, stir their indignation, and legitimate defiant forms of political action. But in the United States, the formal right to the franchise is virtually universal, a condition much celebrated in the political culture. Only those who are aliens, or felons, or not yet of age, or undomiciled are denied the vote as a matter of acknowledged policy. At the same time, the ability of large numbers of people to act on the right to the franchise is impeded by a series of procedural obstructions embedded in the voter registration process. Those obstructions are selective in that they are more likely to interfere with voting by the poor and unlettered than by the better off and educated. Still, they do not bar entire categories of the population, and the method by which people are barred remains obscure. People often fail to register precisely because they do not know much about the requirement or how to complete it, and under these circumstances they do not know just why they do not have access to the ballot. It is in the nature of these barely comprehended procedural obstructions that people tend to blame themselves for their failure to comply. In these cases, the *idea* that voting and elections provide the means for acting on political grievances remains largely intact, even though the means are not in fact available to tens of millions of people. The demobilization of large sectors of the American electorate has thus been secured at relatively little cost to the legitimacy of electoral processes as the prescribed avenue for political change.

At the same time, the constriction of the electorate weakens the complementarities between electoral politics and protest movements. The interactions between movements and the electoral context that encourage the growth of movements, and sometimes lead to movement victories, depend on the existence of voter constituencies with orientations that incline them to be responsive to the appeals of protesters. Thus, protests from below are more likely to arise in the first place when contenders for office are forced to employ rhetoric that appeals to less-well-off voters, and thus give courage to the potential protesters. Such movements are more likely to grow when they are at least somewhat secure from the threat of state repression because political leaders are constrained by fear of adverse reactions by working-class or lower-class or minority electoral supporters. Finally, protesters are more likely to win when the issues they raise stir support among significant numbers of these voters, threatening to lead to voter defections. The complementary dynamic between movements and electoral politics thus depends both on the composition and orientation of movements and on the composition and orientation of significant blocs in the electorate. In other words, the sharp underrepresentation of poorer and minority people in the American electorate creates an electoral environment that also weakens their ability to act politically through movements. This is one important way that massive nonvoting has shaped American politics.

Nonvoting has influenced American politics in other ways as well, and that is why the question of who shall vote has been at the volatile core of American politics for over a century. It may bear on our political future as well.

FRANCES FOX PIVEN
RICHARD A. CLOWARD
September 1987

Why Americans Don't Vote

Chapter 1

The Politics of Nonvoting

The right to vote is the core symbol of democratic political systems. Of course, the vote itself is meaningless unless citizens also have the right to speak, write, and assemble; unless opposition parties can compete for power by offering alternative programs and leaders; and unless diverse interest groups can also compete for influence. And democratic arrangements that guarantee formal political equality through the universal franchise are inevitably compromised by sharp social and economic inequalities. Nevertheless, the right to vote is a basic feature of the democratic polity that makes all other political rights significant. "The electorate occupies, at least in the mystique of [democratic] orders, the position of the principal organ of governance."[1]

Americans generally take for granted that ours is the model of a democratic polity. Our leaders echo this conviction when they regularly proclaim us as the world's leading democracy, and assert that other nations should measure their progress toward democracy by the extent to which they develop electoral institutions that match our own. At the core of this self-congratulation is the belief that the right to vote is indeed firmly established.

[1] Key (1955:3).

But in fact, the United States is the only major democratic nation in which the less well off are substantially underrepresented in the electorate.

The basic facts of contemporary nonvoting are undisputed. The universe of actual voters in the United States is shrunken and skewed compared with the universe of formally enfranchised citizens. Only a little more than half of the eligible population votes in presidential elections, and fewer still vote in off-year elections. As a result, the United States ranks at the bottom in comparison with other major democracies (table 1.1) Moreover, those who vote are different in important respects from those who do not. Voters are better off and better educated, and nonvoters are poorer and less well educated. Modest variations notwithstanding, this has been true for most of the twentieth century, and has actually worsened in the last two decades. In sum, the active American electorate overrepresents those who have more, and underrepresents those who have less.[2]

The contemporary reality of nonvoting notwithstanding, there are reasons in American history for our democratic hubris. The United States was the first nation in the world in which the franchise began to be widely distributed, and this was indeed an achievement.[3] Everywhere in the West, the hopes of peasants, artisans, and the urban poor were fired by the essential democratic idea, the idea that if ordinary people had the right to participate in the selection of their state leaders, their grievances would be acted upon. For just that reason, the propertied classes feared that the vote would give the "poor and ignorant majority" the power to "bring about a more equitable distribution of the good things of this world."[4] The right of ordinary people to vote

---

[2] Pertinent demographic data will be provided in chapter 4.

[3] The exception to this assertion is France, where universal manhood suffrage was won briefly during the Revolution.

[4] This warning was issued by the historian J. A. Froude in an address to the Liberty and Property Defense League in London in the aftermath of the passage of the Third Reform Bill in England. See Brittan (1975: 146).

TABLE 1.1 VOTER TURNOUT PERCENTAGES IN
DEMOCRATIC NATIONS (MOST RECENT MAJOR
NATIONAL ELECTIONS AS OF 1983)

1.	Belgium	95
2.	Australia	94
3.	Austria	92
4.	Sweden	91
5.	Italy	90
6.	Iceland	89
7.	New Zealand	89
8.	Luxembourg	89
9.	West Germany	87
10.	Netherlands	87
11.	France	86
12.	Portugal	84
13.	Denmark	83
14.	Norway	82
15.	Greece	79
16.	Israel	78
17.	United Kingdom	76
18.	Japan	74
19.	Canada	69
20.	Spain	68
21.	Finland	64
22.	Ireland	62
23.	**United States**	**53**
24.	Switzerland	48

Source: Harvard/ABC News Symposium (1984:7). Turnout for the United States is based on the voting-age population; for other countries, it is based on registered voters. Apart from the United States, registration is more or less universal, so these comparisons are roughly correct. Low voting in Swiss federal elections, it should be noted, is a unique case. The federal government there plays a minor role compared with the cantons, and there is little political competition at the national level. See Jackman (1987:409) and Powell (1982:119).

was, in other words, sharply contested. However, the franchise was ceded earlier in the United States because the propertied classes had less ability to resist popular demands. The common men who had fought the Revolution were still armed and still insurgent. Moreover, the American elites were unprotected by the majesty and military forces of a traditional state apparatus.

The political institutions that developed in the context of an expanded suffrage certainly did not remedy many popular grievances. Still, political parties and elections did not merely replicate patterns of class domination. They also reflected in some measure the new social compact represented by the franchise. Contenders for rulership now needed votes, and that fact altered the dynamics of power. In the early nineteenth century, the electoral arrangements that forced leaders to bid for popular support led to the gradual elimination of property, religious, and literacy qualifications on the franchise, and to increases in the number of government posts whose occupants had to stand for election. As the century wore on and the political parties developed systematic patronage operations to win elections, wide voting rights meant that common people received at least some share of the largess—a reflection, if only dim, of the social compact embodied in the right to vote.

But at the beginning of the twentieth century, at the historical moment when the working classes in other Western countries were winning the franchise and even becoming contenders for state power, a series of changes in American electoral arrangements sharply reduced voting by the northern immigrant working class and virtually eliminated voting by southern blacks and poor whites. By World War I, turnout rates had fallen to half the eligible electorate and, despite some vacillations, they have never recovered.

The demobilization of lower-strata voters occurred at precisely that time in our history when the possibilities of electoral politics had begun to enlarge. Indeed, we will argue it occurred because the possibilities of popular influence through electoral politics were expanding. First, as the industrial system grew, government intervened in more areas of economic life, so that the vote bore on a wider range of issues. It is true, of course, that government policies had always played a pivotal role in economic development: policies on tariff and currency, labor and welfare, internal improvements, and especially the subsidization of the railroads, had all shaped the course of American development. But as the twentieth century began, these earlier interventions were overshadowed by the growing scale and penetration of government activities, especially in the Great Depression.

Second, the programs that resulted from government's expanding role in the economy altered both popular political ideas and popular political organizational capacities. Thus, a more pervasively and transparently interventionist state undermined the old *laissez-faire* conviction that economy and polity necessarily belonged to separate spheres[5] and encouraged the twentieth-century idea that political rights include economic rights, and particularly the right to protection by government from the worst instabilities of the market. And expanded state activities created new solidarities that became the basis for political action, including action in electoral politics. For example, government protection of the right to collective bargaining reinforced the idea that workers had rights, promoted the unionization of millions of industrial workers, and made possible a large role for unions in electoral politics; Social Security reinforced the idea that government was responsible for economic well-being and promoted the organization of millions of program beneficiaries, such as "senior citizens" and the disabled; and the enormous expansion of public programs gave rise to a vast network of

[5] Chapter 3 of *The New Class War* (Piven and Cloward 1985) contains an extended discussion of the distinctive political arrangements—including constitutionalism, a complex but flexible federal system, fragmented and bureaucratized government authorities, and clientelism— that contributed to the vigor of *laissez-faire* ideas in the nineteenth-century United States both by obscuring government activities in the interests of business and by creating a realm of government and politics within which politics did indeed seem to be separate from the larger economy.

public employee organizations. In other words, new state programs created new political forces that might over time modify industrial capitalism (in much the way that Marxists thought that a proletariat brought into being by industrial capitalism would over time transform industrial capitalism).[6]

But while the enlarged role of government and the new popular ideas and solidarities associated with enlarged state activities created the possibilty that electoral politics would become a major arena for the expression of working-class interests, that possibility was only partly realized. The reason was that vast numbers of those who might have been at the vortex of these developments were, for all practical purposes, effectively disenfranchised. In Western Europe, the pattern was virtually reversed. There the working classes were enfranchised at the beginning of the twentieth century, and their enfranchisement led to the emergence of labor or social democratic parties that ultimately exerted considerable influence on the policies and political culture of their nations. In the United States, by contrast, the partial disenfranchisement of working people during the same period helps explain why no comparable labor-based political party developed, and why public policy and political culture remained more narrowly individualistic and property-oriented.

These assertions bear on the large debate in the literature regarding "American exceptionalism," which tends to blame the culture of the working class, especially its lack of class consciousness, for the distinctive pattern of political development in this country. But political attitudes are formed in the context of political institutions. We are proposing that the electoral arrangements that evolved at the turn of the century at least partly explain the path of American political development. The disenfranchisement of large sectors of the working class precluded the

---

[6] For the full argument that broad and pervasive interventions by government in the twentieth century generated new political forces, see *The New Class War* (Piven and Cloward 1985).

emergence of a political party that could have stimulated greater class consciousness among American workers by articulating their class interests.[7]

We do not mean by these comments to overstate the importance of the ballot. Voters have limited ability to affect policy, and that limited influence is tempered by the character of the dominant party system and the reigning political culture. Nevertheless, a full complement of working-class voters would have moderated, at the very least, the distinctively harsh features of American capitalist development in the twentieth century. Corporate predations against workers and consumers probably would have been more effectively curbed. Even modestly enlarged electoral influence might have enabled the working class to block the public policies that weakened unions, and inhibited their ability to organize the unorganized. The enfranchisement of blacks together with poor whites would have prevented the restoration of the caste labor system in the South, and it would have precluded the development of a one-party system whose oligarchical leaders wielded enormous power in national politics for most of the twentieth century. And an effectively enfranchised working class almost surely would have prodded political leaders to initiate social welfare protections earlier and to provide more comprehensive coverage in a pattern more nearly resembling the welfare states of Western Europe. In other words, the distinctive pattern of American industrial capitalist development at least partly stems from the fact that the United States was not a democracy, in the elementary sense of an effective universal suffrage, during the twentieth century.

[7] On the role of political parties in forming class consciousness, see Przeworski (1977). The literature on "American exceptionalism" has lately been complicated all the more by a spate of new historical writing on working-class ideology in the antebellum period. A good deal of this new work fastens on the vigor of "republicanism" among American workers, although, considering the varieties of republicanism, it may turn out that this concept is being made to carry too much for this reason alone. See, for example, Dawley (1976); Faler (1981); Montgomery (1981); Wilentz (1984); and Steffen (1984).

. . .

The contemporary business mobilization also illustrates the pivotal role of nonvoters. Numerous commentators have pointed out that American corporations have become more explicitly political than ever before. True, large corporations have always maintained a political presence to guard their particular interests in legislative and bureaucratic spheres, drawing on a repertoire of familiar techniques ranging from personal influence to campaign funding to public relations to vigilant lobbying. The economic instabilities of the past two decades, however, have goaded business leaders into more focused and coordinated political activity. They have tried to shore up sagging and uncertain profits by reorienting policies ranging from taxation to regulation to labor relations to social welfare to military spending.[8] Given the scale of the changes contemplated, this sort of agenda demanded a new and broad-ranging electoral mobilization by business. The usual methods of political influence had worked well enough to promote and protect business interests under more stable economic conditions, but they were not equal to the boldness of the new goals being pursued, which, after all, entailed dismantling the programs won by working people through a history of protest and politics. Accordingly, in the 1970s, American business set out to create a vast political infrastructure capable of conducting national election campaigns. Business leaders revived and financed the sluggish U.S. Chamber of Commerce to reach and influence small businesses to enter the electoral arena in a concerted way; trade associations were similarly activated; new think tanks, such as the American Enterprise Institute and the Heritage Foundation, were established to influence public opinion by

---

[8] The sources on the business agenda are numerous. Overviews are provided in Cohen and Rogers (1983: chapter 5); Edsall (1984); Ferguson and Rogers (1986); Krieger (1986: chapter 7); Davis (1986); Salamon and Lund (1984); and Dolbeare (1984, chapter 5). On the effort to slash social welfare programs, see Piven and Cloward (1985: chapters 1 and 6); and Palmer and Sawhill (1982). On monetary policy, see Epstein (1981). On regulatory policy, see Stone (1981).

articulating and legitimating the business program; meanwhile, corporate leaders also began to coordinate their political contributions in order to centralize control over a rejuvenated Republican party.[9]

These efforts were redeemed in the election of 1980. Victory at the polls made it possible for the Republican-business alliance to claim that their agenda was in fact demanded by the American people. The landslide election was defined as evidence of a broad popular mandate for the ruling-class program. Among other things, Reagan was said to have tapped vast popular resentments against the public policies that had been singled out for attack, as well as vast popular support for tax cuts and a military buildup.

In fact, postelection polls showed clearly that Reagan did not win because of his campaign broadsides against big government,[10] but because of popular discontent with the Carter administration's policies, especially anger over high rates of unemployment.[11] As Schneider sums it up: "The most ideological President in American history was elected . . . in circumstances that were largely devoid of ideology. That is why analysts could

[9] See Edsall (1984).

[10] Even during the 1980 election campaign, surveys repeatedly showed that a majority of respondents were opposed to social program cuts (an opposition that was to grow stronger as the Reagan term continued). Moreover, most people anticipated that, were Reagan to win, he would not in fact cut programs much. See Markus (1982), and Enelow and Hinich (1982). As for the resentment of "big government" that exists, it had different and changing sources. In particular, survey data indicated that the meaning of "big government"—a term that was a euphemism for domestic reform during the New Deal—became much more ambiguous in the 1960s. By the 1970s, liberals were more opposed than conservatives to big government, mainly because of growing concern about the Vietnam War and the widening power of the security agencies. Thus, polling data on attitudes toward big government have to be interpreted with caution. See Nie et al. (1976), and Petrocik (1987a).

[11] Using data from the 1980 National Election Study surveys, Markus (1982) finds no evidence for the contention that the election was a referendum on Reagan's policy positions. The data indicate instead that his election was the result of dissatisfaction with Carter's performance. Similarly, Burnham's (1981a) analysis of exit poll data from the election indicates that the paramount issue among voters who swung from Carter in 1976 to Reagan in 1980 was unemployment. Miller and Wattenberg (1985) make the similar argument that there was no mandate for Reagan's policies. And see Kelley (1986).

find little evidence of a conservative swing in the electorate." [12]
In this respect, the election of 1980 confirmed a trend evident in
presidential elections since the 1930s. Americans believe that
presidents are responsible for ensuring widespread economic
well-being. Judged by this criterion, Carter failed. [13]

These factors and others are important in explaining the
ascendancy of the Republican-business alliance. Even so, and
notwithstanding the formidable corporate mobilization, or Carter's failure to manage the "political business" cycle, [14] we do not
think events would have unfolded as they did were it not for the
truncated shape of the voting universe. The underrepresentation
of the workers and poor people whose living standards were the
target of much of the business program helps to explain the
weakness of partisan political opposition to the Reagan administration's agenda, during the 1980 campaign and after, despite
the fact that public opinion was opposed to much of that agenda
from the start, and grew more strongly opposed to the program
as time went on. [15]

Nonvoting was also decisive in a simpler and more clear-
cut way. The Reagan victory of 1980 was literally made possible
by large-scale nonvoting. Just as polls showed that voters tilted
toward Reagan by 52 percent over Carter's 38 percent, so did
nonvoters tilt toward Carter by 51 percent over 37 percent. [16] In
a close study of that particular election, Petrocik concludes that

---

[12] Schneider (1987:41).

[13] The argument that incumbents are judged by performance was originally put forward by
V. O. Key (1966), and is authoritatively examined in Fiorina (1981). The significance of
economic performance in determining the reelection chances of incumbents in the United
States is not idiosyncratic; it is consistent with political developments throughout the industrialized West. See, for example, Hibbs (1977 and 1982), who shows the critical importance
of the economic performance of the government in recent British elections. As Prime Minister Harold Wilson said in 1968, "All political history shows that the standing of a Government and its ability to hold the confidence of the electorate at a general election depend on the
success of its economic policy" (Hibbs 1982:259).

[14] Tufte (1978).

[15] Pertinent analyses of survey data can be found in Lipset (1985 and 1986); Navarro (1985);
and Ferguson and Rogers (1986: chapter 1).

[16] Petrocik (1987a:253), based on the University of Michigan National Election Study data.

"the . . . margin for Ronald Reagan in 1980 was made possible by a failure of prospective Carter voters to turn out on election day." [17]

Despite the drama of these recent events, and despite the importance that political scientists usually attribute to electoral processes in shaping politics, much scholarly opinion does not attribute important political or policy consequences to the constriction of the electorate. In fact, a fair amount of academic work has been directed to explaining why nonvoting should not be considered a problem at all. In one major tradition, nonvoting is defined as a kind of voting, a tacit expression of consent and evidence of satisfaction. Since many people are so satisfied, their abstention actually demonstrates the strength of the democratic polity. Of course, no one has satisfactorily explained why "the politics of happiness" [18] is so consistently concentrated among the least well off.

Another variant on this theme asserts that nonvoting contributes to the health of a democratic polity, not because the abstainers are necessarily so satisfied, but because mass abstention reduces conflict and provides political leaders with the latitude they require to govern responsibly. A functioning democracy, the argument goes, requires a balance between participation and nonparticipation, between involvement and noninvolvement. [19] The "crisis of democracy" theorists, for example, reason that an

---

[17] Petrocik (1987a:240 and 253) maintains that both the 1980 and 1984 election broke with a pattern in which irregular voters or nonvoters who are "without settled habits and, therefore, sensitive to short-term tides" always surge in the direction of the majority. Petrocik goes on to show that while there was a smaller discrepancy between voters and nonvoters in 1984, "again nonvoters were less supportive of the winner than voters were."

[18] This phrase is taken from the title of an article by Eulau (1956). In the same vein, Orren (1985:52, n. 2) quotes a *Boston Globe* columnist: "Low voter turnout is . . . a symptom of political, economic, and social health. . . . If you'd rather watch 'All My Children' or 'Family Feud' than nip over to the firehouse to vote, then you can't be feeling terribly hostile toward the system." Will (1983:96) also defines much nonvoting as a "form of passive consent." See Jackman's (1987:418) review of this perspective.

[19] See, for example, Almond and Verba (1963: 343–65, 402–69, and 472–505); Eckstein (1966); Dahl (1961); and Huntington (1974).

"excess" of participation endangers democratic institutions by "overloading" them with demands, especially popular economic demands.[20] This rather Olympian view of the democratic "functions" of nonvoting generally fails to deal with the decidedly undemocratic consequences of tempering the demands of some strata of the polity and not others.

A bolder but kindred argument fastens precisely on the characteristics of nonvoters—on their presumed extremism and volatility—to explain why their abstention is healthy for the polity. To cite one classic example, Lipset draws on evidence that nonvoters are more likely to have antidemocratic attitudes.[21] Similarly, George Will, writing "In Defense of Nonvoting," says that "the fundamental human right" is not to the vote but "to good government," and he points to the high turnouts in the late Weimar Republic as evidence of the dangers of increased voter participation, an example widely favored by those who make this argument.[22] Will's point of view is reminiscent of nineteenth-century reformers who proposed various methods of improving the "quality" of the electorate by reducing turnout. Consider, for example, the *New York Times* in 1878: "It would be a great gain if people could be made to understand distinctly that the right to life, liberty, and the pursuit of happiness involves, to be sure, the right to good government, but not the right to take part, either immediately or indirectly, in the management of the state."[23]

Still, whether nonvoting is consequential or not, questions about it have preoccupied political scientists, with the result that

[20] This perspective is set out generally in Crozier et al. (1975); Huntington (1975); Brittan (1975); and Bell (1978).

[21] Lipset (1960:115). Prothro and Grigg (1960) are also pertinent. But see Rogin (1967) for a rebuttal.

[22] Will (1983:96). For the most recent in the tradition of studies that draws the lesson of the dangers of high participation from the fall of Weimar, see Brown (1987).

[23] Cited in McGerr (1986:47). Petrocik (1987a:244) contains a discussion of the literature that claims that new or irregular voters are more volatile.

schools of thought have multiplied. Explanations of nonvoting are roughly of two kinds: those that locate the causes of abstention outside politics, and those that attribute it to political processes of various kinds. The former tradition consists of a long line of studies that ascribe the constriction of the active electorate to the social or psychological characteristics of the nonvoters themselves. People abstain, it is argued, because of their low education, income, or age, which limit the motivation, skills, capacities, or civic orientations said to be prerequisites for participation. Such correlations are real, but the question is whether they illuminate causes. Does something about poorer or younger people lead them to abstain, or does the distinctive character of American political institutions selectively make it less likely that these groups will vote?

This is a key question. In our opinion, cross-national data clearly undermine these social-psychological explanations of nonvoting. Other democracies also have many people with low levels of education and income, as well as large numbers of young adults. Yet nowhere are these demographic factors so dramatically associated with high rates of nonvoting as they are in the United States.[24] Furthermore, explanations framed in such individualistic terms clearly cannot explain the sharp drop in turnout between the nineteenth and twentieth centuries. Indeed, these theories are pernicious as well as wrong. They block popular understanding of institutional barriers to voting and falsely point the finger of blame at individuals.

Other analysts have ascribed low participation to the distinctive emphasis in American political culture on individualism and opportunity. This emphasis presumably prevents the devel-

---

[24] Australia, Belgium, and Italy legally require citizens to vote, and nonvoters are subject to mild penalties, such as small fines, although these sanctions are rarely applied. The legal requirement to vote does not, however, explain the consistently broad difference between the United States and such other democracies as Britain, France, West Germany, Canada, and the Netherlands. See Powell (1986) for an analysis of comparative data. Jackman (1987:414) discusses the uniqueness of the American system.

opment of the polarized group and class identities that would otherwise motivate people to vote. By blurring social cleavages, an individualistic culture also inhibits the emergence of the class-based political parties whose ideological appeals might stimulate voting. There are right and left variants of this cultural argument, with conservative analysts generally approving of what they take to be the distinctive American cultural orientation, while analysts on the left disapprove.[25] Either way, the argument is less than satisfactory as an explanation of nonvoting, for the political culture of individualism, materialism, and opportunity to which it points was presumably more vigorous in the nineteenth century than in the late-twentieth-century era of big organizations and big government. Furthermore, this cultural orientation was more strongly associated with the middle class than with the working class or minorities.[26] But voter turnout was high in the nineteenth century, and fell in the twentieth. Indeed, turnout reached historic heights precisely during the period associated with a flourishing liberal culture of individualism and acquisitiveness. Later, as the world changed and support for untrammeled acquisitive individualism moderated, turnout fell. And it fell most dramatically among those working-class and minority groups on whom the individualist political culture of the nineteenth century had a weaker hold.

Our answer to the question why people don't vote is informed by a different intellectual tradition focusing on how politics patterns electoral participation. Voting and nonvoting are shaped by institutional arrangements that have been forged by a long history of political conflict, including conflict specifically

---

[25] For a perspective from the right, see Phillips and Blackman (1975:39). Burnham's later work turns increasingly to a similar argument (see, for example, 1979:117–18, 1981c:191, 1982a:196–97, and 1982b). These cultural or idealist interpretations are, of course, indebted to Louis Hartz's (1955) classic exposition of the Lockean roots of the American liberal tradition.

[26] Following E. P. Thompson's footsteps (1963), American social historians recently have devoted a good deal of effort to reconstructing the political culture of particular social groups within the working class. Wilentz (1982) contains a review of some of this work.

over the question of who should enjoy the right to vote. That conflict, in turn, was motivated by the recognition that who votes and who does not would have consequences for American politics.

A number of analysts broadly share the position that the shape of the American electorate has large political significance. However, there is a good deal of debate and uncertainty about which of the changes in political institutions that occurred in the late nineteenth and early twentieth centuries best account for the decline of mass voter participation. The main disagreement has been between analysts who emphasize changes in the character of the American political parties and the patterns of party competition, and those who emphasize legal barriers to the suffrage, particularly personal voter registration requirements.[27]

In this book, we also take a position in this debate, but it is a position that draws from both sides. We think the linchpin of the distorted American democracy in the contemporary period is the distinctive system of voter registration procedures. This requires comment because people rarely give much thought to governmental procedures for certifying voters. Existing registration arrangements are taken for granted as natural and inevitable. In fact, American registration procedures are Byzantine compared with those that prevail in other democracies. The major difference is that governments elsewhere assume an affirmative obligation to register citizens. People are certified as automatically eligible to vote when they come of age and obtain identity cards, or government-sponsored canvassers go from door to door before each election to enlist voters. The United States is the only major democracy where government assumes no responsibility for helping citizens cope with voter registration procedures. In 1980, 39 to 40 percent of the American electorate was unregistered, or more than 60 million in an eligible voting-

---

[27] The specific works of these authors will be cited in subsequent chapters. The main proponents of the party emphasis are Schattschneider, Burnham, and Kleppner; legal barriers are emphasized by Campbell, Converse, Miller, Stokes, Kelley, Kousser, Rusk, and Stucker.

age population of 159 million,[28] and two out of three of the unregistered resided in households with incomes below the median. Furthermore, the significance of low registration is suggested by the fact that once people are registered, they overwhelmingly vote. In 1980, more than 80 percent of registrants went to the polls, and the turnout among those with little education and income was only marginally lower.[29] Consequently, when turnout in the United States is calculated *just for registered voters*, the rate here is comparable to rates in other democracies with more or less automatic registration systems (table 1.2).

We hasten to say, however, that we do not think voter registration requirements were historically the singular cause of low turnout (nor are they the singular cause today). The changes in electoral politics that converged to produce that result were indeed complicated; they included shifts in the pattern of party competition and in the organization of the parties, as well as in the rules governing access to the ballot. Those complications have provided the empirical grounds for the diverse points of view in the literature. Nevertheless, we think voter registration requirements were more important than is generally acknowledged. On the one hand, these requirements constituted direct barriers to voting. On the other hand, as these procedural obstacles gradually eroded voter participation among working people, the parties turned away from the issues and campaign stratagems needed to win lower-class support, with lasting effects on our politics.[30] The resulting marginalization of working people not only from political influence but from the political culture created by the parties in turn reinforced their tendency to abstain.

[28] This is the Census Bureau's "civilian non-institutional" definition of the voting-age population, with aliens excluded. See appendix A for statistics on registration levels.

[29] See appendix B for statistics on voting by registrants.

[30] Some evidence is provided by the University of Michigan's National Election Study, which found in 1980 that two-thirds of those who were not registered received neither mail from party campaigns, nor visits from precinct workers; by contrast, only one-third of those who were registered were similarly ignored (Squire, Glass, and Wolfinger, 1984:9).

TABLE 1.2 VOTER TURNOUT IN DEMOCRATIC NATIONS AS A
PERCENTAGE OF REGISTERED VOTERS (MOST RECENT MAJOR
NATIONAL ELECTIONS AS OF 1983)

1.	Belgium	95
2.	Australia	94
3.	Austria	92
4.	Sweden	91
5.	Italy	90
6.	Iceland	89
7.	New Zealand	89
8.	Luxembourg	89
9.	West Germany	87
10.	Netherlands	87
11.	**United States**	**87**
12.	France	86
13.	Portugal	84
14.	Denmark	83
15.	Norway	82
16.	Greece	79
17.	Israel	78
18.	United Kingdom	76
19.	Japan	74
20.	Canada	69
21.	Spain	68
22.	Finland	64
23.	Ireland	62
24.	Switzerland	48

Source: Harvard/ABC News Symposium (1984:7).

Finally, the circle was completed when the political parties that had been shaped within this constricted electorate then defended the barriers to electoral participation that worked to limit the electorate.

In other words, voter registration barriers not only restricted the suffrage, but by restricting the suffrage, they transformed the calculus of the political parties, with pervasive consequences for American political development. In principle, parties strive to select candidates and fashion political appeals that will win majorities. And, in principle, electoral competition should stimulate contending parties to mobilize voters, including new voters. Of course, the parties are subject to many other influences in fashioning campaigns, not least the influence of big-money contributors. But to the extent that voters and their preferences figure in party calculations, the skewed shape of the American voting universe has decisively influenced the practices of the parties. Except under extremely volatile electoral conditions, party organizers turn away from the candidates, the policies, the campaign language, and the logistics that would reach and appeal to the have-nots. Voter registration procedures are thus a main reason that the American political parties have become unhinged from large portions of the potential electorate.

These effects on the parties have in turn had effects on the political attitudes of nonvoters. Parties that do not put forward either the symbols that resonate with the culture of the worse off, or the policy options that reflect their life circumstances, help to explain the weakly differentiated political attitudes of nonvoters revealed in some of the public-opinion data.[31] Considered by itself, this finding is anomalous, for it suggests that sharp socioeconomic differences do not create attitudinal differences. But the opinions elicited by surveys reflect the underdevelopment of political attitudes resulting from the historic exclusion of low-income groups from active electoral participation. In other words, what survey data cannot reveal is the dynamic dimension

---

[31] See Wolfinger and Rosenstone (1980:112–13 and table 6.3). Ranney (1983) reviews the evidence in support of this "no difference" thesis. And see Petrocik (1987a) for a complex discussion that distinguishes between the underlying partisan bias of the nonvoting pool and the short-term factors that influence the preferences of predicted nonvoters. Other analysts think the attitude variations are larger, but Kleppner (1981b:205 and n. 26) is probably correct when he concludes that, given the differences in the socioeconomic characteristics of the voting and nonvoting population, the variations in opinion "are not as great as one would expect."

of politics. Political attitudes would inevitably change over time if the allegiance of voters from the bottom became the object of partisan competition, for then politicians would be prodded to identify and articulate the grievances and aspirations of lower-income voters in order to win their support, thus helping to give form and voice to a distinctive class politics.

To sum up our theoretical perspective, while we agree that there was a multifaceted historical process through which low levels of participation became the rule in the United States, we nevertheless think that over time, voter registration arrangements came to carry much of the burden of sustaining a system of limited electoral participation. State and local officials preside over "voluntary" procedures that place the burden of navigating the often difficult process on the citizen.[32] And elections officials are relatively free to manipulate registration procedures so as to limit voting by poorer and minority groups.

The campaign of 1984 illustrates all of these points. The middle-class bias of the electorate, sustained by voter registration barriers, led the Democratic party to ignore the needs of many working people and thus reinforced the marginalization of many of them from politics. Because an electorate dominated by the better off was taken for granted, party leaders turned away from the possibility of mobilizing a mass opposition to the incumbent Republican regime and its business allies. Of course, even a vigorous opposition probably would not have reversed the outcome. Just as Carter lost in 1980 because he failed to reduce unemployment or halt the decline in real disposable income, Reagan won in 1984 because of a steep upward increase in average real disposable income during the campaign year, and a downward turn in the unemployment rate. For all of the cam-

---

[32] France also has voluntary registration, but French citizens are required to obtain identity cards at the same government bureau that handles voter registration, and that tends to encourage registration. See Jackman (1987:42) and Powell (1986:21).

paign rhetoric of Family, Cross, and Flag, it was almost surely the improvement in the economy that determined the outcome of the election.[33]

Still, the rising tide certainly did not lift all boats. If a good many people were better off, a good many people were also worse off. Poverty had increased; the income gap between the top and bottom was wider; unemployment was no lower than when Reagan took office; anxiety was spreading in the rust belt and the farm belt, even among those who were not yet directly affected, as plants continued to close and farm foreclosures accelerated. If the 1984 presidential outcome was foregone, there nevertheless was a natural opposition that Democratic party leaders did not mobilize and did not lead. They did not try to bring greater numbers of the worse off into the electorate through voter registration (even though the Republican party and the Christian Right invested millions of dollars in voter registration drives during the presidential campaign). And they did not campaign for the votes of those among the worse off who were in the electorate by framing the issues, generating the denunciatory rhetoric, and advancing bold proposals that might have allayed popular economic anxieties. Instead, most Democratic politicians rushed to define the 1980 election as evidence of a "sea change" in public opinion, a shift to the right that the Democratic party could ignore only at the peril of precipitating a long-term realignment toward the Republican party.

Democratic leaders clearly had their reasons. A party constructed on a restricted electorate, and incumbent politicians elected by a restricted electorate, risked serious disturbances to leadership, to funding sources, and to existing constituencies were it to turn seriously to mobilizing the have-nots. Our point now is a simpler one. The performance of the Democratic leadership continued to reflect their taking for granted the underrepresentation of the less well-off, and that reinforced the isolation

---

[33] See Burnham (1985:255, fn. 14) and Beck (1985).

of the bottom strata from electoral politics. As a consequence, and despite the potential stimulus of new grievances and uncertainties, turnout in 1984 remained at a historic low, and the issues of concern to poorer people scarcely emerged in national politics. Meanwhile, local party organizations kept a tight hold on voter registration procedures. In sum, a national party system that over time adapted to the limited and skewed electorate created by voter registration barriers reinforced those barriers by ignoring the people who were beyond them.

This account notwithstanding, we think the events of the last decade also give reason to think that the institutional arrangements that delimit the electorate can be changed. Despite resistance by both political parties, there is mounting evidence that voter registration arrangements may be vulnerable to the currents of political instability and dealignment in the late twentieth century. In the pages that follow, we will try to show why we think that is so. But, of necessity, we must begin earlier, with an analysis of how large numbers of American citizens were marginalized from the electoral system in the first place, and the role of voter registration arrangements in that process.

We begin in chapter 2 with the celebrated nineteenth-century era in which voter participation levels in the United States soared. Our analysis fastens on the distinctive modes of political incorporation which flourished in the United States in the nineteenth century and which made high participation possible—if only by white men—while muting political conflict. We then turn to the period of rapid and disruptive economic changes in the decades after the Civil War, when existing modes of political incorporation were strained by popular discontent, resulting in a series of radical electoral insurgencies of which the Populist challenge of 1896 was the most important. These developments spurred elite-sponsored efforts to regain control of electoral politics, by methods that ultimately led to the demobilization of large numbers of poor rural and working-class voters.

In chapter 3, we discuss the specific changes that occurred in turn-of-the-century electoral politics that drove turnout down. We argue that the decline in party competition associated with the election of 1896 lowered opposition to new rules governing local party organization and access to the ballot. In the South, the drop in turnout was dramatic and precipitous. But turnout fell steadily in the North as well, as electoral "reform" took its toll. By the mid 1920s, the skewed and contracted electorate characteristic of the United States in the twentieth century had been constructed.

With these historical materials in mind, we turn in chapter 4 to the theoretical debates that dominate explanations of nonvoting by political scientists. One group of theorists agrees that changes in American political institutions in the late nineteenth and early twentieth centuries account for nonvoting, but these theorists differ among themselves about just which of those changes were important. Another debate is between these institutional theorists, taken together, and analysts who explain abstention in terms of the social-psychological attributes of those who don't vote. Our perspective is institutional, but we try to show how the debates among the institutional theorists can be superseded in a more comprehensive model that also explains why people with particular social-psychological attributes are more likely to be marginalized from the electoral system.

In chapter 5 we take up the developments that led in the 1930s to a modest but incomplete remobilization of working-class voters during the New Deal. We argue that the partial character of that remobilization, especially its failure to touch the South, had much to do with the conflicts that have since wracked the New Deal coalition. Finally, we show how internal conflict and organizational stasis have prevented the unions and local parties on which the New Deal coalition relied from reaching out to enlist the new ranks of a changing working class composed of women and minorities, with the result that voter turnout has again declined, especially among the worse off.

Chapters 6 and 7 turn to a discussion of the contemporary circumstances which give reason to think that reform of the archaic system of voter registration may finally be possible. One reason is the intense competition for new voters that broke out beginning with the presidential campaign of 1980. Blocs within the parties—the Christian Right, on the one hand, and those associated with the New Politics, on the other—organized voter registration drives of unprecedented scale and effectiveness. At the same time, some state and local officials are showing mild interest in registering poor and minority people by establishing voter registration services in government agencies. We argue that were agency-based registration to spread, it could lead to some form of comprehensive national registration reform modeled after one of the European systems. That prediction is based on parallels with the circumstances that led to the passage of the Voting Rights Act. We close with a discussion of the implications of registration reform for the reconstruction of political parties in the United States.

Chapter 2

Nineteenth-Century Electoral Mobilization and Demobilization

Between the first decades of the nineteenth century and the first decades of the twentieth, the legal right to vote was successively extended to unpropertied white men, then to black men after the Civil War, and finally to women in 1920. But even before this century-long process of formal enfranchisement was completed, a series of legal and organizational changes were introduced into the electoral system that obstructed the actual ability of many people to vote. Throughout the nineteenth century, turnout by eligible voters was high. By the 1920s, however, voting in the South among blacks and most poor whites had been virtually eliminated, and turnout by the immigrant working class had fallen sharply in the North.

The combination of widening formal enfranchisement and narrowing electoral participation is not as paradoxical as it may seem. What explains these contradictory developments was a change in the potential importance of the vote. Under some conditions, the franchise yields people little influence on government; under other conditions, it may yield more. The distinctive methods of organizing voters that emerged in the United States during the nineteenth century produced high levels of participation among the white men who were eligible to vote, but at the same time these methods limited their influence on government. As a result, there was relatively little contention over the right of white working-class men to vote. Toward the end of the century, however, wrenching economic change provoked a series of popular mobilizations that overtaxed the earlier methods of political incorporation that had sustained high electoral participation but limited its influence. Popular demands, especially popular economic demands, began to emerge into electoral politics, and even to dominate some electoral contests. As the possibilities of popular electoral mobilization began to threaten the interests of ruling groups in the late-nineteenth-century United States, they responded by sponsoring something like a democratic counter-revolution. A series of "reforms" were introduced which weakened the ability of local parties to maintain high participation among lower-strata voters, and which impeded voting by lower-strata people. The effect of these changes was to marginalize potentially contentious groups from the electoral system.

In this chapter, we deal first with what we call the tribalist and clientelist characteristics of nineteenth-century politics that made high levels of mass participation possible even while limiting conflict, especially class conflict. Then we investigate how the increasingly issue-oriented and conflictual politics of the decades after the Civil War strained these arrangements. Finally, we describe the crucial election of 1896, in which a Republican-corporate mobilization defeated the Populists, the most important mass electoral challenge of the nineteenth century. With the Populists smashed, the way was cleared for the acceleration of changes in the rules governing voting and in the organization of the local parties. Together, these changes sharply reduced mass participation in the twentieth century, and crippled the ability of popular movements to affect national politics.

The developments described in this chapter had a telling impact on the evolution of American electoral politics in the twentieth century. Still, without a sober assessment of the terms on which mass participation was sustained in the nineteenth century, it is all too easy to be lulled into a nostalgia that mourns the passing of a democratic era that, in fact, never was.

THE "GOLDEN ERA" OF AMERICAN DEMOCRACY

The spirit and vigor of popular politics in the nineteenth century compose the stuff of folklore. Consider Tocqueville's oft-cited impressions in 1831:

> No sooner do you set foot on American soil than you find yourself in a sort of a tumult. . . . A thousand voices are heard at once. . . . One group of citizens assembles for the sole object of announcing that they disapprove of the government's course, while others unite to proclaim that the men in office are the fathers of their country. . . .
>
> It is hard to explain the place filled by political concerns in the life of an American. To take a hand in the government of society and to talk about it is his most important business and, so to say, the only pleasure he knows.[1]

Most political historians echo Tocqueville's characterization: "Political life was rich and vibrant," says Hays, drawing on Handlin's study of Massachusetts for confirmation.[2] "By 1840," Gienapp exclaims, "the tide of political democracy . . . swept all before it."[3]

And the tide drove up rates of voter participation. Property qualifications that had restricted voting in the eighteenth century were steadily lowered in the early decades of the nineteenth, and the electoral-representative system was gradually expanded so that more officials were required to stand for popular election,

[1] Tocqueville (1969:242–43).
[2] Hays (1981:244).
[3] Gienapp (1982:38).

including presidential electors, governors, and many of those in local government.[4] With these changes, the already high voter participation among white men rose to unprecedented levels in an era when the United States was the only democratic polity in the world.[5]

Early in the century, turnout levels were still volatile, surging between 1804 and 1818, and then tapering off during the 1820s.[6] That changed with the election of 1828, when turnout began a steady upward swing, reaching 80 percent of the eligible electorate in the presidential election of 1840. Moreover, stable and high levels of participation penetrated to all levels of the federal system. In the elections between 1824 and 1832, when fifty gubernatorial contests were decided by popular vote, turnout for president exceeded the vote for governor in only sixteen instances.[7] Turnout continued high in the second half of the nineteenth century, ranging from a low of about 69 percent in the presidential election of 1852, just before the electoral realignment that preceded the Civil War, to 82 and 83 percent respec-

---

[4] For a state-by-state review of suffrage restrictions and their impact in the post-Revolutionary period, see Williamson (1960); Campbell (1979: chapter 1); Flanigan and Zingale (1979); Crotty (1977). See also Becker (1968) for a study in detail of the politics that led to the relaxation of suffrage restrictions in New York during the Revolutionary period. And see Burns (1982:362–66) for a more general discussion of the political dynamics through which suffrage restrictions were removed in the early nineteenth century. On voter turnout by state from 1808 to 1828, see McCormick (1960:194, table II).

[5] To Tocqueville (1969:35–36), this was a remarkable development, because nearly universal white male suffrage was won in the United States by the 1830s, and thus "a score of years before the Second French Republic tried to enfranchise all men and two score before the Third Republic actually did it." It was a half century ahead of England and almost a full century ahead of Italy, Germany, Russia, and Scandinavia. Chambers (1967:11) points out that even after the Reform Bill of 1832, the British electorate numbered only about 650,000 in a population of about 16 million. By contrast, in the United States, a population of 17 million in 1840 generated an electorate of 2,409,474.

[6] See Formisano (1974:482); McCormick (1967:95–96). This volatility from election to election notwithstanding, turnout in gubernatorial elections was almost as high as in presidential elections. McCormick (1967:108) reports turnouts of 81.9 percent in Delaware in 1804; 80.8 percent in New Hampshire in 1814; 80 percent in Tennessee in 1817; 79.9 percent in Vermont in 1812; 79.8 percent in Mississippi in 1823; and (an unlikely) 96.7 percent in Alabama's first gubernatorial contest in 1819.

[7] McCormick (1960:295).

tively in the elections of 1860 and 1876. And high levels of voting also continued for lower levels of government. The mean turnout for *all elections* between 1840 and 1860 was 70.3 percent. Turnout in presidential elections during this period ranged from 69 to 83 percent, and it lagged only modestly behind in nonpresidential elections, averaging 67 percent, which is spectacular by modern standards.[8]

TABLE 2.1 PRESIDENTIAL TURNOUT PERCENTAGES, 1840–1896

	South	*Non-South*	*National*
1840	75	81	80
1844	74	80	79
1848	68	74	73
1852	59	72	69
1956	72	81	79
1860	76	83	82
1864	Civil War	76	76
1868	71	83	81
1872	67	74	72
1876	75	86	83
1880	65	86	81
1884	64	84	79
1888	64	86	81
1892	59	81	76
1896	57	86	79

Source: Burnham (1981c:100, table 1). Based on total of all citizens legally eligible to vote, aliens excluded.

Most historians resort to rhetorical hyperbole in describing the nineteenth-century politics that generated such high levels of participation among the eligible white male electorate. There is

[8] Gienapp (1982:20). See Chambers and Davis (1978) for turnout by state in the elections of 1824 to 1844. They argue that turnout variations by state in this period are strongly related to the level of competition and strength of party organizations. McCormick (1960) makes the same argument. See also Formisano (1974:688–89) for a detailed analysis of voter participation in Michigan during this period.

an infatuation with the period, evident in the extravagant images of popular democracy with which it is characterized. Scarcely an account fails to remark upon and celebrate the excitement of nineteenth-century democratic politics: the pageantry, the marching bands, the rallies, the hoarsely shouted slogans, the fury and excitement—in short, the extraordinary popular enthusiasm that marked election campaigns. "There was no spectacle, no contest, in America that could match an election campaign, and all could identify with and participate in it."[9] But there is good reason to be skeptical of the celebratory depiction of nineteenth-century democratic politics.

Tribalism in the Golden Era

To understand the developments that brought the Golden Era to an end, we should identify the modes of political integration that produced high levels of voter participation, and then ask how they changed. Indeed, this period suggests parallels to contemporary politics in economically less-developed regions abroad where democratic forms coexist with and even seem to nurture decidedly undemocratic realities. One such parallel is suggested by the intensity of ethnocultural issues in nineteenth-century politics, a feature we call "tribalism." Just as the politics of contemporary developing nations are often riven by intense tribal identifications and conflicts, so was popular participation in the nineteenth-century United States strongly marked by ethnic and religious divisions.[10]

---

[9] McCormick (1967:108). For a book-length discussion that applauds the spectacular politics of the nineteenth century and mourns its passing, see McGerr (1986). See also Gienapp (1982) and McCormick (1979:282). The spectacular aspect of American politics also impressed foreign observers, although it did not always excite their admiration. Ostrogorski (1964:165) deals with this matter; Rusk (1974) makes some contemporary observations in a similarly sober vein.

[10] Alford (1963:1) makes the point that a democratic polity requires that voters be available for competitive party appeals, which means they are not "tightly integrated into enclaves of traditionalism which reinforces ancestral political loyalties."

The association of religious identification and popular politics was evident from the beginning of the nineteenth century, and religious feelings intensified with the revival movements that swept the North in the 1820s and 1830s. Indeed, Tocqueville's observations of "democracy in America" in 1831 led him to conclude that "religion should be considered as the first of their political institutions."[11] Religion gained unique secular force from the proliferation of church-related voluntary associations through which an essentially civil religion was created, and through which religious crusading and partisan fervor were joined. This ethnoreligious infrastructure provided the vehicle, and rapid immigration and associated labor market competition and conflict provided the stimulus, for the nativist, temperance, and antislavery movements of the midcentury, which in turn strongly marked the party realignment of the 1850s.[12] High levels of democratic participation, in short, were mobilized through overlapping networks of religioethnic associations.

Consistent with these intensely felt ethnoreligious identifications, popular political enthusiasms had what Gienapp calls the "unseemly" features of rival ethnic gangs and thugs who fought to control access to the polls and otherwise participated in the generally inebriated tumult, and whose impact on the exercise of voter choices has received rather casual attention.[13] This pugnacious aspect of popular politics also clearly has its parallels in less economically developed societies, as in the Tillys' descriptions of the battles between gangs from rival villages in preindustrial Europe.[14]

A number of commentators also maintain that ethnic and

---

[11] Cited in Hammond (1983:208).

[12] Gienapp (1982:36–37). The literature that stresses the ethnoreligious bases of partisan identification and cleavage in the nineteenth century is extensive. See Benson (1961); Kleppner (1970:93–100; 1979; and 1981b:114, 139–40); Hays (1967:158–59 and 1981:246); McCormick (1979:282).

[13] Gienapp (1982:46–47). See, for example, the descriptions of political gangs in New York City in Buckley (1987); Bridges (1987); and Asbury (1928).

[14] Tilly, Tilly, and Tilly (1977).

religious identities were intertwined with real differences in social position and economic interest, with the consequence that class, ethnic, and religious identification were mutually reinforcing. Thus Bridges says that the antebellum partisan appeals of the New York Democratic party insisted "that the Democracy was the 'true home of the working classes' " and tried to drive the point home by employing a rhetoric that fused the issues of religion, ethnicity, culture, class, and liberty.[15] Wilentz explains why political appeals of this kind could be made:

> To take a well-studied example: to be an evangelical Protestant in the North in the 1830s and 1840s certainly signified adherence to a broad cultural outlook, a particular moral viewpoint. It also signified something about a person's social position or expected social position in an evolving class society; even more, that "culture," that moral viewpoint, was in part defined and reinforced by changing class relations, in which inherited religious ideals assumed new—and in this case quintessentially bourgeois—meanings and forms.[16]

Sectional passions should be added to these sources of identification and association that encouraged electoral participation. Bensel claims that sectional feelings "constitute the most massive and complex fact in American politics and history."[17] That was so in part because sectional passions were compounded of religious, racial, and regional identifications. It was also in part so because sectional identities were shaped by economic interests— indeed, sectional economic interests often strained against and overwhelmed class allegiances. After all, on the great political questions of the century concerning currency policy, internal

[15] Bridges (1987:106).
[16] Wilentz (1984:50). See also Johnson (1978).
[17] Bensel (1984:5).

improvements, the tariff and slavery, capitalists and workers in the Northeast had a common interest, however else their interests may have diverged; [18] in turn, their common interests differed from those of both rich planters and poor farmers in the South. [19] In the wake of the Civil War, sectional identification intensified. Conflicts of this kind, as they unfold, always create their own reality in the bitter memories of injustices done and losses suffered. The Civil War in the United States complicated and sharpened religious, ethnic, and racial identifications with bloody memories of war and fierce sectional patriotism. The war produced scars, says Burnham, "which took at least a century to heal. There was no town in the North without its memorial to the Union dead; no town in the South without its Confederate counterpart." [20]

Nineteenth-century popular politics did not lack economic or class content, but the political force of class interests was complicated and diluted by sectional economic issues that united industrialists and workers in the North and landowners and tenants in the South. Class issues were also interwoven with ethnocultural and especially sectional identifications. Our purpose here is not to disentangle the relative influences of class, religion, ethnicity, and section, but to make a different point: high levels of mobilization for electoral participation were typically maintained by the overlapping influences of religious, ethnic, and regional identifications. The popular politics organized around

[18] As in the contemporary world, tribalism did not always yield either a simple or neatly ordered politics. For the emerging industrial working class in the North after the Civil War, ethnic and religious identities often strained against what might otherwise be their sectional loyalties, keeping them divided from the dominant northern Republicanism and huddled in what Goodwyn (1978:4) calls urban Democratic "lifeboats" in a sea of Republicanism.

[19] Bensel (1984:4) says, "Although expressed in cultural or religious terms at times, the historical alignment of sectional competition in America is primarily a product of the relationship of the separate regional economies to the national political economy and the world system." In this same vein, Shefter (1986:250) points out that the claims by Republican party politicians that industrial workers shared the interests of their employers on the tariff question was "substantially correct."

[20] Burnham (1981c:151).

these identifications and the conflicts generated by them were intensely felt, and stimulated high participation. But participation on these terms did not lead to challenges to nineteenth-century elites.

Clientelism and Voter Turnout

The popular politics of preindustrial countries are often marked by clientelist methods of organizing participation, as well as by intense tribal identification. Here, too, there are striking similarities between the nineteenth-century United States and some contemporary developing nations. As voter participation expanded, so did the reliance by the political parties on government patronage, and on the clientelist linkages to the electorate that government patronage made possible.[21] The complex federated governmental structure with which the United States entered the nineteenth century exposed the state to penetration by parties that played a central role in coordinating public policy and integrating mass publics.[22] And as in other developing countries, it was clientelist party organizations that emerged to solve the problems of coordination and political integration. Clientelism appears to thrive in situations where formal enfranchisement precedes industrialization and the self-organization of the working class that industrialization makes possible.[23] In the absence of trade unions

[21] Converse (1972:287) also draws a parallel between high turnout in the United States in the nineteenth century and in some Third World contemporary countries, such as Turkey and the Philippines, a parallel he attributes to social intimidation and large-scale corruption. Burnham (1974b:1018–20) takes issue with this argument, but only by attributing rather improbable virtues of political literacy, seriousness, and attentiveness to nineteenth-century voters.

[22] The now familiar characterization of the U.S. political system in the nineteenth century as a "state of courts and parties" is Skowronek's (1982).

[23] Bridges (1987:95) emphasizes the importance of early widespread suffrage in accounting for the spread of machine politics in the United States during the antebellum period. See also Bridges (1984). There are numerous suggestive parallels from our own time, including the reliance on clientelism by the Christian Democratic party in the economically more backward

and working-class parties, voters easily become prey to political operatives who influence them on the basis of preexisting ethnic or territorial loyalties, and enlist their votes in exchange for goods, services, and friendships. In other words, when the franchise is ceded to populations that are unprepared by the experience of industrialization for modern mass politics, those populations are more likely to become the base for clientelist organizations.[24] Also, machine politics is said to take root more readily among people experiencing the social uprootedness associated with economic change, as was true of many people in nineteenth-century American cities.[25]

Clientelism bears directly on nineteenth-century levels of turnout. From the perspective of party entrepreneurs, votes were resources for gaining control of government offices. And control of government offices in turn yielded the patronage on which party leaders depended to organize voters. Reports that celebrate rising turnout and strong partisanship tend to tread lightly on this aspect of nineteenth-century politics. As Formisano says, "Accounts of party formation after 1828 contain perfunctory references to the importance of patronage, but hardly a glimpse of the enormous role played by cadre-men appointed to land

---

mezzogiorno region in Italy, by the New Society movement in the Philippines, by the ruling PRI in Mexico, or the Israeli Likud bloc in its organization of newly arrived Jews from northern Africa and the Middle East.

[24] See Lemarchand (1981); Mouzelis (1985); and Scott (1969). See also Key (1984: chapter 4) for a more general argument about the crucial role of organization in making the votes of the "lower brackets" effective. Eisenstadt and Roniger (1981) make a similar argument about the conditions that encourage clientelism. They go on to point out, however, that these are not simple relations of domination. The very introduction of clientelist arrangements signals that clients have political resources that patrons need to suppress or circumvent. In personal correspondence with us, Shefter makes the strong point that nineteenth-century property owners bore the costs of patronage reluctantly: "Patronage can thus be regarded as a concession to the working class extracted from the middle and upper classes, and the machine can be seen as embodying a class compromise. Thus the impact of mass participation on politics may have been limited in the antebellum period, but it was not completely insignificant."

[25] Huntington (1968:59–64) also relates clientelism to economic development, making the different but consistent argument that the new sources of wealth and power generated by development provide the resources that can be used to establish a clientelist basis for assimilating new groups into the polity.

offices, post offices, customs houses, and the like, in the building of organizations." [26] Some clues to the growing significance of patronage are provided by the growth of government employment, which was the most important way that the functionaries of clientelist party organizations were rewarded and supported. The era after 1830 in which party organization flourished was also an era in which the number of government jobs expanded. Between 1830 and 1860, the number of federal employees increased 3.2 times, while the population grew 2.4 times; state employment also expanded rapidly during this period, largely through extensive public works projects; [27] and federal employment continued to expand after the Civil War, doubling between 1860 to 1880, and then multiplying 2.6 times by 1901. [28] Another form of federal patronage grew even more rapidly after the Civil War as Congress virtually blanketed the northern electorate with veterans' pensions distributed through local Republican leagues. As a consequence, "From New England to Minnesota, hundreds of small towns, as well as broad swathes of rural America, became," Goodwyn says, "virtual rotten boroughs of Republicanism." [29]

If patronage was the fuel of American party politics generally, it was the cities that became the strongholds of patronage

---

[26] Formisano (1974:486).

[27] Gienapp (1982:43).

[28] Polakoff (1981:244). See also Keller (1977:256–57 and 310–12) for a discussion of the uses of federal patronage—particularly the patronage generated by the postal service—in party building.

[29] Goodwyn (1978:5). Veterans' pensions were granted by special acts of Congress, which in the late nineteenth century constituted a substantial portion of the business of the Congress. By 1900, 753,000 veterans and 241,000 of their dependents were receiving pensions, the Pension Office had some 6,000 employees, and the pension program had also generated "an extensive infrastructure of pension and claim agents, pension attorneys (an estimated 60,000 by 1898), medical boards, and 4,000 examining surgeons" (Keller, 1977:311).Bensel (1984:60) draws a close link between Civil War pensions, the tariff, and the broad path of American development: "Because pension recipients allied themselves with the core industrial elite and thus formed a coalition large enough to successfully defend a high tariff as part of the national political economy, the redistribution of this tariff revenue through the Civil War pension system became a major element in the political strategy of development."

politics and (usually Democratic) party "machines," particularly as the nineteenth century wore on.[30] In fact, it is not farfetched to think that the marked local orientation of American popular politics, especially in the nineteenth century, owes something to the strength of locally based machines, both urban and rural. Of course, localism was nurtured by other features of American politics as well: by the simple and unchangeable fact that ordinary people can best organize for politics in the communities where they live and work; by a deep popular animosity toward central government rooted in the suspicion that a remote government inevitably becomes the captive of elites; and by the reality in the United States of a decentralized federal structure in which local government did indeed do many things, although often not the most important things. To all of these conditions that inclined popular politics toward local issues and local government must be added the role of the city machine in delineating alternatives and organizing political participation. And the strength of the city machines, in turn, was made possible by the high degree of decentralization embedded in the structure of the federal system. The authority and resources vested in local and state governments facilitated the growth of decentralized parties with the flexibility to ignore national issues in their campaigns in favor of state and local or even neighborhood issues.[31] Government decentralization also made accessible the patronage resources that permitted local clientelist parties to operate with a large degree of autonomy from the national or even state party organizations. Before 1840, the New York City Democracy had looked to state and federal

---

[30] Scholarly scrutiny of clientelism in the United States has mainly been directed to the political machines that developed in most big cities after the Civil War. See, for example, Katznelson (1981); Banfield and Wilson (1963); Ostrogorski (1964); Bryce (1924); Scott (1969); Miller (1968); Gosnell (1937); Bean (1952); Riordan (1963); and Reynolds (1936). For an exhaustive review of the literature, there is DiGaetano (1951). The urban political machines of nineteenth-century America have become the prototype for the study of clientelism everywhere in the world.

[31] Clientelism implies, accordingly to Mouzelis (1985:343), that the local partron has a certain amount of autonomy vis-à-vis the national organization and leadership.

appointments to support local organization, but by the 1850s, there were seven city departments with substantial payrolls, as well as the resources yielded by multiplying municipal franchises and contracts.[32]

Certainly, the political machines mobilized voters in the big cities, where much of the population was already concentrated by the closing decades of the nineteenth century. They brought "party loyalties to a pitch of almost military fervor and discipline," producing peak participation rates of about 80 percent in the presidential elections of 1876, 1888, and 1896.[33] In particular, the machines mobilized immigrant working-class voters, whose enlarging numbers in nineteenth-century cities might otherwise have caused turnout to fall. The machines kept voter participation high by reaching and enlisting these potential voters, often even before they became citizens, inducing them with friendship, favors, small bribes, by the promise of some protection from the harassment of city cops, or by threatening them with the loss of any of these things. The cadres of machine operatives who "worked" the wards and precincts were themselves kept diligent and loyal with city jobs, real or otherwise, and sometimes with graft. Thus, the votes of the immigrant working-class wards, and often the middle-class wards as well, together with outright fraud, gave the machines control of the municipal and state offices through which they raised the graft and controlled the public jobs that sustained the ward and precinct apparatus.[34] Moreover, just as ethnoreligious political loyalties were often intertwined with class loyalties, so were

---

[32] Bridges (1987:109–10). On the symbiotic relationship between decentralization and clientelism in the United States, see Piven and Cloward (1985:93–95). On the significance of state and local issues in antebellum politics generally, see Gienapp (1982:49–51). See also Benson (1961:292). Gienapp points out that control of the states and state patronage was critical even to national political leaders.

[33] Chambers (1967:14).

[34] The stories abound of voter fraud by methods ranging from bribing voters, to stuffing ballot boxes, to importing outsiders, to voting the names on cemetery stones, to straightforward thuggery at the polling places. Still, for all of the stories, there is not much reliable information on the extent of voter fraud by the machines.

allegiances to the machine intertwined with class feeling. "Is not the pending contest," asked the spokesman of the New York Democracy in 1868, "pre-eminently one of capital against labor, of money against popular rights, and of political power against the struggling interest of the masses?"[35] By these diverse methods, working-class political participation was kept high while working-class political issues were suppressed—a not inconsiderable achievement, especially at a time of massive dislocations caused by burgeoning industrialization, rapid urbanization, and devastating depressions.

The usual account of a spirited democratic politics in the nineteenth century tends to skirt the question of how much that apparent spirit was owed to tribal and clientelist modes of political organization. Burnham's commentaries provide a fair example, if only because he is ordinarily so skeptical and penetrating in his analyses of electoral politics. But there is little of that skepticism in his characterization of the nineteenth-century American voters as primarily "independent yeomen who were thoroughly bourgeois and 'modern,' " mostly literate, and immersed in rich written and oral political communications about "political issues of transcendent importance." The conclusion seems to follow that "the United States was unique in that it had a fully operating set of mass-democratic institutions and values before the onset of industrial-capitalist development. In every other industrializing nation of the 1850–1950 period, modernizing elites were effectively insulated from mass pressures."[36] But this characterization hardly matches the realities of nineteenth-century politics. The existence of issue-oriented and informed democratic publics capable of challenging economic elites cannot be inferred from the fact of high voter turnouts.[37] To do so ignores the evidence that tribalist and clientelist methods of political activation and incorporation insulated American

---

[35] Myers (1971:217).
[36] Burnham (1979:124).
[37] This is also Rusk's (1974) point, and we consider it his most incisive criticism of Burnham.

elites by managing and deflecting mass pressures, at least until the closing decades of the nineteenth century. High levels of popular participation could therefore coexist with tolerable levels of political conflict. After the Civil War, however, a series of wrenching economic transformations strained those methods of incorporating working-class voters and poor farmers, and it was then that popular economic demands emerged into national politics.

THE RISE OF ISSUE POLITICS

In the post–Civil War period, rapid economic growth combined with extreme market instability and the predatory policies of bankers and corporations to promote the rise of popular protests over economic issues. Increasingly, popular demands were directed to the states and even to the national government for action on economic grievances. Foremost among these popular grievances was the deflationary hard-money policy promoted by financiers who held government securities issued during the war. Naturally enough, they preferred that their investments be redeemed in gold rather than in the inflated "greenbacks" with which they had been purchased. The means to this end was the Treasury policy of holding the nation's money supply constant, even while population and production expanded rapidly. The resulting contraction of the currency between the end of the Civil War and the passage of the Gold Standard Act in 1900 drove interest rates up and prices down.[38] It was a tragedy to the nation's farmers, whose debts became steadily more costly, and whose products became steadily cheaper.

The farmers' troubles were worsened by their dependence on the railroads. It was the expanding rail network that had lured

---

[38] Polakoff (1981:245) reports that despite the enormous expansion of economic activity, the currency supply per capita actually declined from $30.30 in 1865 to $27.06 in 1890.

farmers to the prairies in the first place. Once there, the great distances from urban markets left them with no way to transport their products to market except by railroad, and that made them acutely vulnerable to the exorbitant rates charged. Many simply could not survive the combined pressures of low product prices and high interest and shipping costs. Year after year in the decades after the Civil War, more and more farmers were driven by rising debts into the hands of banks and crop lien merchants, and then, as they lost their land, into tenancy or sharecropping, particularly in the South. In response, an extraordinary series of protest movements emerged. By the early 1870s, farmers in the Midwest, their indignation fired by the not unreasonable idea that the railroads, having benefited from huge government land grants and subsidies, ought properly to have been subject to some government regulation, mobilized in organizations called Granges to do battle over high shipping rates. The Grangers did win legislation regulating railroads in a number of states, but over time the power of the railroad interests (and a Supreme Court ruling in 1886 that struck down state laws regulating railroad rates)[39] ensured that these victories were short-lived. Defeated by the political reach and staying power of the railroad interests, the Grange movement lost momentum.

Railroad rates remained high, so did interest rates, and commodity prices continued to fall, especially after the depression of 1873. In the late 1870s, another farmers' movement emerged, this time among the impoverished cotton farmers of Texas, who formed the first of the "Farmers' Alliances." In the following years, Alliance organizers (called "lecturers") fanned out to build chapters among the debt-ridden farmers of other southern states.[40] In time, these Alliances matured into the orga-

---

[39] *Wabash* vs. *Illinois*.

[40] Fully half of the farmers in the South, including the overwhelming majority of black farmers, were tenants or sharecroppers. They, along with poor farmers who still owned their land, were preyed upon by local merchants who extended credit in exchange for liens on the farmers' crops or on their land.

nizational backbone of the Populist movement and of the People's party that the Populists launched.

The Civil War marked a dramatic economic turning point in the Northeast as well, where most of the nation's burgeoning manufacturing enterprises were concentrated.[41] At the beginning of the Civil War, the United States ranked only fourth among industrial nations; by the end of the century, it had become the world's leading industrial power.[42] The transformation was turbulent and costly, especially for the growing number of workers in the new industries. Fierce competition goaded employers to try to lower production costs, mainly by slashing wages. And competition also led to the overproduction that worsened the market collapses that punctuated the era.

These changes simultaneously created an industrial proletariat—at first concentrated in the expanding railroads and the growing steel industry—and the conditions for industrial warfare. On the one side, it was the railroad workers and later the steelworkers who were in the forefront of the industrial battles that erupted in the late nineteenth century. During the devastating depressions of the era, strikes and riots reached unprecedented levels, spreading like brush fires along the newly created networks of rail routes. On the other side, industrialists, pressed by competition and goaded by the predatory ethos of the age, organized themselves into employer associations and mobilized public and private armies to defeat strikes. Their aim was to smash the possibilities of worker power by both breaking unions and mechanizing production in order to lower wages and gain firm control over the production process.[43] The ensuing conflicts, especially in 1877, 1886, and 1894, were among the bloodiest and costliest in peacetime American history.

---

[41] In 1890, three-quarters of manufacturing was located in the northeastern and north-central states, according to Burnham (1974a:672–73 and table 6).

[42] Gutman (1976:33).

[43] See Montgomery (1980); Raybeck (1966); Shefter (1986); Brecher (1974:1–23); Taft and Ross (1969:290–99).

These were desperation strikes prompted by depression and by aggressive employer efforts to cut wages and reorganize production. The ferocity of the workers' response sent waves of alarm through the ranks of America's upper classes. The strikes of 1877, for example, which were met first by militia and then by three thousand federal troops, left twenty-six dead in Pittsburgh, thirteen dead and forty-three wounded in Reading, Pennsylvania, and nineteen dead and more than one hundred wounded in Chicago.[44] Property damage was estimated at about $5 million.[45] Another wave of strikes in 1886 reached a climax in the Haymarket bombing incident and a wave of lockouts, blacklisting, and yellow-dog contracts. In the 1890s, a new and even larger wave of strikes in steel, railroads, and mining again brought out the National Guard and federal troops, culminating in an estimated thirty-four dead in the Pullman strike of 1894, and the massive use of federal marshals to protect railroad property across the country.

These intense economic conflicts spurred recurrent efforts by workers and farmers, sometimes separately and sometimes together, to organize independent electoral challenges. It was probably inevitable that contention would take electoral form, given the vigor of political participation in nineteenth-century America, together with government's enlarging role in promoting corporate growth while breaking strikes and thwarting the demands of distressed farmers. Accordingly, as the level of conflict intensified, the links that bound workers and farmers to the major political parties—and to clientelist and tribalist forms of organization—were strained. As early as 1869, the shoemakers in Massachusetts fielded an Independent party that succeeded in electing two dozen state legislators. In 1872, the Labor Reform party formed by a number of trade union assemblies united in the National Labor Union. Also in the 1870s, farmers backed "antimonopoly" candidates in their fight against the railroads and

---

[44] Brecher (1974:1–23).
[45] Walsh (1937:20).

banks. The efforts of the National Labor Union came to little, but the farmers won important state offices in Illinois and—in coalition with Democrats—in Minnesota, Wisconsin, Kansas, Iowa, and California.[46]

The severe depression that began in 1873 spurred renewed electoral efforts, and in 1876 a farmer/labor coalition emerged under the name of the Greenback-Labor party, which demanded an expansion of the money supply, to be achieved by government resumption of the issuance of the greenbacks that had funded the Civil War. The Greenbacks also called for a shorter workweek, and government labor bureaus, as well as restrictions on immigration and the use of prison labor. In the midterm election of 1878, in the aftermath of the great railroad strike of 1877, the Greenbacks (running as the National party) captured fourteen congressional seats and over a million votes (although some of this support was for candidates who were also backed by one of the major parties);[47] they elected mayors in a number of industrial and mining towns in New York and Pennsylvania; and they won an astonishing 34.4 percent of the vote in Maine, 25.9 percent in Michigan, 23.8 percent in Mississippi, and 23.1 percent in Texas.[48] But as the economy recovered, support for the Greenbacks evaporated, and James B. Weaver, their presidential candidate, won only 3.3 percent of the 1880 vote.

Other antimonopoly and labor parties took the place of the Greenbacks. In the South, where the one-party "Southern Democracy" was not yet firmly entrenched, a series of insurgent electoral efforts in the 1880s demanded repudiation of state debts, the abolition of crop liens and convict leasing, and tax reform. In Virginia, "Readjusters" joined with Republicans to

---

[46] Rosenstone et al. (1984:63). The greater vigor of these third-party movements among western farmers might well have been owed to the fact that nineteenth-century parties were weaker in the West and thus less able to suppress electoral challenges. Shefter suggested this point to us in a personal communication.

[47] Ibid. (65).

[48] Polakoff (1981:251). For a breakdown of the regional basis of Greenback support, see Burnham (1981c:155–56 and table 5.1) and Kleppner (1981b:126–29).

elect a governor in 1881.[49] Electoral challenges also recurred in the North. In the spring of 1884, the new Anti-Monopoly party declared itself, on essentially the same platform as the Greenbacks, but the economy was stronger, and the party's candidate won few votes. Still, third-party efforts persisted. In 1886, the United Labor party in New York City came close to winning the mayoralty election with Henry George as its candidate.[50]

Then, in the early 1890s, the Farmers' Alliances entered the electoral lists. The Alliances came to third-party politics gradually and reluctantly, for the strategy on which their movement had been built ignored and even scorned "politics." The movement's organizing strategy rested instead on building producer cooperatives in an effort to buoy prices and keep the cost of credit down. But as the cooperatives foundered on business opposition, particularly by banks that denied credit, the movement increasingly turned from the cooperative crusade to an electoral crusade against "centralized capital, allied to irresponsible corporate power."[51] The program adopted by the state Farmers' Alliances meeting in St. Louis in 1889 (and endorsed by the Knights of Labor) echoed and expanded upon most of the demands of preceding third-party movements: the abolition of national banks and the expansion of the currency, government ownership of communication and transportation, equitable taxation, and the adoption of the Alliance "subtreasury" plan through which the federal government itself would underwrite the farmers' cooperatives. "Populism," Richard Hofstadter concluded, "was the first modern political movement of practical importance in the United States to insist that the federal government had some responsibility for the common weal; indeed, it was the first such movement to attack seriously the problems caused by industrialism."[52]

---

[49] Polakoff (1981:248).
[50] See Shefter (1986:270–71).
[51] Goodwyn (1978:114).
[52] Hofstadter (1955:61).

With this program, the Alliances entered a number of state electoral contests in 1890, trying to capture local Democratic organizations in the South, and fielding third-party candidates in the West. "Conditions in 1890 were ripe for a political push," [53] as drought in the West added to the perennial problems of the farmers. "Lecturers" moved across the farm states to build support for Alliance-backed candidates running on a program calling for an expanded (and democratically controlled) currency, and regulation of railroad and granary rates. When the returns were counted, they had won fifty-two seats in the House, three Senate seats, three governorships, and majorities in seven state legislatures. [54]

After this heady beginning, the Alliances announced in 1892 the formation of the People's party, convened a national convention, and prepared to enter the presidential campaign behind the candidacy of James B. Weaver, the perennial third-party candidate. This time, however, Weaver won 8.5 percent of the vote, supplanting the Democrats as the opposition party in Nebraska, South Dakota, and Oregon, ousting the Republicans in Texas, Mississippi, and Alabama, and gaining outright majorities in Colorado, Idaho, Kansas, and Nevada. Weaver's twenty-two electoral votes were, in fact, the first to be won by a third party since 1860. Then, in the watershed campaign of 1896, the People's party coalesced with the Democratic party by supporting William Jennings Bryan, the Democratic presidential nominee. With that action, the Populists launched a national election campaign in which economic elites revealed their fear of an enfranchised populace more plainly than ever before in American history.

---

[53] Rosenstone (1984:70).
[54] Ibid. As it turned out, however, the new party had little leverage over its erstwhile candidates once they were elected. See Sundquist (1973:121) and Woodward (1951:241).

THE DEMOCRATIC COUNTERREVOLUTION
AND THE CAMPAIGN OF 1896

In hindsight, the challenge posed by the farmers' movement may seem to have been hopeless, and for several reasons. For one thing, the effort by largely Protestant farmers to build a national coalition with the largely immigrant and Catholic working class ran against the grain of ethnoreligious politics. For another, experience in the United States had already showed how difficult third-party contests were to win, and how elusive the results. From the outset, electoral efforts by the farmers in the South were battered by old-line Democrats who employed frenzied race baiting, as well as force and fraud, to defeat them.[55] Just as serious, in Goodwyn's opinion, was the ingrained loyalty of most southern farmers to "the party of the fathers," a factor that helps account for the reluctance of southern Populists to turn to electoral politics in the first place (and for their eventual alliance with the Democratic party).[56] Then, as the farmers' cause nevertheless gained momentum, it was often the case that southern Democrats simply overwhelmed the Populists by co-opting their issues and their rhetoric. "By the mid-nineties, no stump speech in the South was complete without blasts at the railroads, the trusts, Wall Street, the gold bugs, the saloonkeepers, or some similarly evil 'Interest.' "[57] William Jennings Bryan was just such a master of the rhetoric of the common man, as in the peroration of his address to the Democratic nominating convention in 1896:

> You come to us and tell us that the great cities are in favor of the gold standard; we reply that the great cities rest upon

[55] See, for example, the discussion in Kousser (1974:37).
[56] Goodwyn (1978:142); Woodward (1951: chapters 9 and 10).
[57] Kousser (1974:38).

our broad and fertile prairies. Burn down your cities and leave our farms, and your cities will spring up again as if by magic; but destroy our farms and the grass will grow in the streets of every city in the country. . . . Having behind us the producing masses of this nation and the world, supported by . . . the laboring interests and toilers everywhere, we will answer their demand for a gold standard by saying to them: You shall not press down upon the brow of labor this crown of thorns, you shall not crucify mankind upon a cross of gold.[58]

Such rhetoric helps to explain why the Populists abandoned their third-party movement and endorsed Bryan, the Democratic candidate. But the price of coalition was high. Very little of the bold Populist critique of industrial capitalism, or of its visionary program of economic cooperation, was evident in the ensuing campaign. Even the currency issue was emasculated: if once the Populists had sweepingly called for wresting control of the monetary system from the nation's bankers, the Democratic-Populist campaign demanded only the minting of silver currency.

But industrialists and bankers did not have the benefit, if such it is, of the hindsight that seems to make history as it happened inevitable. Their alarm was palpable, not only because the farmers' movement had spread to reach the still-large proportions of the population in agriculture, but also because of the threat that the campaign might become the vehicle through which a coalition would be forged with discontented industrial workers in the Northeast and Midwest. Nor was the possibility of a farmer-labor coalition entirely a fantasy. The campaign occurred while the country was mired in the major depression that had begun in 1893, and in the wake of the 1894 strike wave, the largest in the nation's history to that time. The Greenback-Labor party had drawn substantial support from voters in

---

[58] Cited in Polakoff (1981:260).

the Northeast in 1878, at a similar conjuncture of depression and class conflict. And beginning in 1886, when the fledgling Texas Alliance had organized a boycott in support of the striking Knights of Labor, the Farmers' Alliances had often worked self-consciously to gain the support of workers. To smooth the way for coalition with the Knights, the National Farmers' Alliance was renamed the Farmers' and Laborers' Union of America in 1889. The meeting in St. Louis in 1892 announcing the formation of the People's party surged with enthusiasm when Ignatius Donnelly took up the rhetorical banner of labor with a ringing denunciation of "corporations, national banks, rings, trusts," not only because they plundered farmers, but because "urban workmen are denied the right of organization for self-protection, imported pauperized labor beats down their wages, a hireling standing army, unrecognized by our laws, is established to shoot them down, and they are rapidly disintegrating to European conditions."[59] The platform adopted by the People's party went on to denounce the Pinkertons, who were, of course, the "hireling standing army."

Of themselves, these pleas for farmer-labor unity probably would not have caused the propertied classes much alarm, particularly since the electoral successes of the Populists had been confined entirely to states in the West and the South. Certainly, the responses by organized labor were not thunderous. The young American Federation of Labor merely endorsed a number of the Populist planks. In 1893, insurgents within the Knights of Labor toppled an increasingly timid Terence Powderly with the demand that the Knights should support the farmers' third-party challenge,[60] but by this time the Knights were overshadowed by the growing AF of L. Still, no one could be sure. Economic depressions had triggered electoral convulsions earlier in the nineteenth century, and the new electoral challenge sought

[59] Goodwyn (1978:168).
[60] Shefter (1986:257).

to tap discontents that had surfaced again and again in the preceding decades. Moreover, popular attitudes were becoming more hostile toward business. Galambos sums up his investigations of public opinion during the period:

> [A]n entire generation of Americans had acquired distinctive attitudes toward big business. Each of the occupational groups studied . . . had become increasingly perturbed about the trusts; all had seen the combination movement spread to a wider range of major industries; all had changed their concept of the corporation in some significant way. The most general pattern that emerges is one of mounting hostility. . . . Neutral attitudes gave way as Americans vented their anger against the trusts and syndicates that were remaking the structure of the industrial economy.[61]

Under these unstable and unfamiliar conditions, the Democratic-Populist challenge was alarming, even horrifying, and to wealthy Democrats as well as Republicans.

Accordingly, corporate interests mobilized, and poured unprecedented sums into Republican coffers for the McKinley campaign, while the Bryan campaign was able to raise only $300,000, a small fraction of the funds contributed by Cleveland's supporters in 1892.[62] The huge railroad conglomerates, such as the New York Central and the Pennsylvania Railroad, took the lead, followed by such corporate combinations as Standard Oil, J. P. Morgan, and New York Life. Some $3,500,000 was raised for the operations of the Republican National Committee alone, which then proceeded to organize a campaign whose scale, says McGerr, was "truly original" in American politics.[63] With virtually unlimited resources to draw upon, a

---

[61] Galambos (1975:112).

[62] See Polakoff (1981:263).

[63] McGerr (1986:140–41). As McGerr goes on to say, this amount does not take account of the funds spent by other Republican operations. The Chicago Literary Bureau, for example, spent $500,000, and "poured out" more than a hundred million documents.

campaign strategy unfolded under the leadership of Mark Hanna, himself a wealthy coal magnate, that was to become the model for the twentieth-century big-money political advertising extravaganza. But the themes that were advertised looked backward rather than forward, resonating with nineteenth-century political culture. Across the land, the newly centralized Republican organization raised the alarm about the threat to "sound money" posed by the Democratic-Populist challenge, a monetary doctrine linked by incantation to national honor and prosperity. And the Republican campaign did not hesitate to appropriate the Flag and "wave the bloody shirt," reminding the nation of persisting deep sectional fissures with marching companies, "sound money" processions, flag-raisings, and a national (but Republican) Flag Day.[64]

The challenge of 1896 was turned aside not only by the sheer weight of the Republican-corporate mobilization, but by weaknesses in the Democratic-Populist fusion as well. In the Metropole, the vast majority of urban workers rebuffed the Populist appeal for a farmer-labor alliance. The Populist coalition with the Democratic party, which had presided over the depression of 1893, the most severe thus far in American history, was surely one reason.[65] Another was the disarray in Democratic ranks in the wake of the depression, as the silverites split with eastern financial interests, which helped to account for the rout of the Democrats in the midterm election of 1894. In addition, urban workers did, in fact, have grounds to think the Republican economic program was in their economic interests. They would share in the increases in jobs and wages associated with protective tariffs and a sound money policy, while the free silver issue and commodity price inflation that came to define the

---

[64] The Republican campaign is described in McGerr (1986:137–45), and Goodwyn (1978:279–83).

[65] Sundquist (1973:132) reports that during 1893 alone, "one-sixth of the nation's railroads, more than six hundred banks and other financial institutions, and some thirty-two iron and steel companies failed."

Democratic-Populist campaign had little meaning to workers in the midst of a depression economy.

Finally, there was the strong and steady hold of tribalism. Whatever the efforts of the Populist leaders to heal the rifts of religion and section, these powerful identifications were deeply rooted in memory and fixed by symbol and association. The farmers remained a movement of Protestants and nativists, now spearheaded by the Bryan of evangelical Protestant oratory, and this must have been alienating to a heavily Catholic urban working class.[66] Similarly, the Republican sectional appeal to memories of the Civil War resonated with the northern workers who had paid the blood price for the war.

All of this helps to explain the Republican victory, won by a substantially larger margin than had decided presidential contests in the preceding decades. McKinley received 7,035,000 votes to Bryan's 6,467,000.[67] More telling, Democratic-Populist support was almost entirely confined to the western and southern periphery of the country. Bryan failed totally in the bid to appeal to urban working-class voters. As Burnham sums it up, the 1892–96 swing to the Republicans was only 2.9 percent in nonmetropolitan areas, but 23.3 percent in metropolitan ones.[68]

The election of 1896 was one of the most decisive in American history, the historic marker denoting the passing of the "populist moment,"[69] and the ascendance in national politics of the conservative wing of the Republican party. At a deeper structural level, it was important because it facilitated the introduction of a series of sweeping changes in American electoral institutions that made possible the near total domination of the Republican

---

[66] For this analysis, see Jensen (1971: chapter 10).

[67] The margin of Republican victory was wide only by comparison with the narrow margins by which presidential contests had been decided in earlier elections during the intensely competitive post–Civil War period. In fact, 1896 was the first in a series of elections in which the presidency was decided by comparatively large majorities.

[68] Burnham (1981c:182).

[69] See Goodwyn (1978 and 1976: chapters 16 and 17). See also Jensen (1971: chapter 10).

party by business in the North and of the Democratic party by planter interests in the South. These changes, taken together, constitute what Schattschneider called "the system of 1896."[70] The system's most important and long-lasting feature was the secular decline in voting that it initiated, a decline that with relatively minor variations has persisted throughout the twentieth century.

THE DEMOBILIZATION OF THE
NINETEENTH-CENTURY ELECTORATE

The movements of the late nineteenth century culminating in the challenge of 1896 signaled that American popular politics was breaking out of the constrained patterns of participation that were both created and limited by tribalism and clientelism. But even as a more issue-oriented popular politics emerged, voting by poor farmers and workers began to decline. As voter participation steadily contracted, the grievances of poor workers and

TABLE 2.2 PRESIDENTIAL TURNOUT PERCENTAGES, 1896–1924

	South	*Non-South*	*National*
1896	57	86	79
1900	43	83	74
1904	29	77	66
1908	31	76	66
1912	28	68	59
1916	32	69	62
1920	22	55	49
1924	19	57	49

Source: Burnham (1981c:100, table 1). Based on total of all citizens legally eligible to vote, aliens excluded.

[70] Schattschneider (1960).

farmers disappeared from the agenda of national politics. By the 1920s, the low point of electoral turnout, businessmen (and planters) not only dominated both parties, but it was business rhetoric that defined the political alternatives open to Americans.

Between the elections of 1896 and 1920, turnout fell from 79 to 49 percent (table 2.2).[71] The southern declines came first, and were more extreme—from 57 percent in the election of 1896, to 43 percent in 1900, to 29 percent in 1904, to a low point of 19 percent in 1924. Blacks and most poor whites virtually disappeared from the polls. The contraction of the electoral universe outside the South was less sharp and less rapid—from 86 percent in 1896 to 57 percent in 1924. The decline was concentrated among the immigrant young, large numbers of whom never appeared at the polls as they came of age.[72] We should note that the northern decline cannot be explained by the low turnout of women who gained the suffrage in 1920.[73] The downward trend began before 1920, and it persisted afterwards,

[71] We should note that the turnout levels in the nineteenth century are very probably inflated by the undercounting of the voting-age population, owing to the crude counting techniques employed by the Census Bureau. Using various retroactive estimations, Shortridge judges that the consequent rate of inflation of turnout might have been 10 percent. When this adjustment is made, the "sharp differences in turnout between the nineteenth century and the twentieth century tend to diminish" (1981:47). The issue is not simply a technical one, since different estimates of nineteenth-century turnout support different explanations of turnout decline. See Rusk (1974:1041) and Converse (1972:290) in their debate with Burnham, whose argument hinges on high turnout in the nineteenth century. In fact, Burnham (1974b:1004) also acknowledges the enumeration problem. We think that Shortridge's proposed qualification is sensible. Underenumeration does not, however, explain the sharp downward trend in turnout from 79 percent in the election of 1896 to an average of 60 percent in the elections of 1912 and 1916, unless one makes the improbable assumption that census procedures were so radically improved in this period as to expand the enumerated voting-age population by fully one-third. It therefore seems reasonable to conclude that while turnout in the nineteenth century may be overestimated, the relative magnitude of the drop in turnout that began in the early twentieth century is not.

[72] See Kleppner and Baker (1980:218–19).

[73] One explanation of the granting of female suffrage is that politicians were confident that mainly middle- and upper-class women would make use of it, thus further diluting the working-class vote.

even when the lower rates of voting by women are taken into account.[74]

The demobilization of the American electorate in the wake of the election of 1896 was to become a massive influence in the shaping of twentieth-century political development. However, the electoral demobilization was gradual, and popular protests continued for a time. There was ample provocation. The pace of industrial concentration that had generated discontent in the North before 1896 did not slow down, and millions of new immigrants poured into the crowded and pestilent cities, and into the maws of the industrial machine.[75] Strikes became more frequent, often leading to local warfare.[76] Moreover, political radicalism among insurgent workers increasingly took form in socialist and anarcho-syndicalist associations, such as the renowned Industrial Workers of the World (IWW).

Furthermore, because turnout fell gradually in the North, the triumph of northern business in the election of 1896 did not entirely suppress electoral challenges. Even third-party efforts reemerged after an interlude of prosperity during the first decade of the twentieth century.[77] In 1912, Eugene Debs's bid for the presidency on the Socialist party ticket captured 6 percent of the vote. Then a resurgence of farmer radicalism in the West, beginning with the North Dakota Nonpartisan League, spread to Minnesota, South Dakota, Wisconsin, and Washington. The Nonpartisan League elected a governor in North Dakota in 1916 and, later, under the banner of the Farmer-Labor party, also elected two senators, two congressmen, and a governor in Min-

[74] Kleppner (1982:69–70).

[75] By 1904, for example, a thousand railroad lines had been consolidated into six great combinations, each allied with either the Morgan or the Rockefeller empire (Zinn, 1980:316).

[76] Zinn reports that while there had been a thousand strikes a year in the 1890s, there were four thousand strikes each year by 1904. See also Montgomery (1979).

[77] Zinn (1980:331). The downturns of 1903 and 1907 were relatively minor, and the more serious depression of 1913–14 was overcome quickly as European war-production orders revived the economy.

nesota.[78] And in 1917, the Socialists scored impressive victories in a series of municipal and state elections.[79]

Nor during this interim was Republican domination entirely secure. True, Republican majorities in the presidential contests of 1900, 1904, and 1908 were substantially larger than they had been during the closely contested elections of the late nineteenth century; and the Republican party dominated the Congress during this period as well. But the language of one-party hegemony with which historians often describe the outcome of the election of 1896 overstates the firmness and durability of Republican control. As early as 1910, the Democrats made something of a comeback, capturing the House of Representatives and twenty-six governorships, including the state houses in Massachusetts, Connecticut, New York, New Jersey, Ohio, and Indiana.[80]

Accordingly, national electoral politics was not, in fact, insulated from currents of popular discontent, at least not until after World War I. Indeed, contemporaries saw these years as a period of extraordinary reform and innovation, and so do many scholars. The rhetoric of progressivism employed by national political leaders from Theodore Roosevelt to William Taft to Woodrow Wilson, together with the string of legislative initiatives they sponsored, constitutes persuasive evidence of the seriousness accorded to persisting popular discontents by national elites. However little these reforms may have changed the lot of working people, national politicians nevertheless felt the need to conciliate. Legislation proliferated: tax reform, railroad regulation, antitrust laws, the outlawing of child labor (later ruled unconstitutional), pure food and meat inspection, the establish-

[78] For a concise discussion of the electoral successes of this generation of farmer insurgents, see Sundquist (1973:168–71).

[79] The Socialist candidate for mayor of New York City, Morris Hillquit, won 22 percent of the vote, and ten Socialists were sent to the New York state legislature. In Chicago, the Socialists won 34.7 percent of the vote, and in Buffalo, 30.2 percent (Zinn, 1980:356). See also Weinstein (1969).

[80] Polakoff (1981:287–88).

ment of the Federal Reserve System and a new and separate government-sponsored system of agricultural credit, a model workmen's compensation law covering federal employees, and federal aid for highways, vocational education, and agricultural extension services. A constitutional amendment provided for the direct election of senators, and another extended the franchise to women.[81]

The propaganda that accompanied this star-studded array of legislation celebrated the aspirations of the popular struggles of the late nineteenth and early twentieth centuries, rather than the doctrine of *laissez faire*. A delegate to the People's party convention of 1908 exclaimed that "Roosevelt's messages read like the preamble of the Populist platform."[82] Four years later, when Roosevelt tried to regain the presidency after the Republican party refused to renominate him in favor of the incumbent Taft, he ran under the banner of the new Progressive party and on a platform calling for social insurance to buffer people against the income losses resulting from industrial accidents, unemployment, sickness, and old age, for the abolition of child labor and convict leasing, for the regulation of interstate corporations and corporate securities, for women's suffrage, and for restrictions on labor injunctions. The Democratic platform incorporated the same themes; it denounced trusts, and called for stricter railroad regulation, a national income tax, and the prohibition of corporate contributions to political campaigns. During the Wilson-Roosevelt campaign, Wilson warned that

> the great monopoly in this country is the money monopoly.
> . . . The growth of the nation, therefore, and all our activities are in the hands of a few men who necessarily, by the very reason of their own limitations, chill and check and destroy genuine economic freedom.[83]

[81] Sundquist (1973:162).
[82] Ibid. (163).
[83] Polakoff (1981:290–91).

Meanwhile, Roosevelt proclaimed himself to be

> for the liberty of the oppressed, and not for the liberty of
> the oppressor to oppress the weak and bind the burden on
> the shoulders of the heavy laden. It is idle to ask us not to
> exercise the power of government when only by that power
> of the government can we curb the greed that sits in the
> high places, when only by the exercise of the government
> can we exalt the lowly and give heart to the humble and
> downtrodden.[84]

Of course, none of this was what it seemed to be. Roosevelt
was a big-business president. Hofstadter points out that "the
advisers to whom Roosevelt listened were almost exclusively representatives of industrial and finance capital—men like Hanna
. . . George W. Perkins of the House of Morgan . . . A. J.
Cassatt of the Pennsylvania Railroad, Philander C. Knox, and
James Stillman of the Rockefeller interests."[85] And Hofstadter
goes on to show that Roosevelt's intention in supporting concili-
atory government interventions was to thwart popular demands
for stronger intervention.[86] Trust-busting legislation broke few
trusts; the new regulatory agencies worked closely with the businesses they regulated; the Federal Reserve System met the demands of the banking industry for a mechanism to regulate
finance in an era of extreme instability, not the pleas of hard-
pressed family farmers.[87] When Congress passed section 20 of
the Clayton Act in an effort to exempt unions from antitrust
injunctions, the Supreme Court subsequently declared otherwise.
And Roosevelt's calls for social insurance, the abolition of child

[84] Ibid.
[85] Hofstadter (1948:222).
[86] Hofstadter (1948: chapter 9). See also Zinn (1980:342–43).
[87] Hofstadter recounts Wilson's rebuff of the bankers' demand for outright control of the
Federal Reserve Board. But he makes clear that this was mostly a matter of allowing Wilson
to feel independent (1948:258–59).

labor, and restrictions on labor injunctions were not to be acted upon for nearly thirty years. The reforms of the Progressive era could be summed up, Kolko thought, as "political capitalism." [88]

While the legislative initiatives of the Progressive era were clearly less than the rhetoric of the period, our central point is that the Progressive agenda as a whole constitutes evidence that business domination of electoral politics was still far from secure. Turnout was edging downward, but slowly. Meanwhile, tribalism and clientelism were also weakening, and as they did, popular discontent with industrial capitalism emerged into national politics in the form of movement struggles and electoral challenges. Their impact could be read in the new language of economic reform spoken by contenders for rulership.

Left interpretations of the Progressive era tend to overlook the extent to which it laid the basis for the popular movements and electoral remobilization that occurred during the Great Depression. The rhetorical acknowledgment of grievances helped legitimate them. And the federal legislation of the Progressive period, however biased toward capital, established a framework of precedents that undermind *laissez-faire* doctrine by exposing it as transparently false. Economy and polity were not the separate spheres they were proclaimed to be. Taken together, these ideological and structural shifts foreshadowed the interventions of the New Deal.

But Progressivism ended, as voter turnout dropped to half the eligible electorate by World War I, and to far less of the working-class electorate. Once turnout fell, elite domination of electoral politics became more or less complete, with the consequence that government postures and policies became increasingly antagonistic to farmers and workers. To be sure, the wartime need for a production mobilization and the lingering credo of progressivism led the administration to placate the in-

[88] Kolko (1977). See also Weinstein (1968).

creasingly mainstream AF of L, whose longtime president, Samuel Gompers, had served as first vice-president of that flagship of progressivism, the business-dominated National Civic Federation. But the jingoism associated with the entry of the United States into the war also provided the occasion for a crackdown on working-class radicalism. A good many insurgent working-class leaders were rounded up and imprisoned, including most of the top leadership of the IWW, as well as many Socialists who opposed the war, including Eugene Debs.[89] When the war ended, the national political climate moved sharply to the right. The strikes that spread in 1919, as workers tried to win higher wages to cope with rapid wartime inflation, were smashed by government firepower. In Seattle, a general strike early in the year was broken by thousands of special deputies and the United States Army and Navy. Calvin Coolidge, governor of Massachusetts, achieved national prominence and the Republican nomination for vice-president after ordering the National Guard to put down the Boston police strike and then firing the entire striking force. Later that year, 350,000 steelworkers struck in an effort to win back the union that had been smashed in 1892. The strike was broken in part by local police and sheriffs' deputies, and by Justice Department raiders who rounded up striking aliens for deportation, while federal troops protected strikebreakers in Gary, Indiana.[90] Some 120,000 textile workers struck in New England and New Jersey, as well as silk workers in Paterson, New Jersey. By summer, cities such as New York and Chicago were alive with strikes, and most of them were broken by force. Then, on January 2, 1920, Attorney General A. Mitchell Palmer took advantage of labor turmoil (and alarm over the Bolshevik revolution) to announce that there was a

[89] On repression during the World War I period, including a proposal to round up radicals and detain them in camps in the central Pacific, see Burns (1985:499–507); Zinn (1980: chapter 14); and Goldstein (1978).
[90] Zinn (1980:372).

radical plot to seize power in the United States, and rounded up four thousand alleged revolutionaries, mainly foreign born.[91]

In the election of 1920, the Republican platform roundly denounced strikes; its only concession to farmers suffering once more from plummeting agricultural prices was to call for the "scientific study of agricultural prices and farm production costs"; and it condemned the League of Nations.[92] Among those still voting, the Republicans won overwhelmingly and Harding took office in the midst of another depression. At a time when European governments were inaugurating unemployment insurance, Harding turned to the high-tariff policies of the nineteenth century for a solution that clearly protected industry more than it protected workers.[93] Then, as farm prices plummeted still further, he announced that "it cannot be too strongly urged that the farmer must be ready to help himself."[94] In 1923, Congress passed the Mellon Plan, sponsored by Secretary of the Treasury Andrew Mellon, which cut taxes in the top brackets by half, from 50 percent to 25 percent, while reducing the lowest bracket from 4 percent to 3 percent.[95]

The 1924 election produced another business and Republican government. The Democrats were in disarray, torn between the combined southern and western wing, whose candidate, William Gibbs McAdoo, tacitly accepted the support of the growing Ku Klux Klan, and the big-city politicians led by Al Smith. The deadlocked convention went through 103 raucous ballots before settling on John W. Davis, a conservative Wall Street lawyer. Meanwhile, the Republicans nominated Calvin Coolidge over

---

[91] On political hysteria in the United States, see Levin (1971).

[92] Polakoff (1981:303).

[93] The Emergency Tariff of 1921 applied mainly to agricultural products, which made little sense since the United States was primarily an exporter of agricultural goods. A year later, the Fordney-McCumber Tariff of 1922 partially restored the high tariffs that had been enacted after the election of 1896, but had been lowered in 1909 under the Taft administration (Polakoff, 1981:305).

[94] Ibid. (306).

[95] Zinn (1980:375).

Robert La Follette by 1,065 votes to 34. The election itself was a landslide, and another business president ascended to power. Coolidge slashed the federal budget, proclaimed *laissez faire* as the guiding doctrine of his regime (the tariff excepted), complacently staffed the federal regulatory agencies that had been created in response to the popular struggles of earlier decades with representatives of industry, and vetoed a proposal for the development of public power at Muscle Shoals, as well as a series of farm bills intended to stabilize crop prices.[96] The corporate forces that had mobilized in the context of 1896 were now in full command.

The domination of both parties by economic elites would have been less complete were it not for the sharp decline in voting. As turnout fell, national politics moved sharply to the right, each development both cause and consequence of the other. We turn now to the question of what it was about "the system of 1896" that explains why that drop occurred. After nearly a century of vigorous participation, how were large sectors of the American electorate demobilized?

[96] Polakoff (1981:315–16).

Chapter 3

How Demobilization
Was Accomplished

A good deal of what has been written in explanation of declining turnout at the close of the nineteenth century fastens on the consequences of the election of 1896—its impact on party competition and especially the impact of the crushing electoral defeat of the Populists. We think the preoccupation with the election is misleading because it presumes that this particular defeat was more telling and enduring than earlier electoral defeats, including the massive reversals that the Republicans suffered only a few years earlier in the elections of 1890 and 1892.[1] It also fails to explain why the subsequent restoration of party competition—first in the North during the 1930s and then in the South in the 1960s—was not accompanied by a return to nineteenth-century levels of turnout. An adequate explanation must look beyond the election of 1896 to the reconstruction of the institutional order of electoral politics that unfolded at the end of the nineteenth century and the beginning of the twentieth. We will be preoccupied with these developments in both this chapter and

---

[1] Converse (1972:301) warns that "in most instances where the division of the vote swerves dramatically in a particular election, the worst prediction for the next election is an extrapolation of the trend."

the next. We turn first to an account of the institutional changes themselves. In the next chapter, we will examine the academic debates about the bearing of these developments on nonvoting.

The impact of the election of 1896 was lasting because it occurred in the context of a series of legal and procedural "reforms" that both reduced the ability of the parties to organize voters and disenfranchised many voters. The elite mobilizations that secured these reforms were not simply a response to the election of 1896, although it is arguable that the election had a galvanizing effect on some of these efforts. Rather, the reconstruction of the legal and procedural underpinnings of party organization and voter participation began before 1896 and continued afterward. This trend can be understood as a pervasive response by American elites to the rising level of conflict and electoral challenge during the closing decades of the nineteenth century. Only by attending to the interaction between the changing patterns of party competition and the rules governing party organization and voter participation can the decline in voter turnout be satisfactorily explained.

THE DECLINE OF PARTY COMPETITION

Party competition virtually collapsed in much of the country, with the result that the parties lost their incentive to enlist voters and people their incentive to vote. Schattschneider underlines this feature of the system of 1896 in the single most influential explanation of the ensuing transformation in electoral politics. Before 1896, the major parties were more or less in equilibrium. To be sure, the sectional alignment that crystallized in 1896 was prefigured in the third-party system created by the Civil War, in the sense that Republican strength was concentrated in the North, and Democratic strength in the South and Border States.

But neither region was exclusively dominated by one party, and national elections were contested on roughly equal terms.[2]

The election of 1896 left the Democratic party greatly weakened in the North and the Republican party virtually destroyed in the South. Burnham shows that in the northeastern and north-central states, Republican presidential pluralities increased from a mean of 3.6 percent in the period 1876 to 1892, to a mean of 21 percent in the period from 1896 to 1928. Moreover,

> There is an enormous increase in noncompetitive Republican bulwarks at the grass roots level. The pattern is not monolithic as in the South. But among the most industrially and socially developed states in the Union, we find one-party Republican hegemony throughout lower New England, Pennsylvania, Illinois, Michigan, Wisconsin, and California. [Later] these states are joined by Ohio and New Jersey. Of the fourteen states of the Metropole, three were one-party Republican bastions in the 1874–1892 period, nine in the 1894 period, eleven in the 1911–1930 period, and four in the 1932–50 period.[3]

Meanwhile, in the South, where party competition had always been weaker, Democratic party pluralities in presidential contests

[2] See Kleppner (1981b:124–25 and table 4.3) for a regional breakdown of party strength in the 1876–92 period.

[3] Burnham (1981c:180). Burnham (1981c:183) goes on to say that the "proportion of geographical areas in which there was relatively close two-party competition showed a strong tendency to decline across the 1896–1930 era. In particular, the near Midwest became much more solidly Republican at most levels of election after World War I than it had been before. By 1924 close Republican-Democratic competition at the presidential level had come to be confined almost exclusively to the Border states and counties immediately adjacent to them, the Appalachian uplands of the South, and the two southernmost Mountain states, Arizona and New Mexico." See also Kleppner (1982:26 and table 2.6) for longitudinal measures of declining competition. Schattschneider (1960:82–83) presents tables showing the singular impact of the election of 1896 itself on sectional party strength. And Carlson (1976:134 and table 4.1) contains a state-by-state accounting of partisan shifts between 1896 and 1930.

increased from 28.9 percent in the period before 1896 to 42.3 percent in the later period.[4] "The resulting party lineup was one of the most sharply sectional political divisions in American political history."[5]

A related change was the increasingly oligarchical character of both parties. Coming after several decades of turbulent agrarian and industrial conflict, the events of 1896 mobilized northern manufacturing interests to participate in electoral politics through the Republican party on a larger scale than ever before. In the South, the decade-long organizing efforts of the Farmers' Alliances provoked commercial, landowning, and financial elites to line up behind the region's traditional Democratic party leaders. Once the Populist organizing campaign had been wrecked, these groups gained undisputed control of southern state governments.[6] Meanwhile, "There seems little doubt that, at some point in the second decade of the system of 1896, a very large class skew in [voter] participation opened up and that it tended to grow across the lifetime of the system."[7]

These changes were mutually reinforcing. The elimination of party competition facilitated internal oligarchy, and sustained it over the longer run. Once electoral contests were reduced to largely internal party affairs in much of the country, at least in national elections, the influence of voters on the calculations of party leaders diminished, and the influence of economic elites commensurately increased. "The results of the big Republican monopoly in the North and the little Democratic monopoly in the South were much the same," says Schattschneider.[8] As the absence of party competition made voters less important to party leaders, "both sections became more conservative because *one-*

---

[4] Burnham (1974c:672, table 6).

[5] Schattschneider (1960:79).

[6] Ferguson's (1983) effort to recast the concept of critical elections as resulting not from electoral realignments but investor realignments is perhaps especially illuminating of this period of party development. See Ferguson (1984) for a further discussion.

[7] Burnham (1981c:192).

[8] Schattschneider (1960:85).

party politics tends to strongly vest political power in the hands of people who already have economic power." [9] Hence, the sectional realignment of 1896 and the accompanying decline of electoral competition buttressed the rising power of corporate elites in the Republican party, and of regional southern elites in the Democratic party.

Schattschneider and Burnham also think that as the parties came more firmly under the control of economic oligarchs in the North and South, issue appeals disappeared from campaigns. (Kleppner holds the parallel view that ethnoreligious appeals softened as well.) We suspect that this is only partly right. While the parties of the system of 1896 did not reflect the class cleavages of a growing industrial society or boldly articulate the issues that divided it, neither did the earlier tribalist and clientelist parties of the nineteenth century. [10] What can perhaps be said is that, as it unfolded, the system of 1896 inhibited the development of a class- and issue-oriented politics that was perhaps becoming possible as the clientelist party system weakened.

These quibbles aside, we think that uncontested elections and internal oligarchy help to account for the atrophy of voter interest often attributed to the system of 1896. [11] Voter disinterest or alienation, in turn, is one explanation of the steady slide in turnout levels after 1896. This is consistent with the widely held

[9] Ibid. (1960:80). Schattschneider's view assumes the absence of effectively contested primaries with a mass electorate. In fact, even after direct primaries were introduced early in the twentieth century, they tended toward a factional politics centered on individuals, with very narrow participation. See Key (1956:169–96).

[10] Thus Kleppner's (1982:148–49) description of the major parties in the decade after the debacle of 1896 does not much distinguish the pre- and post-1896 periods. If anything, it seems a more apt characterization of the party system as it had evolved by the 1920s: "Class-based discontent percolated at the grassroots, but it could not be aggregated by the newly emergent party system. . . . [T]he capitalist consensus limited the scope of partisan disagreement. . . . Since neither major party self-consciously and explicitly represented the economic discontents of the lower strata of society, those group interests remained unpoliticized and unmobilized."

[11] Burnham (1965) in particular stresses the alienation of voters that resulted from the "takeover" of 1896, at least in his earlier work. For a strident attack on this thesis, see Rusk (1974).

view that voter turnout generally falls, and party-voter linkages generally weaken, when competition declines. Thus Burnham describes the alignment established by the election of 1896 as

> a structure of electoral politics marked by a continuous narrowing of organizable general election alternatives. It is, or should be, axiomatic that close relationships exist between the cohesiveness and competitiveness of parties as structures of collective action and the willingness or even the ability of the public to participate in general elections.[12]

And as applied to the United States in the twentieth century by Schattschneider, Burnham, Kleppner, and others, this perspective is sometimes called the *behavioral* interpretation of low voter turnout.

We accept the likelihood that there is a correlation between declining party competition and declining turnout. Still, this explanation is hardly complete.[13] The election of 1896 is frequently described as a landslide that both crushed the Populists and demolished the Democratic party in the North. But why did even a shattering defeat in one election have such pervasive and lasting effects? Why did the voter preferences expressed in 1896 persist? Why was the Republican party able to maintain virtual domination of the North for three decades after 1896, and why was the Democratic party able to maintain even more complete domination of the South until the 1960s? In short, how was the alignment of 1896 institutionalized?

---

[12] Burnham (1981c:190). For a discussion of this relationship that points out some of the ambiguous findings, see Kelley (1967:365–66).

[13] Kleppner, who is a qualified advocate of the party competition or behavioral explanation of falling turnout, also makes this point about the inadequacy of the thesis (1982:73).

THE SYSTEM OF 1896:
THE LEGAL AND INSTITUTIONAL BASES

At least part of the answer lies in a series of legal and institutional changes that began in the closing decades of the nineteenth century and continued into the twentieth century. One set of changes weakened the ability of the local party organizations, especially in the big cities, to enlist working- and lower-class voters. A second set disenfranchised many potentially contentious working- and lower-class voters in the cities, as well as southern blacks and many poor whites in the South. Disenfranchisement was accomplished either by legislating new qualifications for the suffrage or by erecting procedural obstructions, mainly in the form of voter registration requirements. These several legal reforms were interrelated in their effects. Once the local parties were stripped of organizational resources, they were less able to help their constituents hurdle or circumvent the new legal and procedural obstacles to the suffrage.[14] In turn, procedural barriers to working-class turnout weakened the hold of local clientelist parties in the cities and dampened insurgent electoral movements in rural areas, most dramatically in the South. As a result, the groups who had been constituencies for the electoral challenges of the late nineteenth century were gradually purged from the active electorate.

The Assault on the Parties

There are different explanations for the decades-long wave of reforms that weakened the political parties, especially by dimin-

---

[14] Other rule changes that made third-party challenges more difficult also may have inhibited electoral participation, especially in the West. See Argersinger (1980).

ishing their ability to activate and organize lower-status voters. The reformers themselves raised the twin banners of eliminating fraud and inefficiency in city government. These charges had a real basis. Eliminating fraud meant eliminating clientelist parties riddled with corruption and associated with uneducated and rowdy immigrants, and efficiency was understood as government run on business principles in business interests.

However, the deeper reason for the rise of antiparty and anti-suffrage agitation among upper-class businessmen and professionals had to do with the large economic and political changes taking place in post–Civil War America. The rise of business-backed reform can be understood as a defensive response on the one hand to the political disturbances of the late nineteenth century, and on the other as an aggressive effort to gain undisputed control of governmental functions. Business leaders and professionals were unnerved by the hordes of immigrants concentrating in burgeoning city slums, confounded by the strength of the new city political bosses made audacious by their grip on immigrant and working-class voters, shaken by the waves of strikes and riots that began in the 1870s, and then finally jolted by the series of insurgent electoral challenges that culminated in 1896. Nor were industrialists entirely reassured by the victory of 1896, given the scale and persistence of the disturbances associated with the enlarging working class. At the same time, businessmen were prompted by economic expansion to try to assert firmer control of government, especially of those state and local agencies that managed policies important to economic development. In the mid-nineteenth century, government had been involved only intermittently in economic affairs, mainly by dispensing particularistic benefits, such as land grants and favorable tariff rates. But in the decades of rapid and unregulated industrial growth after the Civil War, economic elites began to demand much more from government. These demands anticipated the large role that government on all levels would eventually come to play in a developed capitalist economy—by bringing order to markets, reducing barriers to entry, assuming many of the costs of production, and by alleviating some of the side effects of untrammeled capitalist growth. This was a crucial moment in American development, for the increased dependence of business on the state suggested at least the possibility that new accommodations would have to be reached with the parties and their constituencies. Instead, however, as the need for this array of government interventions began to emerge, the parties, especially local clientelist parties, increasingly came to be seen as a nuisance and an obstruction. American businessmen wanted a widening array of governmental supports without the necessity of dealing with party intermediaries or their voter constituencies. The code words in this effort were efficiency and expertise in government.[15]

Accordingly, during the closing decades of the nineteenth century, the local parties came under progressively more intense assault from a series of business-backed reform movements.[16] The principal targets of the antiparty reformers were the local machines, and the reformers moved on several fronts to weaken them. They formed crusading watchdog organizations to expose corruption and to campaign for efficient government;[17] they fielded reform slates to challenge the machines in local elections; and they mobilized to influence state governments to intervene in city politics. These efforts slowly bore fruit as city and state governments were reorganized. Beginning in the 1870s, public

---

[15] On this point, see McCormick (1981:248); Weibe (1967); and Weinstein (1968: chapter 4).

[16] The several waves of government reform in the late nineteenth and early twentieth century, and the animus toward party organizations, especially toward big-city machines, have been extensively examined. See Weibe (1967); Hays (1958 and 1964); Haber (1964); and Weinstein (1968). Shefter (1978a) distinguishes between the Mugwumps, who advocated a posture of independence toward the parties, and the later Progressive movement, which tried to destroy the parties as an instrument of governance. See also Bridges (1984). There is a debate among historians about whether businessmen or a disgruntled middle class made up the leading edge of these reform campaigns. Hays (1964) and Weinstein (1968) stress the role of business.

[17] McGerr (1986: chapter 4) devotes extensive attention to these extraparty organizations. See his discussion of "educational politics."

jobs gradually were removed from party control by establishing the civil service.[18] Key city functions were reorganized and set up as independent agencies shielded from party influence on the grounds that municipal affairs should properly be run on a nonpartisan basis. And many smaller municipalities whose machine leaders carried less weight in state government simply were put under the control of "expert" city managers or commission forms of government on the grounds that city affairs were properly not political at all.[19] All of this, of course, gradually stripped the urban-based political parties of their patronage resources.[20]

During roughly the same period, a series of electoral reforms—including nonpartisan and at-large elections, the introduction of officially printed ballots (called Australian ballots) during the 1880s and 1890s and, somewhat later, direct primaries—made it more difficult for machines to enlist and control voters. For example, before the introduction of officially printed ballots, each party printed and distributed its own ballot, listing only the names of its candidates, and these were deposited in the ballot box by voters. Party workers could "persuade, cajole, intimidate, and bribe voters to take their ballots as the voters walked to the polling place."[21] Official ballots dealt the clientelist parties a serious blow, since, as Banfield and Wilson say, "the existence of the machine depends upon its ability to control

[18] Shefter (1984:145) suggests a parallel with civil service reform in England. After having been roundly defeated in 1854, reform was rapidly passed on the heels of the extension of the suffrage in 1867, presumably to ensure that the aristocracy and the upper-middle class would not be displaced by the politicians who arose on the basis of newly enfranchised working-class and lower-middle-class voters.

[19] Some three hundred smaller cities were reorganized under a commission form of government between 1900 and 1913, and one hundred were changed to city manager types by 1919, according to Polakoff (1981:277).

[20] Alford and Lee (1968) concluded that "cities without the council-manager form and with partisan elections have higher voting turnout." The difference was large. Median turnout in partisan elections was 50 percent, for example, and only 30 percent in cities with nonpartisan elections. This is consistent with findings reported by Lee (1960). See also Lineberry and Fowler (1967), who concluded that under reformed governments, public policy is less responsive to demands arising out of social conflicts.

[21] Rusk (1974:1901).

votes."[22] And with less ability to control votes, the machine's grip on city and sometimes state governments loosened.[23]

Business-backed reforms gradually weakened the clientelist parties, and diminished their ability to mobilize voters. The alignments in these reform-machine battles were complicated, however. The machines were also closely allied with major business interests, as Lincoln Steffens made vividly clear in *The Shame of the Cities*. The main basis of that alliance was everywhere similar. Machine politicians used their control of public office to dole out franchises, contracts, and the use of the public treasury to businessmen in return for graft. Moreover, clientelist party organizations helped to prevent the political mobilization of working people in opposition to business interests. In other words, the machine provided a method of incorporating working people into politics while keeping their political issues off the electoral agenda, a conclusion reached by Gosnell half a century ago.[24] This may well explain why it was in those rural states where clientelism never took root as strongly that a broad popular movement with a bold political agenda emerged in the late nineteenth century.

Nevertheless, business interests were from the start divided in their responses to the machines. One reason was simply that many businessmen resented the high price machine politicians extracted in taxes and graft, often for indifferent services, or unreliable municipal services and favors. Bridges tells of efforts of New York City businessmen to organize a reform movement as early as the 1850s. The reformers were spurred by the failure of the city council to deliver contracts to businessmen from whom bribes had already been accepted, as well as by rising taxes and the increasingly precarious fiscal circumstances of the city.[25] As the economy and the cities expanded together after the Civil

---

[22] Banfield and Wilson (1963:116).
[23] The definitive study of the Australian or office block ballot is by Rusk (1970).
[24] Gosnell (1937).
[25] Bridges (1987:111 and 1984: chapter 7).

War, the ability of the machines to make some businessmen rich through contracts and franchises expanded. But so did the ire of other major elements in the business community, both because of rising municipal costs and because of the failure of the local parties to deliver efficient and reliable public services and infrastructures. The recurrent reform campaigns in cities across the country during the second half of the nineteenth century were fueled largely by these discontents.

Business interests were also divided in their attitude toward the machines as a reflection of their sharp differences on national economic policy, and particularly the issue of protective tariffs that pitted low-tariff commercial and financial interests against high-tariff industrial interests. Since the national Democratic party opposed tariffs[26] and since the local clientelist parties in the cities of the North were mainly Democratic and were crucial to the fortunes of the national party in the closely contested elections of the 1870s and 1880s, pro-tariff industrial interests had reason to want the machines weakened.[27]

The election of 1896, however, resolved the tariff question in favor of high-tariff industrial interests. At the same time, the Republican sweep dissipated the threat of electoral insurgency from below, and thus made the role of the machine in integrating and controlling the working class less valuable. These developments smoothed the way for the introduction of a new series of legal reforms that struck further blows at the capacities of the party organizations to activate and organize voters.

One change was the introduction of the direct primary in

[26] In the mid-nineteenth century, the major parties had been internally divided on the tariff, but in the elections of 1880 and 1884, the Democratic party gradually adopted a low-tariff position so that the cleavage that divided business interests became a partisan issue. See McGerr (1986:78).

[27] Shefter (1983:467). In personal correspondence with the authors, Shefter makes the additional point that businessmen who supported the national party that was the minority locally —whether Republican or Democratic—were readier to join reform coalitions. For a general discussion of the interrelationship between tariff policy and other key issues of the era, including military pensions, imperialism, and federal intervention in the southern electoral system, see Bensel (1984: chapter 3).

the years between 1903 and 1915. Both V. O. Key and Burnham argue persuasively that the direct primary worked to reinforce one-party domination where it was adopted.[28] And what Burnham calls the "democratic-participatory symbolisms" evoked by the direct primary almost surely made it more difficult for third-party challenges to the dominant parties to emerge.[29]

More frontal assaults on the local clientelist parties also accelerated, usually mounted from the state capitals, where the urban-based clientelist parties could be overwhelmed by business-reformers who staged spectacular investigations of machine corruption. The state legislature redrew the municipal boundaries of New York City in 1898, for example, incorporating the outer boroughs in an effort to swamp the Manhattan-based Tammany organization. Meanwhile,

> The first fifteen years of the twentieth century . . . more precisely, the brief period from 1904 to 1908 saw a remarkable compressed political transformation. During these years the regulatory revolution peaked; new and powerful agencies of government came into being everywhere. At the same time voter turnout declined, ticket-splitting increased, and organized social, economic and reform-minded groups began to exercise power more systematically than ever before.[30]

Very rapidly, investigations of machine-business corruption were initiated in one state after another, involving the life insurance industry in New York, public utility corporations in San Francisco, the railroads in half a dozen states in the Midwest and South, streetcars and utilities in Denver, the liquor industry in Iowa. The result was a battery of new state laws—McCormick

---

[28] Burnham (1981c:166) and Key (1956:169–96). See also Key (1984) for a discussion of the role of the direct primary in the South in promoting a politics of faction.

[29] Burnham (1981c:166)

[30] McCormick (1981:271).

counted 130 laws in selected categories between 1903 and 1908 —regulating lobbying, prohibiting corporate contributions to campaigns, regulating or limiting free railroad passes for public officials, and establishing commissions to regulate railroads.[31]

"Electoral mobilization," in Kleppner's recapitulation, "has always depended on the active intervention of mobilizing agents —political parties."[32] Whatever the limits of voter participation built on the clientelist and tribalist appeals of the nineteenth century, the investment in these appeals by the parties did signal that party leaders needed working-class voters and had the organizational capacity to activate them. But after the turn of the century, the local parties, weakened by relentless reform assaults, were less able to reach voters, by any method at all. The great spectacles and celebrations, the marching bands and parades, that had punctuated earlier campaigns faded away. Even ethnoreligious election appeals lost the force and fire of an earlier era, and Republican campaigns in particular became almost ecumenical.

As party connections to the working-class electorate atrophied, a gradual demobilization of voters occurred. The slide in turnout was one sign. Another, more specifically revealing of the attenuating connection between party and electorate, was the erosion of party-line voting, with the result that a degree of fragmentation began to appear in electoral results that was unknown earlier in the nineteenth century. Republican hegemony in the North in national and especially presidential contests was modified by the simultaneous erosion of the partisanship that had characterized nineteenth-century voting patterns. State and local election results increasingly diverged from national results, so that Democratic victories on the state and local level were not unusual. Burnham characterizes this development as the beginning of the "fragmented" politics of the modern era, by which

---

[31] Ibid.
[32] Kleppner (1982:71). Similarly, Ranney and Kendall (1956) maintain that "a community . . . needs *some* agency or agencies (a) to define the alternatives open to it, [and] to make clear to the voters what is involved in the choice among those alternatives."

he means the dissolution of strict partisanship and the emergence of diverse coalitions at different levels of government.[33] Shefter makes a similar point when he says that the notion of a "one party North" is exaggerated, and points to the vigorous party competition that persisted in New York state politics throughout the period.[34]

Legal and Procedural Disenfranchisement

The closing decades of the nineteenth century also witnessed a wave of legal reforms that had the effect of disenfranchising what McCormick calls "discordant social elements."

> Southern blacks and poor whites, by participating in the Populist movement, and new immigrants, by supporting the most corrupt city machines and flirting with socialism, convinced elites everywhere that unlimited suffrage fueled disorder. Under the banner of "reform," they enacted registration requirements, ballot laws, and other measures to restrict suffrage.[35]

Developments in the South provide the clearest illustration of the impact of legal and procedural changes on voter turnout. Indeed, the model for a new kind of polity that left formal voting rights intact but stripped poorer and less-educated people of the ability to exercise those rights was pioneered in the South. Powerful and transparent economic and political interests underlay the construction of this system. Disenfranchisement was part of the broader effort by the southern planter class to erect a system of political, economic, and social coercion over blacks that would

---

[33] See Burnham (1981c:170–75).
[34] Shefter (1984:143).
[35] McCormick (1979:295).

permit the reestablishment of a quasi-feudal labor system. Experience showed that black enfranchisement interfered with this objective. As late as the turn of the century, blacks were still able to elect representatives to state and local office over much of the South, impeding the uses of the apparatus of state and local government to reestablish the caste labor system. Moreover, black voters could strike alliances with dissident electoral movements, as they had with northern-backed Republicans after the Civil War. Later, as the radical farmers' movement grew and opened new opportunities for insurgent black-white alliances, the pressure for disenfranchisement grew, and was extended to poor whites as well.

From the period of Reconstruction, black voting rights had been countered by reigning Democratic parties and their Bourbon allies with an extraordinary repertoire of inventive techniques ranging from trickery and fraud to outright violence.[36] And although fraud, trickery, and violence went far toward reducing black voter turnout, it apparently did not go far enough. While black voting appears to have fallen, particularly after federal troops were withdrawn in 1877, the evidence is that moderate levels of black participation were maintained, keeping southern Republican parties alive and providing significant potential support for populism in the 1890s.[37] Furthermore, fraud, trickery, and force had their limitations; they were inherently unstable, for their effective deployment depended on vigilant local organization, and they also made the Southern Democracy vulnerable to a national outcry and federal intervention, a danger that persisted long after Reconstruction.[38] "The prospect of federal enforcement of suffrage rights provoked anger, frustration and fear," according to Bensel:

---

[36] For an overview, see Woodward (1968). The techniques pioneered during Reconstruction to obstruct black voting have been described by John Hope Franklin (1969: especially chapter 18). The definitive work on the use of force in deterring blacks from voting is of course V. O. Key (1984: chapters 25–28).

[37] Kousser (1974:17–18, 28, and 78).

[38] Ibid. (46–47).

> The primary purpose . . . was to secure Republican con-
> trol of the national government by recapturing marginal
> areas in the South. Electoral reform simultaneously released
> the Bourbons from the twin threats of federal intervention
> and agrarian class-based radicalism.[39]

Finally, there is some evidence that southern elites simply per-
ferred legal methods of disenfranchisement to other and more
irregular techniques.[40]

The southern solution to the problems posed by the black
franchise was to attach conditions to the right to vote that did not
mention blacks, and so ostensibly would not violate the Fifteenth
Amendment, but which blacks would not fulfill. These disenfranchising devices were not created all at once. Rather, the
campaign occurred in waves. As federal troops withdrew and the
interest of northern reformers in the freedmen waned, the southern states gradually evolved the arrangements that would eventually strip some three-quarters of the population, black and
white, of the right to vote.

> Each state became in effect a laboratory for testing one
> device or another. Indeed, the cross-fertilization and coor-
> dination between the movments to restrict the suffrage in
> the Southern states amounted to a public conspiracy.[41]

Some of the methods were already available. Georgia retained on the books an optional poll tax from the time when the
payment of taxes was a common condition for the exercise of the

---

[39] Bensel (1984:76 and 81). For a description of the heated congressional battles over legislative proposals for federal intervention in southern elections before 1896, see Bensel
(1984:73–88). The last effort to impose federal supervision, known as the "Force Bill," did
not die in the Congress until Cleveland's reelection in 1892.
[40] Kousser (1974:263). Rusk and Stucker (1978:207) disagree with Kousser on this point,
speculating that had informal methods of disenfranchisement been successful, the southern
states would have avoided implementing laws that were susceptible to constitutional challenge.
[41] Kousser (1974:39).

suffrage. In 1877, the state simply moved to make its poll tax mandatory and far more onerous,[42] and turnout dropped precipitously.[43] Shortly afterward, in 1882, South Carolina adopted an "eight-box" law, followed by Florida in 1889, a device that required the voter to deposit separate ballots in each of the boxes marked for different candidates, making it virtually impossible for the illiterate to navigate the balloting process.

> In South Carolina, the requirement that, with eight or more ballot boxes before him, the voter must select the proper one for each ballot, in order to insure its being counted, furnished an effective means of neutralizing the ignorant black vote; for though the negroes, unable to read the lettering on the boxes, might acquire, by proper coaching, the power to discriminate among them by their relative positions, a moment's work by whites in transposing the boxes would render useless an hour's laborious instruction.[44]

The introduction of officially printed ballots, organized by office rather than by party, was similarly confusing to the uneducated. These arrangements anticipated the straightforward literacy tests that were to come later. Meanwhile, the South developed voter registration procedures that were distinctive for the discretion that they granted local election officers in deciding whether potential voters were in fact qualified. These procedures were particularly useful in purging the electorate of blacks and poor whites in anticipation of constitutional conventions where more sweeping disenfranchising laws could then be enacted.[45] As Populist dissidence mounted in the late 1880s, the

---

[42] Rusk and Stucker (1978:211).

[43] Kousser (1974:67 and table 3.2).

[44] Dunning (1901:443). Dunning also reports a remarkable instance of gerrymandering. "In Mississippi appeared the 'shoestring district,' three hundred miles long and about twenty wide, including within its boundaries nearly all of the densest black communities of the state." See Kousser (1974:50) as well.

[45] Harris (1929:157) and Kousser (1974:48–49).

southern disenfranchisement movement accelerated. Mississippi was another pioneer, introducing both a $2.00 poll tax and a literacy test in its constitutional convention of 1890, arrangements that drove voter participation down to 17 percent by 1900.[46] Florida and Tennessee followed quickly after, and then, in 1894, Arkansas fell in line. Kousser offers persuasive evidence of the impact of these disenfranchising measures in simultaneously depressing turnout and reducing support for oppositional Republican or Populist parties in the states that adopted them during the early 1890s, when southern electoral challenges peaked.[47]

The momentum of the disenfranchising campaign accelerated again after 1896, as the earlier measures proved their effectiveness, and as the resistance offered by southern Populists and their poor white constituencies dissipated. The fact that national Republican leaders seemed to lose interest in protecting the electoral base of southern Republicanism once the party's national dominance was assured by the 1896 sweep of the North probably encouraged the disenfranchisers. The rising wave of race-baiting after Bryan's defeat also helped pave the way by appealing to the racism of poor whites in an effort to win their support in completing the legal system of disenfranchisement.

Accordingly, after 1896, the remaining southern states followed the path laid out by Mississippi, introducing poll tax laws where none yet existed, or making existing poll tax measures more restrictive by raising the amount of the tax or by making it retroactive. In Texas, a poll tax had first been proposed in 1875, on the ostensible grounds that it would eliminate "irresponsible voters." But Texas was the birthplace and organizing center of the Farmers' Alliance, and it was not until 1902, when the Populists had disappeared, that a constitutional amendment es-

---

[46] See Phillips and Blackman (1974:8).
[47] Kousser (1974:41 and table 1.5).

tablishing the poll tax was approved, this time frankly presented as a white-supremacy measure.[48] By 1904, turnout in Texas had plunged to 30 percent from its peak level of 80 percent twenty years earlier.

After the debacle of 1896, the southern states also acted rapidly to add literacy test barriers to poll tax barriers. To overcome the opposition of the poor and illiterate whites who would also be disenfranchised by these measures, complicated loopholes were introduced that could in principle refranchise some of those who were being disenfranchised. Thus "good character" clauses were added that permitted voter registrars to make exceptions, or clauses permitted registrars to accept "understanding" of some portion of the state constitution as a substitute for literacy, or grandfather and "fighting grandfather" clauses permitted exceptions to be made for those whose grandfathers had voted, or whose grandfathers had fought for the Confederacy. But these gestures to overcome the opposition of poor whites were usually allowed to lapse. In any case, the loopholes did not work and were probably not intended to work. Most poor whites were unwilling to risk the humiliation of failing the new voter tests.[49]

TABLE 3.1 RELATIONSHIP OF POLL TAX AND LITERACY TEST LAWS
TO PRESIDENTIAL TURNOUT IN SOUTHERN STATES, 1892–1916

	Absence of *Literacy Test*	*Presence of* *Literacy Test*
Absence of poll tax	72	57
Presence of poll tax	40	24

Source: Rusk (1974:1043). Cell entries are presidential turnout means computed over all years, 1892–1916, for states having the legal combination listed.

---

[48] McDonald (undated:112–13).

[49] A witness cited by Pendleton (1927:459) offered this description of how poor whites reacted: "It was painful and pitiful to see the horror and dread visible on the faces of the illiterate poor white men who were waiting to take their turn before the inquisition. . . .

No one disputes that the southern system "worked." In the 1880s and 1890s, turnout in the South had regularly exceeded 60 percent, and sometimes reached 85 percent.[50] Phillips and Blackman provide some dramatic examples of the change. In Arkansas, turnout dropped from over two-thirds to just over one-third between 1884 and 1904; in Mississippi, from almost 80 percent in 1876 to less than 17 percent in 1900; and in South Carolina participation plummeted from 83.7 percent in 1880 to 18 percent in 1900.[51] As the system of legal barriers was put in place, the black vote dwindled and then disappeared, and white turnout shrank as well. In Kousser's words, "The security of the black belt and the Democratic party had been purchased at the cost of abandoning popular government."[52]

TABLE 3.2 SOUTHERN PRESIDENTIAL TURNOUT PERCENTAGES
BY RACE: 1876–1892; 1900–1916; 1920–1924

South	1876–1892		1900–1916		1920–1924	
	White	*Black*	*White*	*Black*	*White*	*Black*
Black-belt counties	75	44	47	5	27	0
White counties	62	79	53	0	35	0
Total	69	60	50	2	32	0

Source: Kleppner (1982:53 and 65, tables 3.6 and 4.4). Black-belt counties defined as 30 percent black.

Scholarly debate over the causes of turnout decline in the South turns on a rather narrow dispute having to do with the

---

This was horrible to behold, but it was still more horrible to see the marks of humiliation and despair that were stamped on the faces of honest but poor white men who had been refused registration and who had been robbed of their citizenship without cause. We saw them as they came from the presence of the registrars with bowed heads and agonized faces; and when they spoke, in many instances, there was a tear in the voice of the humiliated citizen." Of course, this was only one of the ways in which poor southern whites were victimized by their own racism.

[50] Kousser (1974:236).
[51] Phillips and Blackman (1974:8).
[52] Kousser (1974:103).

relative weight of force and fraud on the one hand, and legal barriers on the other hand. On the larger points, there is in fact no dispute: millions of blacks and poor whites were disenfranchised, and legal barriers mattered in that process. The boldness of the disenfranchising movement in the South makes the motives of the disenfranchisers and their techniques clear. The South also provides strong clues, we think, to developments in the North: "The South is properly viewed as an extreme rather than a wholly deviant example of processes more generally and diffusely at work."[53]

Indeed, southern elites learned many of their arguments for disenfranchisement from reformers in the North, just as reformers in the North learned some of their methods from the South. The decades after the Civil War, when techniques for disenfranchising blacks and poor whites were being perfected in the states of the Confederacy, were also the decades when something very much like a democratic counterrevolution swept across the North, leaving in its wake a new system of rules governing electoral participation.

Limiting the suffrage was a solution that came easily to the minds of northern reformers. Restricting the vote to the better sorts of people would work toward restoring firm control of government and politics to business and professional leaders. Otherwise, the *Nation* warned in 1877, immigration would lead to "the severance of political power from intelligence and property."[54] Nor at the time could this sort of solution have seemed so farfetched. It was after all still early in the "age of democracy." As late as 1828, fourteen states continued to impose property or tax-paying restrictions on white male suffrage; Connecticut, Louisiana, and New Jersey retained these restrictions into the 1840s, Virginia until 1851, and South Carolina through the Civil War. Dorr's Rebellion against suffrage re-

[53] Burnham (1974c:1054).
[54] Cited in McGerr (1986:46).

strictions in Rhode Island in 1842 had in fact ended in a draw
that established different property tests for native-born and naturalized citizens.[55] And the democratic counterrevolution gained
momentum in the United States at a time when most European
workers had not yet won the right to vote, so precedents elsewhere offered no defense of the franchise.

The straightforward attack on the right to vote for the
unpropertied remained largely rhetorical, however, perhaps because it was so unlikely to receive the support of politicians who,
pending the success of the disenfranchisers, would have to risk
the ire of the unpropertied at the polls. In 1875, Governor
Tilden of New York appointed a bipartisan commission to reform city governments that recommended restricting the franchise in municipal elections to taxpayers and rent-payers, with
property and rental payment floors graduated by city size. In
New York City, it was proposed to restrict the franchise to those
with more than $500 in property, or those with annual rental
payments over $250. The Tilden Commission recommendations
were received enthusiastically by New York City businessmen,
including the Chamber of Commerce, the Stock Exchange, the
Produce Exchange, and the Cotton Exchange, all of whose representatives rallied to its support, along with a roster of promi-
nent and wealthy New Yorkers. But the strategy was too obvious,
and too drastic in the effects it promised to have, particularly on
Tammany Hall, which led the opposition and worked to defeat
legislators who supported the plan. The Tilden Commission plan
ultimately failed.[56]

Other and more circumspect routes to the same end were
explored. Seven nonsouthern states increased the length of their
residency requirements,[57] and eleven states repealed older laws

---

[55] Kleppner (1982:8); Williamson (1960); Riker (1965:38).

[56] McGerr (1986:49–50).

[57] "Durational residency requirements of a year or more were a feature of most state codes
since the 1780s when," according to Riker (1965:57–58), "they were invented precisely
because universal suffrage seemed imminent, to substitute for land ownership as proof of an

or constitutional provisions that had permitted immigrants to vote if they declared their intention to become citizens.[58] Educational requirements were another and broader solution, and one that matched the reformers repeated rhetorical calls for a more intelligent electorate.[59] Moreover, there was something like a modest precedent in the literacy requirements that existed on the books in Massachusetts and Connecticut (although these had not been enforced). There were soon to be stronger precedents in the South, where seven states imposed literacy requirements between 1892 and 1910. Accordingly, eleven states in the North and West imposed literacy requirements between 1890 and 1926, aimed, says Kleppner, at the lower class, and especially at naturalized voters.[60] In 1953, Riker summed up the use of literacy tests:

> The real political purpose, so artfully concealed, is to deprive of citizen rights certain minorities believed to have a low literacy rate. Eighteen states have adopted the test, seven to disfranchise Negroes, five to disfranchise Indians and Mexicans and Orientals, and six to disfranchise European immigrants.[61]

Riker goes on to give the example of New York, where the administration of literacy tests during the 1920s disfranchised almost 20 percent of the people who took them.[62]

But residency requirements or literacy tests were of them-

'interest' in the election of local officials." These restrictions persisted until the Voting Rights Act amendments in 1970, which reduced the residence requirement for presidential elections to thirty days, with the practical effect that thirty days became the requirement for all elections.

[58] Kleppner (1982:57–58 and 60). Between 1848 and 1890, eighteen states adopted these alien-with-intent laws (Rusk and Stucker, 1978).

[59] McGerr (1986:47) and Kleppner (1982:59).

[60] Kleppner (1982:10).

[61] Riker (1965:59–60).

[62] Ibid.

selves not sufficient to achieve the ambitious goal of restricting electoral participation, especially in circumstances where local party organizations were intent on recruiting voters, literate or not. Nor indeed were any new rules likely to be very effective without a procedure to implement them. An administrative mechanism was needed that would sort out those who were eligible from those who were not. The obvious mechanism was a voter registration system, arrangements that were in fact devised to serve a double purpose. On the one hand, these systems implemented newly restrictive rules and tests; on the other hand, they also provided a potentially flexible and selective administrative mechanism to make it more difficult for some to vote and easier for others.

The effort to restrict the suffrage focused more and more on the procedures for certifying eligible voters, or voter registration. In fact, Massachusetts had required registration as early as 1800, and Connecticut and Maine also adopted early registration systems.[63] And there had been episodic efforts to impose registration requirements in other states, although these efforts frequently failed, or the systems were weak or indifferently applied, at least until the closing decades of the nineteenth century. Between 1876 and 1912, however, almost half the northern states introduced amendments to their constitutions providing the authority for voter registration requirements. Others already had such authority, or simply legislated it without constitutional provision.[64] By 1929, when Joseph Harris compiled his review of voter registration in the United States, all but three states (Arkansas, Texas, and Indiana) had instituted registration procedures, and these states would soon fall in line.[65]

A system for registering voters seems at first glance a rea-

---

[63] Carlson (1976:105).

[64] Phillips and Blackman (1975:8).

[65] There exists no adequate political history of voter registration. Harris (1929) is a fairly thorough compilation of the main legislative developments. The review that follows also draws on a paper by Hayduk (1986).

sonable development. It was, after all, simply a means of compiling a list of those who were eligible to vote, a procedure that became more necessary as the population grew, and as the vote fraud perpetrated by the clientelist political parties became more common. In practice, however, the way the lists were compiled had a great deal to do with who was likely to be on them, and who was likely to be omitted. The procedures for certifying voters had, in other words, political significance, a fact recognized from the earliest days of a mass suffrage. For that reason, the procedures have always been the object of conflict. An attempt to introduce an amendment to the New York constitution in 1821 providing for a registry of eligible voters provoked the charge that men would be compelled to make an extra journey, perhaps of some great distance, with the result that "a few should rule the many, who have a desire that aristocracy shall triumph but honest republicans will never take such pains."[66] The amendment failed, by a vote of 60 to 43.[67] Similarly, when Pennsylvania enacted its first registration law in 1836, requiring the assessors in the county of Philadelphia to make up a list of qualified voters, and providing that no one would be permitted to vote who was not on the list, there were protests in the constitutional convention the following year. The law, it was charged, was designed to reduce the Philadelphia vote, and to cut down the vote of the poor.

> When the assessors went around, the laboring men were necessarily and of course absent from their homes, engaged in providing subsistence for themselves and their families; and not finding the men at home, did not go again. When the election came on these men . . . were spurned from the ballot boxes. They were told their names were not on the registry, and that, therefore, they had no right to vote. . . .

[66] Cited in Harris (1929:70).
[67] Ibid. (69–70).

But how was it with the rich man? The gold and silver door plate with name was enough, and there was no danger that the assessor would overlook that.[68]

These early objections only hint at the variable political consequences of different registration procedures. In fact, compared with the personal voter registration arrangements developed later, these first "nonpersonal" registration systems were relatively benign, for they placed the burden of compiling lists of eligible voters on town or county officials.[69] However, as political insurgency spread in the late nineteenth century and the movement to reform the franchise gathered momentum, voter registration arrangements became not only more widespread, but also increasingly restrictive. The trend was toward ever more onerous procedural requirements: from nonpersonal registration lists compiled by local officials to personal registration lists that required citizens to appear before those officials at given times and places; from permanent registration to periodic and even annual registration; to earlier closing dates for registration, so that campaigns no longer served to stimulate voters to register;[70] and toward more centralized administration of voter registration that not only removed registration to less accessible and less familiar sites, but also was more likely to remove it from the control of local politicians with an interest in maintaining existing patterns of voter participation.[71]

Logically enough, the big cities were marked from the beginning as the target of these increasingly restrictive registration requirements. Partisan motives, class interests, and animus against the machines combined to explain the urban focus. Dem-

---

[68] Cited in ibid. (68).

[69] Carlson (1976:155, table 4.11) compares turnout in counties with nonpersonal and personal voter registration systems in early-twentieth-century elections, and shows that turnout was consistently lower in counties with personal registration systems.

[70] See Kelley et al. (1967:367) on the impact of closing dates on rates of registration. See also Gosnell (1927:104).

[71] Harris (1929:186).

ocratic strength (outside of the South) was based on the immigrant working class and the political bosses, and they were based in the cities. McGerr quotes Theodore Dwight Woolsey, a liberal reformer and past president of Yale, in 1878: "The cities are to be dreaded. . . . They take the lead in all commotions, they have less wisdom and stability, but more energy and political fanaticism." And historian Francis Parkman agreed: "It is in the cities that the diseases of the body politic are gathered to a head, and it is here that the need of attacking them is most urgent. Here the dangerous classes are most numerous and strong, and the effects of flinging the suffrage to the mob are most disastrous." [72]

Thus Pennsylvania's early nonpersonal system of registration applied at first only to Philadelphia, and each time the registration system was made more restrictive, it was Philadelphia that was singled out for the new procedures. [73] In 1906, the state legislature amended the registration procedure again, to require annual personal registration in Philadelphia, Pittsburgh, and Scranton. [74] When New Jersey Republicans succeeded in legislating a permanent system of personal registration in 1870, their earlier legislative victory having been repealed by the Democrats, they applied the system to the seven cities in the state with populations of more than twenty thousand. [75] Subsequently, after a series of revisions, the registration system was changed so that voters in cities over fifteen thousand had to register in person each year.

[72] Cited in McGerr (1986:48).

[73] Even so staunch an advocate of registration as Harris (1929:80–81) was confounded by the system that had developed in Philadelphia by 1929 as a result of the accumulation of restrictive procedures: "No one may register who has not paid a poll tax, occupation tax, or some other form of state taxation within a period of two years, and to pay the poll tax, one must be listed by the assessor. In Philadelphia it is notorious that the assessors' lists are grossly inaccurate and inflated, and serve no useful purpose. The poll tax required in Philadelphia is only fifty cents, and payment serves to qualify one for two years, but many persons are omitted by the assessor and find themselves unable to register."

[74] Carlson (1976:107).

[75] McCormick (1953:149–53).

The climactic national electoral challenge of 1896 only gave greater impetus to efforts to strengthen registration requirements, while the landslide Republican victory over much of the North smoothed the way politically by weakening the Democratic opposition. Harris summarizes the development:

> In the period from 1896 to 1924, when the turnout declined almost steadily, state after state enacted registration laws which typically required registration annually and in person of all voters in the nation's large cities; the registration procedures of this era have been described . . . as "expensive, cumbersome, and inconvenient to the voter."[76]

Kleppner makes the same point:

> Beginning in the 1890s, stronger types of voter-registration systems replaced the weak ones that had been used earlier in some states. The key feature of this change was the imposition of a personal-registration requirement, a provision that shifted the burden of establishing eligibility from the state to the individual. By 1920, 31 nonsouthern states had put some form of personal registration requirement into effect.[77]

Thus, for example, Massachusetts had been more or less content with its registration system of 1800, which remained unchanged until in 1896 the citizens of Boston were made subject to a personal periodic registration requirement, at a central location.[78] And in New York, where the first registration law passed in 1859 had authorized precinct officers to prepare lists, the 1894 constitution required personal annual registration in

[76] Harris (1929:89).
[77] Kleppner (1982:60).
[78] Carlson (1976:105).

cities over five thousand. In 1898, a state agency was created to detect election fraud, and for the first few years it focused almost exclusively on registration fraud in New York City.[79] Delaware moved from permanent registration to biennial registration in 1899, and in 1896 Maryland required annual registration in the city of Baltimore, where the police also purged the lists each year by means of a house-to-house canvass.[80] Annual purges of this type, which were also instituted elsewhere—in Boston and Milwaukee, for example[81]—are especially revealing of the purposes of the new voter registration arrangements. Where once the door-to-door canvass had been used to add electors to the list, now it was used exclusively to eliminate them.[82]

Finally, the very intricacy inherent in variable registration systems operated by state, county, and municipal officials was important, for the execution of these complex arrangements inevitably gave officialdom the latitude for uneven and selective enforcement of the new procedures. Literacy tests, for example, could be administered differently in different places, and differently for different people. The new voter registration apparatus also permitted the introduction of a series of informal barriers, having to do with the days and hours that voter registration was available, where the offices were located, how people were informed of where and when, and the manner in which they were treated by the officials who administered the procedures. In-

---

[79] Harris (1929:76).

[80] Carlson (1976:110).

[81] Harris (1929:89).

[82] Burnham's (1981c:167) suggestion that the reliance on personal voter registration systems in the United States owed something to the weakness of state bureaucratic caspacities in this country is inconsistent with the historial evidence, which shows that increasingly elaborate bureaucratic machinery did in fact exist, although it was used to impede voting. Thus he says that "elsewhere in the West (including neighboring Canada), it was early accepted that it was the state's task to compile and update electoral registers" because of the existence of state bureaucracies capable of carrying out such a task or a "consensus that such a bureaucracy should be created." But American registration systems were also initially based on the presumption that registering people was a state responsibility; only later were they changed to shift to the citizen the obligation of getting one's name on the register.

evitably, over the long run, these informal barriers tended to exclude those who were less educated and less self-confident, and in any case were often administered so as to secure that effect.[83]

The new procedures gradually took their toll, and voter turnout dropped, specifically as a result of voter registration. Kleppner, who thinks the decline in electoral competitiveness is the principal explanation of falling turnout, nevertheless concludes that voter registration requirements accounted for between 30 and 40 percent of the turnout decline where they were in force.[84] Burnham comes to a similar conclusion, conceiving of these obstacles as one of the ways in which the rules of the game were intentionally changed to limit access to the ballot at the end of the nineteenth century. He credits the new requirements with responsibility for part of the decline in turnout that occurred, although he thinks the effect less important than "behavioral" depressants of turnout. In a statistical comparison (similar to Kleppner's) of counties with personal registration with nonregistration counties between 1890 and 1910, Burnham finds that the turnout decline in the registration counties is "only" 14.5 percent greater.[85] Overall, however, Burnham concludes that about a third of the decline in voter turnout that occurred in the early decades of the twentieth century was attributable to rule changes, and particularly to voter registration.[86]

---

[83] Campbell et al. (1960:152) make this point about southern systems; it is informal barriers, rather than legislative restrictions, that account for variations in turnout among southern blacks.

[84] Kleppner (1982:61–62). His conclusion is based on a comparison of turnout rates in areas covered by personal registration requirements, and areas in which there was either no registration or a nonpersonal registration system. It should be noted that Kleppner concludes that the impact of personal voter registration was substantially weaker in the Metropole than in the Periphery, especially after 1900. See also Kleppner and Baker (1980).

[85] Burnham (1974b:1011, and see also 1970: chapter 4, and 1979).

[86] Burnham (1981c:191) is also pertinent; he rephrases his estimate of the turnout decline due to voter registration "as much less than one half." Carlson (1976: chapter 4) contains a systematic comparison of turnout in counties and states with personal registration, nonpersonal registration, and no registration in the presidential elections from 1912 to 1924. Carlson also goes on to reexamine these data controlling for a series of socioeconomic vari-

. . .

Because the several main features of the system of 1896 worked together, each reinforcing the other, we think attempts to estimate the separate effects of each aspect of the system can be misleading. We will turn to this problem, and to the theoretical disputes that have arisen in assessing these relative effects, in the next chapter. For now, our point is simpler. The several transformations in the institutional framework that governed electoral participation—a decline in party competition, weakened and reorganized parties, and new rules restricting access to the ballot —worked together to depress turnout.[87] In chapter 4, we show how this integrated perspective brings together the several main strands of thought that purport to explain the class-skewed electorate in the United States.

---

ables. But for reasons that we will explain shortly, it is the simple correlations that are most illuminating.

[87] Not surprisingly, given the general demobilization of the electorate, the fall in turnout is even steeper in off-year elections. And it was steepest in the South, where, in the off-year elections between 1922 and 1926, turnout fell to 10.6 percent. See Kleppner (1982:37).

Chapter 4

Explanations of Nonvoting

There are two important debates about nonvoting. One is among theorists who share the view that sweeping institutional changes in the late nineteenth and early twentieth centuries account for the contraction of voter turnout, but disagree about whether changes in party and voter behavior, or legal changes, were the more important. They also disagree about which political forces produced behavioral or legal changes. The second debate is between these institutional analysts and the large number of scholars who consider that nonvoting results from one or another of the characteristics of the nonvoters themselves, or what for convenience we have labeled the social-psychological school. We will examine each of these debates in turn, and then try to show how the evidence drawn upon to sustain the several arguments can be integrated into a comprehensive explanation of electoral constriction. Voter registration procedures play a pivotal role in such an explanation, but their impact can be fully understood only by examining how they interact with party behavior and with the social characteristics of nonvoters, especially the attributes associated with race and class.

THE DEBATE ABOUT THE
INSTITUTIONAL CAUSES OF NONVOTING

Analysts who emphasize changes in party and voter behavior have generated a debate with those who emphasize legal and procedural changes. The main issue is whether the decline of party competition and the consequent voter estrangement or the legal and procedural changes in electoral machinery, especially the introduction of the Australian ballot and voter registration procedures, caused declining turnout. Walter Dean Burnham is surely the unchallenged leader of the first school. His work is heavily influenced by Schattschneider's earlier analysis, which stressed the significance of the collapse of party competition in much of the country in 1896, together with increasingly oligarchical parties, in accounting for diminishing voter involvement. For Schattschneider, the expansion of the electorate early in the nineteenth century had been "largely a by-product of the system of party conflict." The rise of nonvoting, in turn, resulted from "the attempt to make the vote meaningless":

> Abstention reflects the suppression of the options and alternatives that reflect the needs of the nonparticipants. . . . Whoever decides what the game is about decides also who can get into the game.[1]

The relevance of this perspective to the interpretation of the system of 1896 is obvious. As party competition disappeared in much of the country, "votes decline in value because the voters no longer have a viable party alternative."[2] This perspective has

---

[1] Schattschneider (1960:100–101 and 105).
[2] Ibid (80).

also been influential in Paul Kleppner's extensive and authorita-
tive studies of nineteenth- and early twentieth-century electoral
politics.[3]

Analysts who propound what is sometimes called the "legal-
institutional" theory attribute turnout decline and volatile voting
patterns to changes in laws and procedures.[4] This view is associated with the influential work of Campbell, Converse, Miller,
and Stokes, as well as that of Kelley, Kousser, Milbraith, Rusk,
and Stucker, all of whom emphasize aspects of electoral law and
machinery as major determinants of electoral behavior. Thus,
Campbell and his colleagues reported in *The American Voter*, on
the basis of data from the 1950s, that variations in registration
and voting requirements were important determinants of differences in state turnout levels.[5] Earlier, Campbell and Miller had
reported that straight ticket or split ticket voting was significantly
affected by the type of ballot.[6] And a few years after *The American
Voter* was published in 1960, Miller reported that variations in
voting rates were strongly associated with residence requirements, registration procedures, closing dates for registration,
poll tax requirements, and the ballot form.[7] Subsequently, in
1967, Kelley, Ayres, and Bowen published a study of variations
in turnout rates in 1960 in 104 of the largest cities with the
stunning conclusion that 78 percent of the variation among cities
could be explained by variations in the percentage of citizens
who were registered.

Converse and Rusk in particular have vigorously promoted
the legal-institutional interpretation as a sweeping alternative to

---

[3] For a summary, see Kleppner (1981a). See also Jensen (1971). While both Kleppner and
Jensen clearly have been influenced by Burnham, their work concentrates on the ethnoreligious bases of nineteenth-century politics.
[4] The phrase "legal-institutional" is taken from Rusk's characterization of his own work. See
Rusk and Stucker (1978:199).
[5] Campbell et al. (1960: chapter 11). These authors also consider individual social characteristics, namely, education and motivation, to be important determinants of turnout.
[6] Campbell and Miller (1957).
[7] Miller (1963).

Burnham's political-behavioral interpretation.[8] The argument, like most important arguments, is rooted in large differences in underlying interpretations of American politics. But much of the debate has been limited to rather narrow questions such as the extent of fraud in nineteenth-century electoral politics. The legal-institutional adherents argue that the voting decline was in substantial part illusory, a result of reforms such as the Australian ballot and voter registration that deflated voting returns by reducing the numbers of coerced or fraudulent ballots cast, and that this was, in fact, what the reformers who promoted the legal reforms were trying to accomplish, much as they claimed. The decline in turnout, in other words, was at least partly an artifact of more honest elections. In addition, these analysts allow that the changes in electoral machinery that reduced fraud, such as the introduction of voter registration, also had the unintended consequence of reducing turnout by making it more difficult to vote and more difficult for the parties to enlist voters.

The argument that fraud prompted the reforms, and that lower turnout is in large part evidence of the elimination of fraudulent ballots, depends on the assumption that voter fraud was in fact pervasive in the nineteenth century, as Converse and Rusk insist that it was. Burnham and Kleppner similarly insist that fraud was an episodic rather than an endemic problem, and that the decline in turnout was the real and deliberate outcome of political changes, notably reduced party competition. This dispute is certainly not readily resolved by reference to available facts, since much of what passes for data on fraud consists of anecdotal charges by contemporaries, including the reformers themselves. While such charges cannot be dismissed out of hand, we must regard them as the opinions of highly motivated observers. Moreover, the bearing of fraud on turnout is complicated,

[8] The best expositions of the contending positions in this debate are to be found in a series of articles published together in the *American Political Science Review* (September 1974); see Burnham, "Theory and Voting Research," together with the comments of Converse and Rusk, and Burnham's rejoinder.

as Argersinger points out, by the fact that fraud also took the form of intimidating or of deterring voting, or of stealing ballots, which deflated turnout.[9] (It is even possible, of course, that these two forms of fraud canceled each other out in affecting overall turnout.)

The dispute about fraud and turnout only hints at the large differences in interpretations of American political development that animate the debate. In particular, Converse and Rusk oppose the Schattschneider and Burnham thesis that the electoral changes of the late nineteenth century reflected the politics of class conflict. Rusk states the issue forthrightly when he proceeds to attack Burnham as something of an "economic determinist" who accounts for the decline of voting as a response to a "capitalist conspiracy" by businessmen and Republicans whose "capture of the electoral system" in 1896 led to the alienation of voters from the political system.[10] In the same vein, Converse and Rusk express the opinion that "the idealistic forces of reform [were] bent on cleaning up fraud" just as they said they were.[11] Business involvement, Converse asserts, was only "spotty." Instead,

> The forces of good government who as "idea men" generated the proposals, struggled to publicize them, and remained their most energetic and reliable core of support through the process of adoption included mainly intellectuals, journalists, ministers, and other professionals.[12]

According to this view, the reformers promoted the legal changes, principally voter registration, that reduced corruption, although the "unintended effect . . . was to put up an additional

---

[9] See Argersinger (1985–86:684–85). Argersinger observes cogently that there is a wide tendency to underestimate voter fraud, simply because a good deal of academic work hangs on the validity of nineteenth-century electoral data, but concludes nevertheless that fraud was common. For a discussion of the problem of evidence, see Allen and Allen (1981:153–93).

[10] Rusk (1974:1028–45).

[11] Converse (1972:286).

[12] Ibid. (297).

barrier to the vote, eliminating many honest votes on the part of marginally involved citizens."[13]

However, if the role of class forces in explaining either political-behavioral or legal-institutional changes is put aside, the debate between the schools loses much of its cogency, and indeed scarcely seems to be a debate at all. The theories, as Kleppner and Baker point out, are "not mutually exclusive, either logically or behaviorally."[14] After all, it is in politics, including party politics, that legal arrangements and administrative procedures are forged. It was Schattschneider who said that politics is, in fact, mainly about rules, "about procedure rather than substance."[15] In this sense, political and legal variables are related, but political variables take pride of place; they are the independent variables. However, it was also Schattschneider's point that rules, once institutionalized, change politics—the "rules of the game determine the requirements for success"—which is why they are the focus of so much political contention in the first place.[16]

One difficulty scholars have experienced in interpreting American politics has always been that the grand strategy of politics has concerned itself first of all with the structure of institutions. The function of institutions is to channel conflict; institutions do not treat all forms of conflict impartially, just as football rules do not treat all forms of violence with indiscriminate equality.[17]

Or to put the same point another way, political and legal-institutional variables are interactive, and they are each both independent and dependent variables.

[13] Converse (1974:1040).
[14] Kleppner and Baker (1980:205–26).
[15] Schattschneider (1960:72).
[16] Ibid. (48).
[17] Ibid. (72).

Burnham and Kleppner have in fact moved part of the way toward such an integration of political changes and rules changes. Burnham's earlier work tended to relegate voter registration to a marginal role, emphasizing instead the narrowing of political options associated with the system of 1896 as the principal explanation of declining turnout.[18] By 1970, however, perhaps in response to the findings reported in the interim by Kelley, Ayres, and Bowen (showing strong correlations between aggregate registration and turnout levels by city), Burnham allowed that voter registration requirements "counted for something," although not for much:

> By putting first things first, one concludes that the systemic forces at work during these periods were far broader in their scope and far heavier in their impact than any single change in the rules of the game or, in all probability, of all such changes put together.[19]

In the years since, Burnham has gradually come to attribute greater statistical weight to personal voter registration requirements in accounting for the drop in turnout. Voter registration requirements not only "count for something," they count now for quite a bit more. Voter registration has become "a highly significant intervening variable,"[20] but a variable that itself can only be understood as a consequence of the political changes associated with the system of 1896:

> The most compelling reason for rejecting the legal-structural change theory—or more precisely, for subordinating it to its proper role in a more comprehensive set of propo-

---

[18] See Burnham (1965:7–28).
[19] Burnham (1970:90).
[20] Burnham (1974b:1012).

sitions concerning the etiology of major electoral change—
is that, from beginning to end, Professors Rusk and Converse have treated this intervention as though it were an
uncaused cause, a kind of external intervention into the
history of men.[21]

What Burnham must really mean is that he does not consider the
causes outlined by Converse—that the reformers were merely
acting on their ideals—to be credible. This, however, is another
way of restating the large underlying dispute about the role of
class forces in American politics.

To establish the preeminence of politics over rules, Burnham repeatedly returns to data showing that turnout also dropped
in counties that had no personal voter registration.[22] Converse's
response is to postulate that the heightened political controversy
over vote fraud during the 1890s and 1900s could have led to
curtailment of the more blatant forms of vote corruption, and
hence to lower turnouts, even where registration was not imposed.[23] This sort of county-by-county comparison, varieties of
which are also employed by Kleppner and Carlson, has the virtue
of bringing empirical data to bear on the problem of estimating
the impact of voter registration procedures. But it also grossly
simplifies the dynamics through which political and rule changes
came to affect turnout levels, a simplification that Burnham's
discussion does not go far enough toward remedying.

It is easy to grant the contention that rule changes originate
in politics, that they are "produced by concrete men acting out
their idealogical biases in concrete legislative form."[24] But it is
more complicated than that. The new rules were, to be sure,
shaped by the mobilized economic elites represented for Burn-

[21] Burnham (1974c:1054).
[22] Burnham (1974b:1005 and 1007).
[23] Converse (1974:1024–25).
[24] Burnham (1974b:1004).

ham by the national Republican party, "the political vehicle of industrial capitalism."[25] They were also shaped by state and local political parties competing under specific state and local conditions. Moreover, once rule changes were formally initiated, their implementation was mediated by local political parties in contingent and variable ways, so that the impact of rules on turnout cannot be inferred from their mere existence. And, finally, the relationship between the rules and politics also worked the other way. Once the rules were inaugurated and implemented, depending on how they were implemented, they in turn had political consequences.

Thus, early voter registration laws emerged out of conflicts in which state and local parties were very active contenders, if not the principal contenders. Converse, notwithstanding his general conviction that idealistic reformers were the main political actors in voter registration reform, describes the "heated political controversy" generated by the registration issue in the period from 1860 to 1900:

> Minority groups in the largest urban centers typically used the Democratic Party as a vehicle to challenge the constitutionality of laws that forced them into an elaborate registration procedure but required nothing of their small-town and rural compatriots. Meanwhile, of course, the Republicans were painfully and often explicitly aware of how sharply their rural vote base might shrink with the extension of controls on voting to the countryside, and fought tooth and nail to preserve their artificial legal advantage. Many of the wanderings into and out of statewide registration laws that occurred in some states were a simple reflection of the momentary ascendancy of one or the other of these competing powers.[26]

[25] Burnham (1974a:688).
[26] Converse (1972:286).

The sources of these local partisan conflicts are clear. State Republican parties stood to gain from disenfranchising urban and working-class voters, and northern Democratic parties stood to lose, not only because the laws were aimed at the cities where the Democrats were stronger, but because the immigrant and working-class voters who were more likely to be affected were the key to Democratic power in the cities. McCormick makes just this point in describing the legislative battles in New Jersey, where the first registration law was passed in 1866, after the Democrats lost control of both houses of the legislature:

> The Democratic press attacked the registry laws on the grounds that they made voting "troublesome, inconvenient and expensive." Too, it was contended that the laws kept from the polls the poor working man who could not afford to take time off from his job to register. Republican spokesmen insisted that the laws had worked well and that the Democrats disliked them because they could no longer flood the polling places with floaters and repeaters.[27]

As it happens, the Democrats regained control of the legislature in 1868 and abolished the new registration law (over a veto by the Republican governor), but when the Republicans returned to power, they restored registration.[28]

The first observation to be made about these early battles over registration is how aptly they illustrate Schattschneider's point that the grand strategy of politics concerns itself above all else with the structure of institutions. It follows that the parties themselves always try to shape the rules under which they compete, including the rules governing voter participation:

---

[27] McCormick (1953:149).
[28] Ibid. (149–50). See also the discussion of the history of voter registration laws in Harris (1929: chapter 3).

Election machinery always has been something more than an instrument through which the will of the voters could be made known. It has been the means of influencing the verdict of the electorate. Any change in the machinery affected the fortunes of the major factions contending for political power. . . . No factor is more constant in explaining the development of election machinery than this one.[29]

The second observation is that during this early phase in the development of voter registration procedures, the state and local parties were the main actors, and they cannot be defined simply as surrogates for class actors at this point in American party history. Of course, there was a good deal of class animus among the promoters of registration reform, especially toward the immigrants who were rapidly becoming majorities in some of the biggest cities and who provided the social base for the political machines that were beginning to provoke business reform campaigns. Nevertheless, the motives of the contenders in these registration battles derived as much from party advantage as class advantage, since economic elites were divided in their partisan allegiances until the elections of 1894 and 1896. In other words, the state legislative battles over voter registration that began in the 1860s were motivated in part by raw calculations of party fortune.[30]

However, no matter the outcome of these legislative conflicts, the impact of early voter registration laws (particularly the weaker forms of registration) was negligible[31] because the local parties were competitive and vigorous. The legal expansion of the suffrage earlier in the nineteenth century had made high

---

[29] McCormick (1953:215–17).

[30] Some of these legislative battles are described in Harris (1929: chapter 2).

[31] McCormick (1953) makes this point. While changes in election machinery were motivated by efforts to affect the electorate, the reforms in New Jersey actually had slight effect during the period of 1870 to 1900. We think the answer to this apparent puzzle is that new and obstructive procedures took their toll on electoral participation only very gradually, and only in the context of changes in party organization and the pattern of party competition.

participation possible, and the development of strong mass parties in turn sustained participation.

> Political parties—as organizations and as objects of habituated loyalties—were critical intermediaries in the process of mobilizing a mass electorate. Party formation in the 1830s and 1840s intersected with a changed legal environment to stimulate electoral participation.[32]

Most historians of the "second party system" agree.[33] But the role readily conceded to the parties in creating and sustaining the mass electorate of the nineteenth century bears on the way voter registration was implemented. So long as the local parties were tied to voter constituencies at risk of being disenfranchised by the new laws, they had ample motive to resist, amend, or circumvent the new registration procedures when they faced electoral challenge. And so long as the local parties were organizationally strong, they also had the capacity to resist, amend, or circumvent them. *In other words, the impact of voter registration laws and procedures cannot be assessed without taking into account the motives and capacities of the political parties involved in implementing them.*

The image of machines in American folklore is of all-powerful organizations. Had they been all powerful, machine politicians would have had little incentive to mobilize high voter turnout. The folklore is wrong, however. The clientelist organizations rarely gained undisputed control, and when they did it was usually not for long. In many cities, local bosses competed

---

[32] Kleppner (1982:28 and 33). Kleppner points out that strong parties succeeded in sustaining high participation despite such lingering barriers to the suffrage as residency requirements, poll or registry taxes, and inconvenient polling places.

[33] For example, Formisano (1969:688) points to the large impact of party organization in driving up turnout in the 1830s and 1840s: "Historians sometimes get confused about whether organization caused voter participation or vice versa, missing the point that both are dependent as well as independent variables." Chambers and Davis (1978:188–89) try to estimate the relative impact of competition and party "organizational inception" on turnout during approximately the same period.

among themselves. Even the legendary New York Democracy was rent by factionalism for much of its reign, and it was also challenged from without by periodic reform efforts, including in 1885 by a labor mobilization behind the candidacy of Henry George. It was not until the late 1880s that Tammany succeeded in centralizing its control of the local Democratic party.[34] Moreover, from the beginning, the clientelist parties confronted opposition from reformers who also entered the electoral lists and sometimes won, at least for a time. So long as machine control was contested, turnout of working-class voters remained crucial to machine success, and the machines exerted themselves to enlist voters and help them hurdle whatever barriers they confronted.

Accordingly, just how the new requirements worked out in practice depended very much on the vigor of local political parties, and particularly on the clientelist parties that dominated electoral politics in the cities where the immigrant working class was concentrated. Whatever the intentions of the registration reformers, where local parties were strong and closely linked to the immigrant working class, ways were discovered to overcome the new restrictions, just as ways had been found to overcome earlier restrictions, such as naturalization laws.[35] Indeed, the evolution of voter registration requirements, from nonpersonal to personal, from permanent to periodic and even to annual registration, and from local to centralized administration, can be understood as a reflection of the ongoing political contest over registration. As particular registration arrangements fell under the control of local party functionaries, efforts were in turn made in the state legislatures to "reform the reforms," so to say, in a continuing struggle for party advantage.

However, after the election of 1896 and the weakening of party competition on the state level throughout most of the country, effective partisan resistance to registration statutes largely

---

[34] Shefter (1978b:263–66).
[35] See Shefter (1986:268) for a description of the "naturalization frauds" of 1868 in which hundreds of immigrants at a time were naturalized by Tammany judges.

dissipated. Registration laws spread rapidly, and became more restrictive. Even so, it was not so simple a matter as enacting restrictive laws. What continued to matter in practice was the organizational capacity of the local parties to shape implementation. When the New York state legislature established an Office of Superintendent of Elections in 1898, the legislature apparently meant to target New York City registration practices. Tammany was still vigorous, however, and managed to dominate the office until it was abolished in 1921.[36] Similarly, a tough Pennsylvania registration statute directed at Philadelphia in 1906 did not affect the city's turnout; "the ring" continued to produce higher turnouts than in a majority of the thirty-seven Pennsylvania counties that did not require personal registration.[37] In the 1902 gubernatorial election, eight of the machine-controlled Philadelphia wards produced a turnout rate of 105.3 percent, with the machine's candidate winning 85.4 percent.[38]

Still, the tide was turning. The clientelist parties came under assault in this period not only from partisan contenders, but from businessmen reformers as well. After 1896, the largely Democratic machines lost ground in the state legislatures, and they also lost the protection that once was yielded them by the national power of the Democratic party in an intensely competitive period. As these business reform campaigns gained momentum, the local parties were stripped of some of the resources they had used to sustain their cadres, to reach voters, and to overcome registration barriers. Consequently, the gradual weakening of the clientelist parties worked in tandem with more restrictive registration laws to steadily lower turnout, especially among the worse off.

With these points made, we return to the proposition that rules, once implemented, change politics. As voter registration restrictions took effect little by little, the linkages that bound the

[36] Harris (1929:76).
[37] Burnham (1974b:1006).
[38] See Burnham (1979:138, fn. 31).

parties to their working- and lower-class constituencies withered. Calculations of electoral advantage turned party strategists away from the worse off, who voted less, and toward the better off, who voted more. This tendency meshed nicely with other developments that were changing the local parties, including the contraction of clientelist resources, and the rise of business influence. Once this shift in orientation and constituencies had occurred, the parties tried to sustain it in order to avoid the threats to incumbency and to internal stability that new and unpredictable voters entailed. Consequently, *the parties themselves became the defenders of the voter registration procedures that ensured their stability and protected incumbents.* As early as 1917, the machine and the reformers switched sides in Chicago, with the machine defending more cumbersome registration procedures against the Chicago Bureau of Public Efficiency's efforts at simplification.[39] Thus, the local parties became the guardians of a contracted electoral universe, using the voter registration restrictions that had helped to create that constricted electorate in the first place. In the late nineteenth century, the local parties helped voters hurdle electoral barriers because they depended on a broad electorate, but as the parties lost ground to the disenfranchisers, they adapted to a narrow electorate by taking up the defense of electoral barriers.

As the connections between the parties and the electorate were reconstituted so that working-class groups were far less important, party appeals changed. In the mid-nineteenth century, clientelist parties employed the boisterous rhetoric of class in building popular support, along with strident ethnic and religious appeals. And in the decades after the Civil War, there were at least some signs of the emergence of appeals based on issues, including economic issues, partly in response to the insurgent third-party challenges that injected broad issue appeals into electoral contests. The campaign of 1896 underlined the possi-

[39] Harris (1929:83–84).

bility of the emergence of issue politics. "Perceptions of 'hard times' dominated . . . and strongly influenced the decisionmaking process of large numbers of voters. Older ethnoreligious antagonisms did not suddenly evaporate . . . [but] as economic worries came increasingly to the forefront of consciousness, they crosscut the older lines of conflict and decreased their salience."[40] As the links that bound the local parties to a working-class constituency became attenuated, however, party appeals based on class identity and class interests gradually disappeared. Electoral contests were eventually neutered of class rhetoric, with the result that the marginalization of working-class voters from electoral politics that resulted in the first instance from the combination of registration barriers and the breakdown of clientelist ties was not overcome by the emergence of electoral contests whose symbols and substance resonated strongly with working-class experience, except under the exceptional conditions of the Great Depression campaigns of the 1930s.

Under these political conditions, voter registration procedures depressed turnout. Without the parties as intermediaries to help voters complete registration procedures, the "costs" of registration rise. And without appeals that resonate with the identity and interests of working-class groups, the benefits of voting shrink.[41] In short, rules do indeed originate in politics, and their implementation is conditioned by complex features of the political situation, including the new political conditions the rules themselves helped to produce. Voter registration arrangements helped to create a party system severed from the working class. In a politics of weak linkages and hollow appeals, registration became a larger barrier to participation.

We argued earlier that a singular emphasis on the crushing of party competition associated with the election of 1896 ultimately fails as an explanation of the long-term decline in turnout,

---

[40] Kleppner (1982:74). See also Harris (1929:179–268) and Jensen (1971:238–68).

[41] "Every rational man decides to vote just as he makes all other decisions: if the returns outweigh the costs, he votes; if not, he abstains" (Downs, 1957:260).

if only because it cannot explain why low turnout became a permanent feature of twentieth-century political life, persisting throughout the twentieth century, long after party competition was restored to most of the country. In our opinion, it was the combined effects of changes in the local parties and the introduction of new rules that marginalized potentially disruptive elements from the electorate. This helped to stabilize the tendency toward one-party sectional domination associated with the election of 1896. Moreover, the changes in the rules and in the parties that secured that result continued to depress turnout, even after party competition intensified in much of the North in the 1930s, and in the South in the 1960s. One-party sectionalism is a thing of the past, to be sure, but other aspects of the system of 1896 persist.

One final comment. Schattschneider and Burnham do not rest their case solely on the collapse of party competition. They think the collapse of party competition went hand in glove with the increasing domination of both parties by economic elites, with the consequence that potential voters were alienated because their interests were ignored.[42] There is surely truth in the view that business influence on party programs and symbols dampened political participation by large numbers of minorities, the poor, and blue-collar workers. Still, that was not the whole of it. The singular domination of electoral politics by business was in turn sustained by institutional barriers that excluded large proportions of the have-nots—of the groups who were made to bear the costs of business policies.

---

[42] Burnham made this argument with particular boldness in 1965 and 1970. In subsequent work, however, he also makes what would seem to be the inconsistent argument that most Americans agreed with the political directions of the system of 1896.

INSTITUTIONAL VERSUS
SOCIAL-PSYCHOLOGICAL EXPLANATIONS

In the main, however, analysts have not cast the problem of nonvoting in institutional terms. Rather, the scale and persistence of nonvoting in the twentieth century encouraged scholars to fasten on the question of what it is about nonvoters themselves that accounts for their failure to participate. Something approaching a theoretical consensus has developed, albeit a consensus broad enough to permit a flourishing academic debate about a virtually endless number of variations and permutations of the general thesis. Notwithstanding the variety of specific propositions advanced, the overall line of reasoning is simple: the key to the puzzle of why so many people do not vote lies in one or another of their attitudes and preferences, or their lack of necessary resources. Thus, people fail to vote because of a sense of political ineffectiveness,[43] or they lack a sense of civic obligation,[44] or they feel little partisan attachment,[45] or they possess few educational resources,[46] or they exhibit some combination of these factors.[47] Aldrich and Simon speak of this large body of research as having become, by the 1970s, the "normal science" of nonvoting."[48]

Thirty years ago, Lazarsfeld, Berelson, and Gaudet, writing in *The People's Choice*, set the direction for this sort of interpretation when they concluded that "three quarters of the non-

---

[43] Schaffer (1981).

[44] Almond and Verba (1963: especially chapters 11 and 12) and Verba and Nie (1972: 125–37).

[45] Campbell et al. (1957 and 1960).

[46] Wolfinger and Rosenstone (1980).

[47] Abramson and Aldrich (1982) emphasize both partisanship and political efficacy as determinants of turnout.

[48] Aldrich and Simon (1986:293).

voters stayed away from the polls deliberately because they were unconcerned. . . . A long range program of civic education would be needed to draw such people into the orbit of political life."[49] Or in the economistic language of the rational choice analysts, people abstain because, given their attitudes, the "costs" of voting outweigh perceived benefits.[50] The assumption underlying these studies is that attitudes determine behavior, and attitudes toward politics determine the decision whether or not to vote.[51]

This is no doubt true, at least in the sense that we would expect people who do not vote to express attitudes that are in some measure consistent with their behavior. But where do these attitudes come from? The tendency in the dominant literature is to search for the origins of subjective orientations in such characteristics as socioeconomic status or age.[52] Some analysts treat these demographic characteristics as significant in their own right because they are associated with differential access to the resources that make electoral participation easier and more gratifying, particularly access to skills and information. Perhaps the most influential current argument has been set out by Wolfinger and Rosenstone, who claim that educational levels exert a stronger influence on voter turnout than either income or occupation because education

[49] Lazarsfeld, Berelson, and Gaudet (1948:47).

[50] The economic model of the decision whether or not to vote is associated with the rational choice school, particularly with Anthony Downs's (1957) economic model of political choice. There is, however, a major dispute as to whether the preferences that govern the voting decision have to do with the outcome of the election, or with the process of voting itself. Or, in other words, whether the motivation is instrumental or expressive, whether voting is an investment to realize an end, or valuable in its own right. See also Riker and Ordeshook (1968) for an early development of the expressive view of voting. And see also Shienbaum (1984). However, something like this view was advanced as early as 1924 by Schlesinger and Eriksson. See also Lipset (1960:205) for a similar explanation of nonvoting.

[51] Aldrich and Simon (1986:271–301).

[52] Verba and Nie (1972:126–27) call this the "baseline" model: "Individuals of higher social status develop such civic orientations as concern for politics, information, and feelings of efficacy, and these orientations in turn lead to participation."

increases cognitive skills, which facilitates learning about politics. . . . Better educated people are likely to get more gratification from political participation. . . . Finally, schooling imparts experience with a variety of bureaucratic relationships: learning requirements, filling out forms, waiting in lines, and meeting deadlines.[53]

The overall thrust of this corpus of work is to direct attention away from political and institutional explanations of nonvoting in favor of psychological or social explanations. Berelson, Lazarsfeld, and McPhee called the tune in 1954 when they cautioned against "purely political explanations for nonparticipation. . . . Nonvoting is related to persistent social conditions having little to do with the candidates or issues of the moment."[54]

Of course, it is obvious that less educated or poorer or younger Americans in fact vote less. But the social or psychological differences between voters and nonvoters do not constitute explanations of nonvoting. As we have already said, such attributes as low education or low income or youth do not have a comparably depressing impact on voter turnout in the democracies of Western Europe. Not did education (or income or occupation) much depress turnout in the United States during the nineteenth century. What these correlational analyses cannot explain is why turnout levels reached historic highs in the nineteenth century, when educational levels were low, and why they then fell in the twentieth century, when educational levels rose.[55]

These observations virtually compel one to conclude that

---

[53] Wolfinger and Rosenstone (1980:88). Campbell et al. (1960:476) also think low educational levels deter participation because the less educated cannot deal with the overflow of political information. Other demographic factors, such as residential mobility, have also been put forward as explanations of nonvoting. See Alford and Scoble (1968); Verba and Nie (1972, chapter 13); Cavanaugh (1981).

[54] Berelson, Lazarsfeld, and McPhee (1954:32).

[55] We are hardly the first to make this observation. Schlesinger and Eriksson pointed out over a half century ago (1924:164) that educational levels had skyrocketed since 1890, while turnout had plummeted. See also the comments of Orren and Verba in the Harvard/ABC News Symposium (1984:14).

whatever relationship exists in the contemporary United States between turnout and political attitudes or demographic characteristics is specific to the contemporary American electoral system. Of course, the general notion that turnout is conditioned by political context, no matter the attitudes or resources of the potential electorate, is commonplace. Everyone would agree that attitudinal or demographic predispositions can be offset by more intense political stimuli.[56] This is why we correctly expect higher turnouts in more important electoral races, or in more closely competitive races, or at moments when group consciousness rises, or when electoral races are associated with sharply divisive issues.[57] It is what Verba and Nie mean when they acknowledge that other forces may moderate the bias toward lower participation by groups with lower socioeconomic status, and with political attitudes that discourage participation:

> If there were more class-based ideologies, more class-based organizations, more explicit class-based appeals by political parties, the participation disparity between upper- and lower-status citizens would very likely be less.[58]

Similar reasoning is often employed when the supposition that low socioeconomic status depresses political participation is projected backward to the nineteenth century, as when Chambers and Davis take for granted that high voter participation in the lower social and economic portions of the electorate could only have been made possible by much stronger political stimuli.[59] In

---

[56] See Kim, Petrocik, and Enokson (1975:107–31) for an effort to disentangle the effects of rules, party competition, and socioeconomic characteristics in comparing contemporary turnout among the states. Their comments (1975:110 and fn. 22) on the methodological problems of attempting to model these relations so as to permit the discovery of interaction effects between contextual variables and individual characteristics are especially interesting.

[57] Phillips and Blackman (1975:38–39) make this point.

[58] Verba and Nie (1972:340).

[59] Chambers and Davis (1978:177–78). See also Kleppner (1982:34–36) for a historical commentary that gives qualified weight to such individual characteristics in the nineteenth century.

these hybrid arguments, a political context that generates greater stimulus and more organizational cohesion merely qualifies the dominant social-psychological model derived from contemporary American data.[60]

This simply is not good enough. It is an effort to cope with the empirical contradictions that the dominant model confronts while preserving the basic assumption that voter participation can be explained by personal characteristics rather than by political institutions. The point is not that the political context sometimes *offsets* the effects of demographic or social-psychological factors on turnout, but that the political context *determines* whether these factors will have a significant effect on participation, and just what those effects will be. The evidence strongly suggests that who votes and who does not has no inherent relationship to either variations in attitudes or socioeconomic status. The reasoning that assumes that an intense politics in the nineteenth century offsets the influence of socioeconomic or attitudinal factors is a tortured effort to sustain the "normal science" model. What the data show instead, according to Kleppner, is "the virtual absence of age and socioeconomic biases in the nineteenth century"; indeed, he finds that in broad regions of the country, "there is more evidence that electoral turnout was an inverse, rather than a direct, function of economic condition."[61]

The challenge to the "normal science" model generated by cross-national evidence is, if anything, even more compelling. Burnham cites a startling comparison: turnout in Sweden by propertied middle-class voters is no higher than by manual workers (90 percent versus 87 percent in 1960), but in the United States the propertied middle class turns out half again more than the working class (77 percent versus 52 percent in

---

[60] Verba and Nie (1972:126–27).
[61] Kleppner (1982:34–36). We should note, however, that Kleppner (1982:149) nevertheless holds a hybrid position. Gienapp (1982:61) makes a similar, though less categorical, point, asserting "sound reasons to reject the assumption that education played as important a role in past politics as it does today."

1972). When education is considered as a determinant of turn-out, the Swedish data show no difference between the voting rates of the most and least educated (97 percent versus 95 percent in 1979), but in the United States the most educated vote at twice the rate of the least educated (82 percent versus 44 percent in 1976).[62] Similarly, about 90 percent of Italians with five years or less of formal schooling voted in 1968, while only 38 percent of Americans with comparable educational levels did.[63] Powell's cross-national findings are particularly compelling. Using the same measures employed by Verba, Nie, and Kim,[64] he found a substantial correlation between turnout and socioeconomic status in the United States, but none in ten other countries.[65] More-over, except for the youngest age group, correlations between age and turnout were quite weak in these countries, as they also appear to have been in the nineteenth-century United States.[66] And most persuasive, the attitudes associated with status or age, regarded by analysts using the dominant model as the interven-ing variables explaining why demographic status depresses turn-out, are *not* correlated with cross-national differences in turnout. Indeed, Americans as a whole rank very high on attitudes that are said to facilitate turnout. They are more intensely partisan, feel themselves to be more efficacious, and are more interested in politics. Turnout should therefore be higher, not lower. Powell sums up his findings:

> Using a combination of aggregate and comparative survey data, the present analysis suggests that in comparative per-spective, turnout in the United States is advantaged about

---

[62] See Burnham (1979:114).

[63] See Burnham (1982a:169 and table 5).

[64] Verba, Nie, and Kim (1978).

[65] Powell (1986:29). The standardized beta coefficient was .33 in the United States, but only .05 in ten other nations.

[66] Kleppner and Baker (1980:218–19) provide data suggesting that the system of 1896 involved "the development of a different set of age-cohort-with-turnout linkages, and that this difference was especially marked among the young of immigrant parentage."

5% by political attitudes, but disadvantaged 13% by the party system and institutional factors, and up to 14% by the registration laws.[67]

In short, the social-psychological model confounds causes and consequences.[68] Features of the electoral system affect different groups differently. Legal and administrative barriers to voting impinge less on the well-off and well-educated than they do on the poor and the uneducated. Party strategies to activate and enlist voters are similarly selective in their impact on different groups, and so are the ideological appeals generated by candidates and parties. As Burnham says, "When politics matters . . . people behave as though it matters."[69] The lack of motivation associated with the apathetic attitudes of nonvoters is not the cause of their marginalization from electoral politics, although it may be one of the outcomes.[70] Similarly, people with lower levels of education vote less in the United States because the political system tends to isolate them, and not because less education is an inherent impediment to voting. Apathy and lack of political skill are a consequence, not a cause, of the party structure and political culture that is sustained by legal and procedural barriers to electoral participation. The political system determines whether participation is predicated on class-related resources and attitudes.

There is a historical irony in the emergence of the social-psychological model as "normal science." The institutional arrangements that combined to narrow the electoral universe were constructed by regional elites who worked over time to refashion

[67] Ibid. (17–19).
[68] The general suggestion that independent demographic variables ought to be reconstructed as dependent social and economic variables to understand the behavior of voters and parties is made by Hays (1981:265).
[69] Burnham (1974b:1019).
[70] Powell's (1986 and 1982)) comparative data speak only to aggregate national attitude measures, and do not contradict other studies which show that nonvoting is correlated with attitudinal measures of political alienation within the United States.

the legal and party basis of mass electoral participation. They were activated by political problems created by an urban immigrant working class, by insurgent western farmers, and by both white dirt farmers and blacks in the South. They crafted the step-by-step development of institutional arrangements to narrow the electorate precisely to demobilize the groups whose politics were threatening and disruptive. Not only were blacks and poor whites disfranchised in the South, but voter registration arrangements were targeted specifically at the northern cities where the immigrant working class was concentrated. Literacy tests, stricter naturalization procedures, and burdensome voter registration procedures were not so likely to bar the rich as they were the poor, or the well educated as they were the uneducated.[71] Not only do a good many social scientists manage to ignore these developments by treating the racially and class-biased effects of these arrangements as causes, but they are encouraged to do so by the witless use of multiple correlational analyses. The prime example is the attempt to discover whether the inauguration of voter registration arrangements affected turnout *when urbanization, income, and education are controlled.* But urbanization, income, and education cannot reasonably be employed as control variables, since they in fact predict the likelihood that stringent voter registration procedures exist in the first place. Voter registration was intended to discourage voting in big cities, and by the poor and less educated. The effects of restrictions cannot be disentangled—indeed, they are necessarily obscured—by introducing urbanization, income, or education as controls.[72] This is

---

[71] Kleppner (1982:66–68) provides data on turnout changes in the Metropole between the late nineteenth and early twentieth centuries that show that the impact of registration procedures on turnout increased as per capita wealth decreased.

[72] Carlson's (1976) otherwise excellent study of the impact of registration requirements early in the century is a regrettable example of this widespread modeling error. He establishes that turnout was significantly lower in counties with personal voter registration requirements than in counties with no registration or with nonpersonal registration in the presidential elections between 1912 and 1924. But when he then controls this finding by demographic, party competition and urbanization variables, it disappears! As a result of this "nonfinding," the contribution his research makes to the literature has not been recognized.

just another way in which the political underpinnings of voter exclusion are made to disappear in favor of an analysis that searches for an explanation of nonparticipation in the nonparticipants.

Chapter 5

The New Deal Party System: Continuities and Breakdown

By the 1920s, low levels of electoral participation had become a central fact of American political life. During the decades since, successive cohorts of tens of millions of nonvoters constituted the most unstable element in American politics. At different times, fractions of these marginalized populations were drawn into the electorate, or allowed to drop out of it, and these successive expansions and contractions of the voting universe have played a critical (if often unacknowledged) role in the dynamics of electoral change.

The metapolitics of participation had three distinct phases. The first is associated with the New Deal, though it began in 1928 with a partial remobilization of northern working-class voters stimulated by the intense ethnocultural conflict evoked by Al Smith's candidacy against Hoover. The participation of these working-class voters in the Democratic party expanded further during the New Deal, and was sustained by the extraordinary programmatic and structural innovations of the decade that, among other things, created a party apparatus to enlist working-class voters. The constrictions on electoral participation established by the system of 1896 persisted through all of these developments, however, shaping the Democratic party that emerged from the New Deal realignment. As a result, voter turnout among working-class voters did not rise as much as it might have, signaling that the previous patterns of legal restrictions and skewed party-electoral linkages had been modified but not overturned. Perhaps even more important, the southern wing of the system survived the upheavals of the New Deal period intact, with the consequence that blacks and poor whites remained effectively disenfranchised there. Meanwhile, the role of the South in national affairs enlarged because it was key to the majority status of the Democratic party. Consequently, the South could exert a powerful conservative weight that tempered the influence —and at least indirectly the Democratic allegiance—of the northern working class.

The second phase saw the breakdown of one-party politics in the South, and the resulting partial breakup of the New Deal electoral coalition. This phase too can be understood as a series of challenges to the terms of electoral participation associated with the system of 1896. The civil rights movement raised one set of challenges and ultimately created the political conditions that forced reluctant national Democratic leaders to intervene in the southern system to secure the partial reenfranchisement of southern blacks, although at great cost in white southern support. Political modernization in the South also resulted in the reenfranchising of less-well-off southern whites, many of whom entered the electoral system under the banners of the Christian Right's remarkable late-twentieth-century revival of tribalist politics. These events completed the collapse of the one-party South, and led to a revival of the Republican party.

The third phase in the politics of participation unfolded in the North, where support for the New Deal was also weakening. Most explanations emphasize working-class defections prompted by the conflicts that emerged in the 1960s, particularly over race and the issues associated with the New Politics. We think, however, that there was a deeper and more long-lasting problem. The apparatus created by the New Deal leadership during the

1930s to reach and hold its new working-class constituency consisted largely of revived clientelist local parties, and a network of new party-linked labor unions. However, after World War II, as the composition of the working class gradually shifted from industrial workers to include large numbers of minorities and women in the emerging service sector, this apparatus for mobilizing voters became progressively less effective, paralyzed partly by organizational stasis and partly by antagonisms between its old working-class constituents and the new working class.[1] The Kennedy and Johnson administrations tried to reach past malfunctioning local parties and city bureaucracies by intervening in the cities with new "Great Society" programs. But the voting apparatus itself remained firmly under the control of state and specifically local parties. One result was that the partial remobilization of the working class that had made the construction of the New Deal coalition possible was gradually reversed. Voter turnout again began to decline, and once again it declined most among the less well off.

THE NEW DEAL: REALIGNMENT AND
INCOMPLETE REMOBILIZATION

The origins of the New Deal realignment are often located in the presidential contest of 1928, when the Democrats nominated Al Smith—New York machine boss, Catholic, and wet.[2] Intense feelings about religion, immigrants, and Prohibition dominated the election, and large sections of the South actually defected to Hoover rather than vote for "a subject of the Pope."[3] Mean-

---

[1] See Mollenkopf (1983) for a similar analysis of the Democratic party's electoral problems, although not applied to levels of participation.
[2] Key's (1955) classic article on critical elections locates the beginnings of the New Deal realignment in 1928.
[3] Sundquist (1973:177).

while, Catholics and immigrants rallied to Smith, the first Democratic presidential contender since Cleveland to carry the ten largest cities.[4] It was, in short, a contest, and it was about matters of cultural identity that stir passions. For the first time since 1896, turnout rose significantly; it jumped from 19 percent to 23 percent between 1924 and 1928 in the South, and from 57 percent to 66 percent in the North (table 5.1). It is testimony to the persistence and force of the ethnocultural attachments that figured so largely in the nineteenth-century politics that the contest of 1928 actually produced a larger jump in turnout than the realigning elections of 1932 and 1936.[5] But a contest between Protestants and Catholics did not, of course, break the pattern of Republican and business control of the national political dialogue that had unfolded with the system of 1896. John J. Raskob, a General Motors executive, became chair of the Democratic National Committee; business slogans dominated the rhetoric of both parties; and Smith was routed, winning only 87 electoral

TABLE 5.1 PRESIDENTIAL TURNOUT PERCENTAGES, 1924–1940

	South	*Non-South*	*National*
1924	19	57	49
1928	23	66	57
1932	24	66	57
1936	25	71	61
1940	26	73	62

Source: Burnham (1981c:100, table 1). Based on total of all citizens legally eligible to vote, aliens excluded.

[4] Polakoff (1981:317).

[5] However, the data do not support the thesis, advanced by Kleppner, Jensen, and others, that the primary ethnocultural division in 1928 was between pietists and liturgicals. This was a straightforward conflict between Protestants and Catholics. See Lichtman (1979) for an exhaustive study of the voting data. The surge was actually larger among Republican voters than among Democrats, which also suggests a reaction by Protestants against Catholics. Of course, the religious basis of this electoral contest makes it quite different from the realigning elections of the 1930s. See Burnham (1982a:177).

votes, while Hoover ascended to the presidency with the largest Republican congressional majority since 1920.[6]

When the crash of 1929 hit, entire industries were stricken, whole towns devastated.[7] But people did not turn to electoral politics for solutions; in 1930 and 1932, there was no additional turnout rise *at all* in either the North or South. In the depressions of the 1870s and 1890s, by contrast, economic catastrophe had drawn people to the polls. Turnout had jumped in the midterm elections of 1874 and 1894, each of which came on the heels of a major depression.[8] The dislocation and distress occasioned by the depression of 1929 were probably more severe, if only because so much of the country was by that time urbanized and industrialized and totally exposed to market fluctuations. Still, the system of 1896 gradually had restricted the participation of the less well off, and popular economic grievances had disappeared from party agendas by the 1920s. Those who voted spurned the incumbent regime, to be sure, and Roosevelt carried all but a few states in the Northeast. But this expressed a reaction by voters of all strata against a president and a party that had presided over the economic calamity:

> In 1930 and 1932 the available political alternatives failed to stimulate political consciousness among the deprived or to increase greatly their interest in electoral politics. Neither major party effectively gave meaning to and mobilized economic discontent. What occurred in these elections was a decisive rejection of the party of "hard times" and of its

---

[6] There were some small signs in the farm belt, however, that severely depressed agricultural conditions in the 1920s were moving votes into Democratic columns. Smith carried forty-five counties in Illinois, Iowa, Minnesota, and North Dakota. See Sundquist (1973: 174–76).

[7] Bernstein (1970:255–56) reports that by January 1930, 30 to 40 percent of the male labor force in Toledo was out of work. By the end of 1930, half the textile workers in New England were unemployed; and the Metropolitan Life Insurance Company discovered that one-quarter of its policyholders in forty-six cities were jobless.

[8] Kleppner (1982:85).

most visible officeholder, Herbert Hoover. The anti-Republican swings that shaped those outcomes extended to virtually all categories of voters, but they did not restructure the fault line of partisan combat.[9]

The usual view is that the upturn in voting that eventually occurred among the less well off was a response to the depression and the New Deal. Of course, in some sense that has to be true; something about the 1930s galvanized higher voting participation, and little of political consequence in the 1930s was unrelated to the depression and the New Deal. But the rise did not begin until the midterm election of 1934—five years after the collapse—and turnout rose again in both 1936 and 1940. What the timing of rising turnout makes clear is that it was not a simple response to economic distress. Moreover, while the New Deal initiatives helped to motivate new voters to try to contend with the registration process, these initiatives themselves have to be explained.

The role of popular movements is missing in most accounts of the emergence of rising turnout in the 1930s. To be sure, New Deal reforms helped increase turnout in the North in ways that we will describe. But the reforms themselves were forged by the interaction between political movements and electoral politics.[10] The Roosevelt administration reached out to people in the middle and the bottom of American society because its hand was forced by popular mobilizations and the uncertain electoral repercussions that they produced. Even the 1932 campaign appeals, which restored to national politics a rhetoric celebrating the common man and denouncing the economic royalists that had been absent since the Progressive era, and the fact that Roosevelt came to office prepared to inaugurate some relief measures and

[9] Ibid. (98).
[10] The interaction of protest movements with the electoral context is the main theme of the analysis of twentieth-century movements in Piven and Cloward (1977).

to buoy commodity prices by imposing controls on agricultural production, were influenced by early waves of popular protest. That said, however, the new administration's initial plans were mainly oriented to reviving business by bringing order to the financial markets, and by adopting a plan for industrial price and production controls proposed by the U.S. Chamber of Commerce. The protest movements caused sufficient disruption and electoral dissension to change that. The movements transformed vague campaign promises into contentious issues with which the Roosevelt administration had to cope, or risk both escalating disruptions in the streets and factories, and disaffection among elements of its still insecure electoral constituency. Popular protests compelled the administration to inaugurate massive relief programs, to support legislation giving workers the right to collective bargaining, and to initiate sweeping social security legislation. The New Deal programs, in short, were at least partly a response to an electorate galvanized by movements.

The movements in turn were also energized by the comparative responsiveness of the new administration: they were not simply a reaction to economic calamity. Protest emerged and spread because of the new political possibilities suggested by the partial erosion of the system of 1896 and the instabilities associated with electoral realignment. Those possibilities were not just vaguely sensed. They were evident from the changed rhetoric of political leaders, and from the early initiatives they took to appease popular unrest. The campaign promises, Roosevelt's overwhelming victory, and the dramatic legislative initiatives during the first hundred days encouraged people to think that public issues had some bearing on their private troubles.

The sense of popular power and programmatic possibility that was communicated by politicians who were trying to ride out the currents of electoral instability helps to explain the emergence of what were surely the largest protests of the unemployed in American history. People marched and demonstrated for "bread or wages" and battled the police to stop evictions in many of the major cities of the country.[11] The emergency relief measures of 1933, initiated within weeks of Roosevelt's inauguration, were a response to these protests, and to the alarm they generated among politicians generally, not least among panicked local government officials whose efforts to provide unemployment relief were leading to local fiscal disaster. A Social Science Research Council bulletin put it this way:

> By the time the new federal administration came into power in 1933, the pressure for more money had become so nearly unanimous that it was politically desirable for congressmen and senators to favor large appropriations for relief; candidates were elected often on a platform which predicated adequate relief appropriations by Congress.[12]

The changed climate also stirred other hard-pressed groups —workers, the aged, farmers, and farm tenants. Rural mobs resisted farm foreclosures; the aged campaigned for government pensions to the battle hymn of "Onward Townsend Soldiers"; mass encampments of displaced tenant farmers demanded government aid; and, as the economy finally began showing feeble signs of recovery in 1934, industrial workers erupted in strikes and sit-downs to win collective bargaining rights. These popular actions were incited by the hopes that the New Deal stimulated. In turn, mass action transformed hope into demands and galvanized voters around those demands, thus shaping the New Deal programs and rhetorical appeals. By raising issues and polarizing alternatives, the dynamic between movements and the New Deal almost surely helped sustain and enlarge voter turnout, particularly in the elections of 1934 and 1936. However, the larger

---

[11] See Piven and Cloward (1977: chapters 2 and 3), as well as Bernstein (1970) and Schlesinger (1957). See also Goldfield (1985) for a judicious review of the diverse political forces accounting for New Deal labor legislation that nevertheless emphasizes the importance of mass protest. Ferguson (1984) describes the divisions between business and the New Deal.

[12] White and White (1937:84).

impact of movements on turnout was indirect. The combination of electoral instability and protest forced the New Deal administration to intervene in the structure of the federal system, in the economy, and in the lives of ordinary people in ways that Roosevelt and his brain trust had almost surely never contemplated, and this too affected turnout. In the American federal system, the impact of national policies on the everyday life of most people had always been obscure. This was no longer so. Now new federal programs overrode state and local governments to reach out directly to the citizenry; or federal program dollars (and New Deal popularity) were used to press sometimes reluctant state and local governments into collaboration. Kleppner describes the resulting change in the relationship of masses of people to the national government:

> Never before had so many citizens experienced the effects of federal actions so directly or been able to see their consequences so concretely. Federal relief agencies—the Civil Works Administration, the Federal Emergency Relief Administration, and the Works Progress Administration—provided jobs for over seven million adults, as did the National Youth Administration for over seven million young Americans. The Home Owners' Loan Corporation helped refinance one out of every five mortgages on private urban dwellings in the country. The Social Security Act created a system of old-age insurance and established a federal-state system of unemployment insurance. The Tennessee Valley Authority and the Rural Electrification Administration brought electric power to millions of rural homes and farms.[13]

The vast new federal or federally funded programs not only linked program beneficiaries to the Roosevelt wing of the Dem-

---

[13] Kleppner (1982:100). See also Leuchtenberg (1963:53, 120–32, and 157–58).

ocratic party but also created organizational vehicles to mobilize voters from the bottom. Thus, the various relief programs provided part of the foundation on which the Democratic party's apparatus to recruit votes was rebuilt:

> Econometric analysis of state-by-state relief expenditures shows that political considerations (like closeness of the vote) far overshadowed poverty in explaining the distribution of billions of dollars of relief money. Historians examining the situation by states and cities concur that politicized relief, especially as channeled through Democratic organizations, played a major role in rebuilding the Democratic coalition. At one time or another during the decade, somewhere between 40 and 45 percent of all American families received federal relief. Gallup polls show that families receiving politicized relief (WPA, CCC, NYA, and related programs) voted much more heavily Democratic than did poor people not on relief. In August 1936, for example, reliefers were 82 percent for Roosevelt; the lowest one-third income group was 70 percent; and the highest third, only 41 percent.[14]

Some of the main intermediaries in establishing these links between working-class voters and the Democratic party were the old political machines, which in many places had become debilitated by municipal fiscal crises (as well as by the longer-term effects of decades-long reform campaigns). With federal program monies, however, they could be reinvigorated. Roosevelt collaborated with the local clientelist parties,[15] and they in turn supported the New Deal: "Far from rendering the machine[s] obsolete, Roosevelt reinvigorated [them] for at least another

[14] Jensen (1981:205–6). The reorganization of federal agencies to facilitate the institutionalization of linkages to a new constituency during the New Deal is discussed in Shefter (1978a:39–41) and Mollenkopf (1983: chapter 2).
[15] See Mann (1965).

decade." [16] The most famous instance was the New Deal relationship with the Chicago machine—initiated in return for Mayor Anton Cermak's support at the 1932 convention—where federal funds made possible the centralization of the fractious ward-based Chicago bosses. (By the same token, control over the distribution of federal benefits could be used to punish enemies. Thus, Roosevelt used relief and public works programs for New York City to help destroy Tammany Hall and the base of Al Smith, his archrival. Tammany was already reeling from a series of investigations of corruption initiated by Roosevelt while he was governor. Then, in 1933, Roosevelt's allies collaborated in fielding a Democratic competitor to the Tammany candidate who divided the Democratic vote in the mayorality contest and threw the election to Fiorello LaGuardia, the reform-Republican candidate. LaGuardia's subsequent firm hold on the mayoralty was at least partly due to the liberal allocations of federal monies to New York City. Taken together, these actions were probably fatal —or as near fatal as any particular set of measures ever had been —to the hardy "New York Democracy.") [17]

The unions came to constitute a parallel infrastructure to mobilize voters. After Roosevelt reluctantly ceded industrial workers government protection for the right to organize, the national Democratic party developed strong organizational ties to the new CIO unions. In many places, the unions functioned as local parties, turning out their own members for the Democratic slate, and organizing campaigns in their localities. As early as 1936, the CIO threw itself into the effort to reelect Roosevelt by staging rallies, paying for radio time and leaflets, and spending nearly $1 million in the industrial states of New York, Pennsylvania, Illinois, and Ohio. In addition, the constituent unions of the CIO contributed $770,000 to Roosevelt's cam-

[16] Jensen (1981:210).
[17] For a close study of the Chicago machine during the depression, see Gosnell (1937). On FDR and the machines, see also Dorsett (1977).

paign fund, most of it from the mine workers' treasury, a sum that dwarfed the AF of L's political contributions, which had totaled a mere $95,000 over the entire previous thirty years.[18] In subsequent elections, the CIO commitment to the Democratic party became firmer. In 1940, union delegates figured prominently in the national Democratic convention, and Roosevelt ran strongest in the industrial counties where the CIO was concentrated.[19] In 1944, every constituent CIO union endorsed Roosevelt, the CIO campaign contribution was raised to $1,328,000, and an apparatus involving tens of thousands of workers was created under the newly launched Political Action Committee.

If the timing of the rise in turnout supports the view that new voters were drawn to the polls by the interaction of popular protest and the New Deal programmatic and mobilizing initiatives that protest had forced, the changing social composition of the active electorate provides additional support. Turnout increased most among the lowest economic categories—those hard hit by unemployment and the recipients of relief assistance. It rose more among immigrants and those of immigrant parentage. "Overall," Kleppner concludes, "the increased turnout resulted from new mobilization among immigrant-stock voters, the young, those toward the bottom of the economic ladder, the unemployed, reliefers, and citizens" who had not voted in the 1920s.[20] And as turnout rose, the electorate polarized along class lines. These two developments were related in the sense that both were ultimately responses to the politics of protest, and to the initiatives that protest had forced. In 1932, Roosevelt outpolled Hoover among every category of voters, including the highest-

---

[18] See Pelling (1962:166). See also Schlesinger (1960:594) and Greenstone (1969:49).

[19] Schattschneider (1960:49) reports on polls taken at the time that showed CIO members voting 79 percent and 78 percent Democratic in the elections of 1940 and 1944. And Bernstein (1970:720) reviews an analysis of election results in 1940 in sixty-three counties and fourteen cities that showed the strength of the Roosevelt vote paralleled the concentration of CIO members.

[20] Kleppner (1982:89).

income category. By 1936, however, "businessmen switched to Landon while workers went the other way"[21]: Roosevelt ran 29.1 percentage points behind the Republican candidate among high-income voters, and his lead among voters on relief rose to 68.8 percent.[22] In early 1940, the *Public Opinion Quarterly* summarized Gallup poll data showing that 64 percent of upper-income respondents preferred the Republicans, while 69 percent of lower-income respondents preferred the Democrats.[23] Similarly, table 5.2 shows sharp class differences in response to the question from the same poll: "In politics, do you consider yourself a Democrat, Independent, Socialist or Republican?"

TABLE 5.2 PARTY IDENTIFICATION PERCENTAGES, 1940

	Republican	*Democrat*	*Independent*	*Other*
Total sample	38	42	19	1
Professional	44	29	25	2
Business	48	29	22	1
White-collar workers	36	40	22	2
Skilled workers	36	44	19	1
Semiskilled workers	33	47	18	2
Unskilled workers	27	55	16	2

Source: Sundquist (1973:202). Based on a Gallup poll question asked in early 1940.

Not surprisingly, as electoral polarization along class lines increased and voting levels rose, the turnout gap between the well off and the poor narrowed.[24] These developments indicated that several important changes had occurred in the electoral ar-

---

[21] Jensen (1981:212).

[22] Ibid. (103).

[23] These data are reprinted in Sundquist (1973:202).

[24] Kleppner (1982:105) claims that in 1936 the difference in turnout between the top income group and the lowest had narrowed to 7 percent. However, Jensen (1981:211 and table 6.5) reports data for 1940 and 1942 (from the American Institute of Public Opinion Poll no. 294, April 1943) that shows a much wider gap of 18 percentage points in 1940 and, as is typical, an even wider gap in the off-year election of 1942.

rangements associated with the system of 1896, and especially in the pattern of partisan competition and party-constituency linkages. Economic collapse toppled the Republican party from its position of dominance in much of the country. The ensuing electoral instability, combined with popular protest, oriented the Democratic party toward the urban working class, and even prompted at least a partial reconstruction of organizational linkages to the working class.

But the party mobilizing apparatus of big-city political organizations and unions was limited in its reach and, as we will soon note, riddled by contradictory political pressures. Meanwhile, other elements of the system of 1896 persisted, and inhibited the extent of party recomposition. In particular, voter registration barriers partly choked of the surge in turnout among those who suffered most from the economic collapse and benefited most from the New Deal concessions. It has become commonplace to speak of soaring turnout during the mid-1930s. But considered in the light of the extraordinary economic and political events of the period, the increase in turnout was not what it might have been. Nationally, voting rose from 57 percent in 1932 to 61 percent in 1936, and to a peak of 62 percent in 1940.[25] Given the momentous political events of these years—the cataclysmic depression, the spread of mass protest movements, the extraordinary New Deal policy initiatives, and the

[25] There is a considerable academic debate about whether the New Deal Democratic majority was constructed from the entry of previous nonvoters, or the conversion of former Republicans. Anderson's (1982:9) position is that the New Deal realignment resulted from the mobilization of previous nonvoters in the big cities: "[T]he Democratic party, beginning in 1928, changed its bases of support largely by appealing to the hitherto politically uninvolved groups such as women, young people, and the foreign-stock urban working class." For the view that it resulted from converting Republicans, see Erikson and Tedin (1981) and Sundquist (1973: chapter 10). Among others, Burnham (1982a:179) challenges Anderson, concluding on the basis of a detailed analysis of California data that a little more than half of the Democratic gains in 1932, and about a third of the increment in the 1936–40 period, came from new registrants rather than former Republicans. This does not quite justify Burnham's (1982b:181) conclusion that "no such thing as a huge implicit or potential Democratic majority existed among the 'party of nonvoters' until *the Great Depression and the New Deal created one*" (emphasis in original).

exceptional effort to enlist voters—why didn't many more people flock to the polls?

We think the surge that might otherwise have occurred was restrained by the elements of the system of 1896 that did not change. In particular, the restrictions on the franchise associated with literacy tests, residence requirements, and voter registration procedures persisted. Indeed, voter registration requirements had spread in the course of the preceding decades, as *more and more counties* were covered by state registration laws.[26] Literacy tests and residency requirements barred some people outright from voting, no matter the political stimuli of the era. The administrative barriers of the voter registration process were more flexible, for the better educated or more confident or highly motivated might overcome them. And many people did overcome them. Nevertheless, there is persuasive evidence that personal voter registration requirements continued to inhibit access to the ballot to many others, if only by discouraging them, and thus dampened the electoral mobilization of the 1930s. According to Kleppner's analysis, the difference in turnout between counties with and without personal voter registration requirements in the urban and industrial Metropole was about 8 percentage points.[27] Thus the intense politics of the decade did raise turnout, but less than might have been the case had the restrictive electoral machinery of 1896 not been in place. The electoral universe remained skewed, and that is surely a main reason that

[26] In 1900, only 30 percent of the counties outside of the South had registration requirements, although of course these were more likely to be urban and populous counties. By 1930, 52.5 percent of the counties required voter registration, and by 1940, 59.2 percent (Kleppner, 1982:86).

[27] Ibid. (86–87). Kleppner (1982:155) himself seems somewhat undecided about the significance of this obstruction, arguing that the "more powerful constraint . . . was the reigning ideological consensus on the central principle of political economy—the preservation of a capitalist mode of production." The New Deal, in other words, mobilized fewer nonvoters than it might have because it was constrained by the ideologically ambivalent and "morselized" character of majority opinion. However, as we have been at pains to argue, the legal obstructions that had contracted the electoral universe, and delinked the parties from "discordant elements," also meant that the dominant ideological consensus went unchallenged.

the class reorientation of the Democratic party was as partial and short-lived as it was.

Another reason is also traceable to persisting features of the system of 1896. The electoral mobilization that spread across the country in the 1930s never reached the one-party South. Turnout had risen from 18 percent in 1924 to 23 percent in 1928 in response to the ethnocultural challenge of the Smith campaign. But there was no upsurge in the 1930s: turnout rose by a mere 3 percentage points over the decade, reaching 26 percent by 1940. Neither the protest movements nor the New Deal electoral organizing efforts of the 1930s penetrated the southern political oligarchy, and the arrangements that disenfranchised blacks and most poor whites were not shaken.

FDR thus constructed a peculiar electoral coalition between an underrepresented northern urban industrial working class and southern white elites. True, the outlines of that coalition were long-standing. The Democratic party had harbored the big-city machines and southern oligarchs in uneasy coexistence since the late nineteenth century, and the party had sometimes been rent by conflict between these constituencies, especially in the 1920s. But two things were different in the 1930s. A national Democratic party dependent on southern support now held national power. And the urban working class had become both more assertive and a more important element of the coalition than it ever had been before. Accordingly, the party tried to craft programs that would knit together the diverse constituencies that made up its new voter majority while suppressing conflict between them. The relief and public works programs that we usually think of as oriented to the urban working class were also a lifeline to the devastated South:

> During the Depression the "colonial" economy of the South was ravaged far beyond the comprehension of most contemporary northern residents. The prostrate condition of the periphery led its congressmen to support progressive taxa-

tion (which raised comparatively more revenue from core industrial regions) and vast relief programs (which, while they favored the North, still redistributed income to the South because they were financed through progressive tax schedules). On these policies, both the plantation elite and northern labor could agree.[28]

And just as the lifeline to the urban working class bolstered big-city machines, the lifeline to the impoverished South bolstered the state and local parties. At the same time, to mute conflict between the northern and southern wings, the administration of many of the New Deal programs was decentralized. This is what Bensel calls "cooperative federalism." Federal authority in some of the new programs was limited largely to fiscal support of state and local initiatives; other programs were located in independent agencies, spun off from federal oversight to enable them to bend to local interests; or vast legislative powers were delegated to existing executive agencies so as to avoid intractable conflict on the floor of the Congress. New Deal public works or relief or labor programs could thus be tailored to the requirements of the southern system. This means that the programs did not interfere with

> [t]he cheap and captive labor pool that segregationist institutions provided for rural plantation owners and low-skill manufacturing industries. . . . For this reason, agriculture and most seasonal activities such as canning and cotton ginning were exempted from minimum wage and union legislation.[29]

The New Deal, in short, did not challenge segregation, the plantation system that kept sharecroppers in bondage to the plant-

---

[28] Bensel (1984:151–52).
[29] Ibid. (233).

ers through constant debt, or the low-wage rates on which southern manufacturing depended. Roosevelt even refused to sign an antilynching law. In these ways, the New Deal helped to entrench the Southern Democracy associated with the system of 1896, a system that rested on the legal disenfranchisement of the vast majority of blacks and poor whites.

These arrangements also set narrow limits on the political development of the national New Deal coalition. The persisting one-party system in the South meant that its congressional representatives had the seniority to dominate the committee system in the Congress, with the result that a bipartisan congressional coalition of southern Democrats and Republicans continued to hold national Democratic policies hostage for at least the next four decades. And over the longer run, it also meant that the market strength and organizational capacities of northern workers would be undermined by the low-wage labor system in the South, which the "cooperative federalism" of the New Deal left untouched.

The limits on the possibilities of electoral politics inherited from the system of 1896 worked together. Because participation by the working class and the poor in the North continued to be constrained, Democratic control of the urban North was contingent and uncertain, and the party could not aspire to national power without the support of the South. This made the party doubly dependent on the South. It depended on southern support in the Congress for its legislative agenda, and it depended on southern votes in presidential contests. In the absence of these severely limiting conditions, it seems reasonable to surmise that the Democratic party that emerged from the New Deal might have come to resemble a European social democratic party. Of course, other things were also supposedly different in the United States, including the vigor of a popular culture of individualism, and the single-minded greed of American business. Still, popular political attitudes change as party formations change, and business is sometimes defeated. If party leaders had been confronted by a full complement of working-class voters in the cities, and a full complement of impoverished black and white laborers and tenants in the South, who can be sure that a labor-based political party would not have emerged?

DEALIGNMENT AND PARTIAL REMOBILIZATION IN THE SOUTH

It was inevitable that the New Deal coalition would be torn asunder by the strains inherent in its accommodations to the South. National conflicts over racial and sectional arrangements were rooted in the modernization of the southern economy. On the one side, New Deal policies favored the industrial development of the South, a bias that was first observable in the decisions of the World War II War Production Board.[30] This bias persisted in the postwar period because the seniority of southern representatives enabled them to influence the location of military installations and the allocation of defense contracts for the next forty years. At the same time, federal accommodations to the South in labor and social welfare legislation ensured that wage rates remained low, and attractive to northern investors.[31] Taken together, these developments produced a greatly enlarged southern middle class, and helped spur a Republican revival.

On the other side, southern agriculture became more capital-intensive during and after the war, again partly as a result of

[30] Ibid. (181–82).

[31] On the changing class structure in the South, see Wright (1986). The dispersal of branch plants to the South is said to have brought with it northern executives and technicians who were Republicans. See Converse (1972:313–14) and Campbell et al. (1965: chapter 12) for data on the impact of the migration of better-off whites into the South on patterns of partisanship among white southerners. However, Petrocik (1987b:45) disagrees, asserting that the Republican shift occurred entirely among native southerners. In either case, the long-term dilution of Democratic partisanship as a result of changes in the southern class structure should be distinguished from defections by southern whites over the race question, particularly in presidential contests.

federal agricultural policies that were dominated by southern congressmen. Millions of black and white tenants, day laborers and sharecroppers, as well as small farmers, were steadily forced off the land. The displaced whites largely remained in the South, but about half of the displaced blacks migrated to the big cities of the North, where they became voters and constituents of the urban and northern wing of the Democratic party.

In other words, key constituent blocs of the New Deal electoral coalition were being transformed. Northern urban blacks had become Democrats in 1934, largely in response to the help extended to them by New Deal welfare programs, as well as the symbolic assurances associated with Eleanor Roosevelt's cultivation of black leaders. But their numbers were not large, and they only mattered in close elections. The migration northward meant that steadily growing numbers of blacks concentrated in the big cities, where those who voted could sometimes determine how the big industrial states swung in presidential contests. Harry Truman's attempt to conciliate blacks by appointing the U.S. Commission on Civil Rights just prior to the 1948 campaign was an early sign that northern black votes were beginning to matter to national Democratic politicians, and especially to presidential contenders.[32] And when four state delegations from the Deep South walked out of the Democratic convention that year because some of the recommendations of the Civil Rights Commission were incorporated in the Democratic platform, it was an early sign of the pending hemorrhage in the

---

[32] The fact that Truman was fending off Henry Wallace's third-party challenge from the left in a close election may have forced the civil rights issue into national politics rather earlier than would otherwise have been the case. Truman was also prodded by the possibility of Republican competition for northern black votes (a factor that influenced Democratic strategy on civil rights into the 1960s). However, Clark Clifford, Truman's chief campaign strategist, warned that unless Truman acted, the Republicans would offer a legislative program to appeal to blacks, including a Fair Employment Practices Commission, an anti-poll-tax bill, and an antilynching bill. See Yarnell (1974:35–69); Bernstein (1970); Berman (1970); and Vaughan (1972).

New Deal's southern support. Truman survived, but with only 53 percent of the southern white vote compared with FDR's 85 percent in 1936.[33]

Just as Roosevelt's rhetorical appeals to hard-hit working-class voters had raised hopes and stimulated protest, the gestures of national Democratic politicians toward the enlarged numbers of northern urban blacks in denouncing the southern system helped to raise hopes and stimulate protest. Increasingly liberal national rhetoric on the race issue, especially on voting rights in the South, ignited the civil rights movement in the mid-1950s. The result was over a decade of wracking conflict that began in the South, and then spread to the North. National rhetoric about civil rights for blacks, and the 1954 Supreme Court ruling against segregated schools, goaded southern politicians and white segregationist organizations into a "movement of massive resistance" challenging the authority of the federal government to intervene in the southern system.[34] But these events also incited southern blacks to demand federal intervention, beginning with the Montgomery bus boycott in 1955 and continuing with more boycotts, lunch counter sit-ins, freedom rides, marches, and voter registration campaigns, all of which defied caste rules and provoked massive confrontations with southern mobs and police. Throughout the 1950s, the Democratic party vacillated over civil rights, trying to hold its traditional southern white constituencies and the growing number of black voters in the North. Events would soon force a choice.

As the conflict escalated, southern electoral tactics to keep the national Democratic party from acceding to demands for civil rights legislation intensified. The Dixiecrat revolt in 1948 had deprived the Democratic ticket of the votes of Alabama, Louisiana, Mississippi, and South Carolina. Thereafter, southern political leaders turned to a strategy of "presidential Repub-

[33] Ladd (1985:5).
[34] Bartley (1969) and Tindall (1972).

licanism," encouraging their constituents to vote both for Republican presidential contenders and for Democratic congressional and state candidates. In 1952 and 1956, the resulting southern defections cost the national Democratic ticket four states in the Outer South—Florida, Virginia, Tennessee, and Texas—as well as Louisiana in 1956. Furthermore, the increasingly unsuccessful national Democratic strategy of trying to placate the white South by dragging its heels on effective civil rights legislation began to provoke defections among the enlarging number of blacks who were gaining the franchise as they migrated to the northern cities. Stevenson won 80 percent of the national black vote in 1952, but only 60 percent in 1956, and his "states' rights" position on civil rights was surely a main reason. Kennedy fared somewhat better after having campaigned specifically for black votes, winning 68 percent of their ballots, but he lost Florida, Tennessee, and Virginia, as well as Alabama and Mississippi, whose electors were unpledged.

By the early 1960s, the scales began to tip against the white South and in favor of civil rights. The allegiance of many of those white southerners who were in the active electorate seemed to be lost, and incipient black defections portended trouble in the northern strongholds of the Democratic party. In the context of the demonstrations in Birmingham, the march on Washington, and a summer in which the U.S. Justice Department recorded 1,412 separate demonstrations, Kennedy moved to strengthen civil rights legislation making its way through the Congress, and Johnson followed through after Kennedy's assassination. The first civil rights bill in almost a century with effective enforcement provisions was signed into law on July 2, 1964. Lyndon B. Johnson went on to win a landslide victory, no doubt benefiting as the successor to a slain president, and from the weakness of the Goldwater candidacy. Aside from Goldwater's home state of Arizona, Johnson carried every state except four in the Deep South. The landslide notwithstanding, the results were ominous for the New Deal coalition. As Evans and Novak pointed out shortly afterward, "Behind the statistics was a revolution in American politics. The first Southern President since the Civil War captured 90 percent of the Negro vote and lost the Deep South by large margins."[35]

If the election of 1964 again showed the extent of white southern defections, it also revealed something quite new: the southern black vote was emerging as a major factor in the region's politics. As criticism of the southern system by national political leaders mounted during the previous two decades, and as black protest emerged, the proportions of blacks who were registered to vote in the South also had begun to increase, from 4.5 percent in 1940, to 12.5 percent in 1947, to 20.7 percent in 1952, to 29.1 percent in 1960 and 35.5 percent in 1965,[36] just before the passage of the Voting Rights Act. Rising turnout, furthermore, was correlated with "a new surge of political awareness among southern blacks. In less than a decade, the proportion of apoliticals had fallen from 28 percent to about 3 percent."[37] Blacks were becoming voters, and staunch partisans of the national Democratic party that was championing the civil rights cause. (Conflict also stimulated increases in white turnout, from an average of 54.9 percent in the 1952–60 period, to 59.6 percent in the 1964–80 period, and there was a slight tendency for a larger rise among lower-stratum whites.[38] However, the events that led to increased white turnout were also leading many of these voters to defect from the Democratic party, at least in presidential contests.)

Had it not been for black support, the Democratic party would have lost four additional southern states in 1964 (Arkansas, Florida, Tennessee, and Virginia). These developments almost surely influenced Johnson's subsequent support for the Voting Rights Act of 1965. Nearly a century before, the Repub-

[35] Evans and Novak (1966:481).
[36] Kleppner (1982:116).
[37] Converse (1972:6).
[38] Kleppner (1982:120–21).

lican party had similarly recognized that the black vote was crucial to the party's fortunes in the South. The Force Bill of 1890, which would have permitted federal supervision of southern elections under certain conditions, was an early version of the Voting Rights Act, and it had the support of President Benjamin Harrison:

> [T]he primary purpose of the legislation was to secure Republican control of the national government by recapturing marginal areas in the south. The president viewed federal protection of the black vote as the only way to promote a Republican revival in the region and believed that such a revival would create a permanent majority for the protective tariff.[39]

As it happened, the Force Bill failed because too many Republicans were unwilling to risk disrupting the South, which had by then become a stable environment for northern commerce and investment. By 1965, the national Democratic party was in a position similar to the Republican party a century before with regard to the South, and the black movement had helped bring it there. If it was to hope to hold southern states in presidential elections, it needed the votes of blacks to replace the white Democrats whose numbers were being depleted both by defections over the race question and by the tendency of the upwardly mobile to join a modern and Republican middle class. In this sense, the Voting Rights Act widened and institutionalized electoral changes that had already been set in motion by economic change and by the civil rights movement.

The eventual result of this series of developments was to erode the one-party South that had survived from the system of 1896 to undergird the New Deal coalition. As party competition grew in the South, national Democratic leaders had no choice

[39] Bensel (1984:76).

but to support legislation overturning the more blatant methods of disenfranchisement that had prevailed in the South since the late nineteenth century. Southern registration levels leaped upward after federal intervention in southern electoral systems was first authorized under the Voting Rights Act.

Subsequent elections confirmed these changes. Carter, the first president from the Deep South since before the Civil War, failed to win a majority of white southern votes in 1976, and he won only one-third of white southerners in his 1980 reelection bid.[40] Mondale did worse, winning only 25 percent of the southern white vote in 1984. Between 1980 and 1984, fully half of the Republican party's gains among whites came from the South, as did half of the party's gains in the House of Representatives (it captured four Democratic seats in Texas, three in North Carolina, and one in Georgia, while giving up a seat in Arkansas).[41] Fifty years ago, 117 of 120 southern seats in the House of Representatives were held by Democrats; only 85 of 124 were in 1986.

Meanwhile, the Democratic party's ability to compete in the South depended increasingly on the black vote. In 1986, when the Democrats won five new Senate seats in the South (and control of the Senate), it was largely because of the lopsided support of newly enfranchised blacks.[42] In the southern region as a whole, blacks compose only about 20 percent of those who vote, but they generally vote 90 percent Democratic, yielding an 18-point advantage to the Democratic party, according to Petrocik.[43] To offset that advantage, the Republican party must carry at least 65 percent of the white vote. Republican victories in the South over the last decade depended on just such margins. In 1984, for example, the Republicans won a U.S. Senate race in Mississippi even though 30 percent of the voters were black and

[40] Ladd (1985:5).
[41] Sundquist (1985:10–11).
[42] Except Florida, where the black population is relatively small.
[43] Petrocik (1987b:52).

they voted 80 percent Democratic, giving their candidate a 24 percentage point advantage. The Republican candidate won by garnering 81 percent of the white vote. The question remains, nevertheless, whether southern whites will dependably produce such lopsided Republican majorities. The Republican losses in the 1986 southern U.S. Senate races showed that it may be difficult to offset the black Democratic vote. The third column of table 5.3 shows the black Democratic advantage in these races, and the fourth column shows the huge white pluralities with which the Republicans nevertheless lost.

TABLE 5.3 SOUTHERN DEMOCRATIC VICTORIES IN 1986 U.S. SENATE RACES DESPITE LARGE WHITE REPUBLICAN PLURALITIES

	Blacks as Percentage of Voters	% Black Democratic Vote	% Black Democratic Advantage	% White Republican Vote
Senate races				
Alabama	21	88	19	61
Georgia	24	75	18	59
Louisiana	29	85	25	60
North Carolina	16	88	14	56

Source: Petrocik (1987b:49 and table 4).

Petrocik concludes that the "Republicans lost the Senate races in the South not because the realignment [among whites] of the past two decades was reversed, but because the parallel effort to effectively enfranchise Southern blacks has been successful."[44] Moreover, southern black registration levels do not yet equal white levels. Of all groups in the country, black southerners are the most likely to overreport registration.[45] Mississippi is a case in point. Blacks in that state reported to the Census Bureau in 1984 that they were registered at the extraordinary

[44] Ibid. (49).
[45] See appendix A.

level of 86 percent (the national black reported rate was 66 percent). In a special study of Mississippi, Lichtman reported that the actual black registration level in 1984 was only 54 percent compared with a 79 percent white rate.[46] The full impact of the southern black vote, in other words, is still to be felt.

In sum, the one-party South is history.[47] The southern pillar of the New Deal inherited from the system of 1896 has crumbled. Meanwhile, deep cracks were appearing in the northern pillar as well.

DEALIGNMENT AND DEMOBILIZATION IN THE NORTH

Unless the Democratic party could compensate for eroding support in the South by strengthening its base elsewhere, the breakdown of the sectional accommodation that had been part of the system of 1896 threatened to be fatal to the party's grip on national power. But instead of deepening and enlarging, the party's support in the North became weaker and more uncertain, even as the dimensions of its southern problem unfolded.

The evidence was apparent as early as the 1960s. The main problem was that the American working class was changing, and the Democratic party was not. The old white male working class based in the mass production industries was declining relatively and absolutely. A new working class, concentrated in the service sector, more geographically dispersed, and resting heavily on women and minorities, was emerging. But as the recomposition of the working class swiftly proceeded, the Democratic party and its mobilizing apparatus of unions and local parties lagged behind. Their failure to enlist the ranks of a recomposing working

---

[46] Lichtman (1987).

[47] It is also significant that the realigning processes set in motion by the rise of southern black voting had a critical impact on the conservative coalition that has dominated the Congress since the New Deal, as we note in the Epilogue.

class was not much noticed, however. Instead, commentators directed their attention to a second problem: the rising tide of defections among the old industrial working class. Because this latter process has generated so much discussion, we will consider it first.

Dealignment

During the 1940s, the Democratic party commanded overwhelming majorities among industrial workers. That support wavered during the Eisenhower elections of 1952 and 1956, then rallied again in the elections of 1960 and 1964, but has not been sustained (table 5.4). A main line of explanation attributes these defections to weaknesses in the American party system itself, which is said to be undergoing a process of "fragmentation" or long-term dealignment. The evidence summoned in support of this diagnosis includes the rising numbers of independents, increasing volatility in partisan identification or voting, and the trend toward split-ticket voting. According to Pomper, one-third to two-fifths of the electorate now disclaim ties to the parties, and the proportion of the electorate voting on purely partisan grounds has declined markedly, from 42 percent in 1960 to 23 percent in 1972.[48] Jensen says that the percentage of "strong" partisans dropped from an average of about 36 percent between 1952 and 1964 to 24 percent in later years, while independents rose from 15 percent in the 1940s to about 40 percent in 1974. Using different measures, which show a less extreme trend, Norpoth and Rusk report a decline in partisanship during the 1964–76 period from 75 to 63 percent.[49] And the proportion of ticket-splitters rose from about one-fourth of voters in 1940 to two-thirds in the 1970s.[50]

[48] See Pomper (1977:34).
[49] Norpoth and Rusk (1982).
[50] Jensen (1981:220–21).

TABLE 5.4 PERCENTAGE OF WHITE MAJOR PARTY VOTERS
WHO VOTED DEMOCRATIC FOR PRESIDENT BY
UNION MEMBERSHIP, CLASS,
AND NON-SOUTH

	Union Member	Working Class	Non-South
1944	67	64	—
1948	79	76	—
1952	53	52	39
1956	50	44	36
1960	64	55	46
1964	80	75	65
1968	50	50	42
1972	40	32	33
1976	60	58	46
1980	48	44	36
1984	50	42	37

*Source: Extrapolated from Abramson, Aldrich, and Rohde (1986: figures
5-2, 5-3, and 5-4). Based on National Opinion Research Center polls, which
are susceptible to substantial overreporting of voting.*

Everyone more or less agrees that partisanship is eroding;
the debate is about why.[51] Some analysts attribute it to the long-
term decline of party organizations in the United States—Burnham, for example, traces the decline to the "anti-partyism" and
electoral fragmentation he thinks were ushered in by the system
of 1896.[52] Others think the decline of parties and partisanship
originated more recently. Thus Pomper contrasts the present
plight of the parties, particularly at the state and local levels,
with the legitimacy, resources, and control over candidate recruitment that they commanded at the end of World War II.[53]

[51] For several views, see Miller and Miller (1977); Converse (1976); and Nie, Verba, and
Petrocik (1976).
[52] Burnham (1974a:678–79, 720; 1981b; and 1981c).
[53] Pomper (1977:21–41 and 1975:163) also thinks there is a "countervailing trend": while
state parties are losing strength and coherence, the national parties are gaining. Nevertheless,

And Jensen thinks that 1968 was the Democratic party's "last hurrah," because it was the last nominating convention that party leaders were able to control.[54]

Dealignment is said by others to be the result of the intense conflicts that swept through American society in the 1960s and 1970s. "Issue polarization over Vietnam, the racial question, law and order, new life styles, and moral questions have prompted large-scale voting defections to George Wallace in 1968 and Richard Nixon in 1972," according to Norpoth and Rusk.[55] Converse points to similar "chaotic" political events in trying to account both for voter volatility and for the lower sense of efficacy reported in survey data.[56] These explanations are not, of course, mutually exclusive. It is reasonable to suppose that the decline of party organization and the diminishing ability of the parties to orient voters and command their allegiance have left the electorate more exposed to the currents of disturbance generated by specific conflicts.

We agree that the parties are weaker, or at least that their hold on the electorate is weaker. And sharp political conflicts do precipitate voter reactions. Nevertheless, the focus in most of these analyses on the past two decades is somewhat misleading. A series of longer-term changes have gradually produced an electorate that votes on the basis of issues rather than partisan allegiances.[57] This long-term development in turn is compounded of the decline of parties, and especially the decline of clientelist and tribalist party linkages to the electorate, and the expansion of

---

he thinks the decline of partisanship that he documents points to a "nonpartisan electoral future."

[54] Jensen (1981:219). As late as 1968, only 40 percent of the delegates to the nominating convention were chosen by primary elections.

[55] Norpoth and Rusk (1982:526).

[56] Converse (1972:329–30).

[57] The documentation of the emergence of an issue-oriented and ideologically consistent electorate is explored most comprehensively in Verba, Nie, and Petrocik (1976). See also Nie and Andersen (1974, especially 573–78 and 581–85). Most studies use survey data from the 1950s as their base line.

the role of government over the course of the twentieth century. Inevitably, as government increasingly penetrates the economy and other facets of everyday life, questions of government policy have become more salient in popular electoral politics.[58] And the issue-oriented popular politics generated by the expansion of government and the decline of parties ebbs and flows in response to particular conflicts that emerge in the political system. In the 1930s, issue politics intensified, as it did again during the last two decades when American society was indeed rent by a series of intense conflicts over race, economic policy, foreign policy, environmental issues, gender roles, and matters of culture or life-styles.

If the decline of partisan allegiance and the salience of issues are affected by rising conflict, then two sources of conflict are usually emphasized in accounting for voter volatility generally, and defections from the Democratic party in particular. The first is the spread of racial turmoil to the North, probably an inevitable development given the growing numbers of blacks (and Hispanics) in the northern cities and their growing weight in the Democratic party. After all, the electoral influence of northern black voters was a main precondition for the emergence of a civil rights movement in the South. Blacks in the North (as well as Hispanics) also had deep grievances of their own, arising from the poverty and discrimination they confronted. By 1963, in the wake of the confrontations in Birmingham, and even while the massive march on Washington was being planned, blacks in the northern cities joined in demonstrations to demand decent jobs, integrated schools, community control of public services, better housing code enforcement, and an end to the demolition of black neighborhoods. Protests escalated from demonstrations and

---

[58] This perspective is developed in Piven and Cloward (1985). For the point that the decline of partisanship and the rise of issue orientations are no longer independent of each other, see Rusk (1974:1047). However, Pomper (1975 and 1977) sees the rise of issue politics as a by-product of the decline of partisan allegiance. Thus, for him the declining command of the partiesover key resources ultimately causes electoral fragmentation.

marches and sit-ins emulating the southern movement, to rent strikes and riots, and to intermittent street warfare. The national Democratic party, and especially Democratic presidents, responded to these troubles in the heart of its northern base with a series of new social welfare programs under the auspices of the Great Society. But if concessions to urban blacks could no longer be avoided, they were nevertheless costly, for they aroused the ire of big-city Democratic leaders and provoked resentments in the white working class. The rest of the story is familiar. The national Democratic strategy to win and hold the political allegiance of the new urban minorities became mired in racial conflict. As the 1960s drew to a close, the issues of school busing, affirmative action, and crime in the streets generated mounting resentment among white working- and middle-class Democratic constituencies in the cities. The forces that drove "the lower middle class" away from the Democratic party, Galston says in a thinly veiled allusion to the race problem, included "a deep-seated antipathy to many of the party's efforts on behalf of the disadvantaged."[59] The results of the election of 1968, held in the wake of several years of urban rioting and federal concessions, reflected this antipathy as many of the white working-class urban voters most exposed to the race conflict in the North began to defect from Democratic columns.

Another line of argument blames the intense conflicts of the period and their fragmenting or "dealigning" consequences for the Democrats on the rise within the party of middle- or upper-middle-class activists who championed such New Politics issues as peace, the environment, and racial and gender equality. Schneider writes regretfully that in the old days, "a political party was a big tent, with room inside for all kinds of people. The Democratic Party included southern white racists, blacks, urban bosses, and liberal reformers." These good old days are gone, however; the tents have gotten smaller, and the reason is

[59] Galston (1985:23).

the "liberal activists, union organizers, and radical nuns" who administer "litmus tests" in order to certify that political candidates are of the true faith.[60] Their lofty causes notwithstanding, the new activists are often charged with less than noble motives. They presumably represent an enlarging "new class" of educated professionals who have a self-interested stake in the expansion of government bureaucracies that employ them, and especially the federal bureaucracies, which supposedly accounts for their alliance with minorities, and for their diverse "causes"—such as environmental regulation or social welfare expansion.[61]

As the story is usually told, this elite stratum of activists both promoted and benefited from the McGovern reforms adopted in 1970 that elevated them in the party and put their causes at the center of the party agenda at the expense of more representative union and party leaders, and at the expense of older New Deal–style issues to which working-class voters respond.[62] As a result, the so-called "new class" and its causes brought disarray to the Democratic leadership, and prompted disaffection among the Democratic rank and file. A good many analysts, whose perspectives are as otherwise different as those of Edsall and Huntington, define the rise of this "elite" stratum as responsible for alienating white working-class voters.[63] The New Politics activists certainly did alienate many party regulars, and probably many members of the old working class as well.[64] Still, the use of the term "elite" to describe them is an obfuscation.

---

[60] Schneider (1987:45–46).

[61] For a rather overworked interpretation of this sort, see Shefter (1978a:245). See also Ginsberg and Shefter (1985:11–12). Kleppner (1982:157) also more or less adopts this interpretation.

[62] George McGovern chaired the Commission on Party Structure and Delegate Selection, which set the rules for the 1972 Democratic convention.

[63] See Edsall (984:159 and chapter 1) and Huntington (1985:63–78).

[64] It was by no means clear that this alienation was permanent. Opinion polls in the 1980s showed there was, in fact, wide public support for the causes associated with the New Politics, including disarmament, environmental regulation, minority and women's rights, and expanded social programs. For comprehensive reviews of the survey data on these issues, see Navarro (1985) and Lipset (1985).

The activists drew their influence from the increasingly restive ranks of minorities, women, and youth in the electorate, many of whom were employed in the expanding service sector, and especially in public agencies. These activist spokespersons were, as is to be expected, middle class and educated, but they surely were not higher in the class structure than the regular Democratic power brokers,[65] and many of those for whom they spoke were worse off than the old Democratic working class. To be sure, a good number of the new activists had been drawn to politics by the civil rights and antiwar movements (and drawn into public service by the Great Society programs). But their subsequent political development can be understood as an early if somewhat inchoate effort to give voice in Democratic circles to the vast numbers of women and minorities entering the rapidly changing work force, and attempting to enter public life.

There is no question, however, that the demands of the new activists caused fissures in the Democratic party. Their issues competed for attention and prominence with more traditional Democratic commitments, and their fights for internal party democracy weakened the control of traditional party leaders, including those who were union-based. If the McGovern candidacy of 1972 is taken as the high point of the New Politics, then there is also evidence that white working-class voters reacted against the new activists. The Democratic ticket won only 32 percent of the working-class vote, and only 40 percent of the vote among union families, by far the most dismal showing since the formation of the New Deal coalition.

The exclusive focus on the flamboyant battles associated with race and the New Politics, however, turns attention away from another more important source of working-class defections: the

---

[65] Lipset (1986:223) makes the point that while privileged, this educated stratum is less conservative than elites have been in the past. For a very different outlook, in which the New Politics activists are defined as reformers who temporarily opened the Democratic party to popular influences, see Karp (1984).

Democratic party's increasing unwillingness or inability to respond to the economic aspirations of either the old working class or the new. During the long-term postwar economic boom, the main basis for the party's appeal to its core working- and lower-class voters was the promise of steady economic growth through international expansion and Keynesian macroeconomic management.[66] It was a formula consistent with the interests of the party's union constituency in the mass production industries, and with the interests of those corporations that were coming to be allied with the Democratic party. The dividends of the tremendous economic growth of the two postwar decades thus made possible a kind of business-labor accord.[67] American corporations struck a truce with unions where they already existed, conceded wage increases that at least maintained organized labor's share of an expanded economic product, and acquiesced in government policies that ensured relatively low unemployment rates as well as modest social welfare protections. In the 1960s, in the wake of demonstrations and riots, major business leaders even went along with a renewed expansion of social welfare programs, and some actually took the initiative in efforts like the Urban Coalition, which sought to bring peace to the cities through modest concessions for blacks. Living standards improved for the great majority, and so long as economic growth continued, the New Deal coalition was viable.

But when rising real incomes became problematic in the

[66] The apparatus that made possible the fantastic expansion of the U.S. economy and its penetration of the world economy is familiar. It included the Marshall Plan, which revived the European economies and made them major markets for American goods, at least for a time; the Bretton Woods agreement, which fixed and stabilized international exchange rates and established the dollar as the currency of international trade; the International Monetary Fund and the World Bank, which regulated credit; and the General Agreement on Tariffs and Trade, devoted to lowering tariff barriers. See Ferguson and Rogers (1986:49–50).

[67] For discussions of the "pro-growth coalition," and the business-labor accord it made possible through the wage and social welfare dividends of growth, see Gold (1977); Wolfe (1981); Bowles and Gintis (1982); Bowles, Gordon, and Weisskopf (1984); and Cohen and Rogers (1983). Mollenkopf (1975) originated the phrase, "pro-growth coalition," in his study of the politics of postwar urban development.

early 1970s, the political accommodations based on them faltered and then collapsed, and dealigning tendencies intensified. The first signs of economic trouble were evident in the late 1960s, when U.S. corporate profits began to decline. Investment in new plant and equipment soon followed suit, and so did overall growth rates. Analysts dispute the reasons for the ensuing period of slow economic growth and economic instability, or the relationship of domestic economic problems to the changing competitive position of American firms in the world economy, or even whether the economic problems that the conventional indicators described are real.[68] But whatever the reality and the reasons for it, by the early 1970s, especially in the wake of the price shocks generated by the Arab oil boycott, the pie seemed to have stopped growing, and corporate America announced that it was no longer willing to live by the business-labor accord.

The subsequent turnabout is by now legendary. American business became much more resistant to wage increases, despite the inflation triggered by the Vietnam War. Nonunionized workers were hurt first and most, and their numbers were enlarging, as more and more of the new jobs in the economy were concentrated in the lowest-paid service sector. The wage differential between the old industrial working class and the new working class began to grow.[69] But the old industrial working class was not protected for long. As the decade wore on, corporations that had more or less accommodated to unionism and steadily rising wages mobilized to fight wage increases or improved working conditions, to demand wage givebacks, and to smash existing unions. The blame for economic malaise could

---

[68] For a critique of the economic indicators which support the widespread view that growth has been slowing and investment declining in the United States, see Block (1987).

[69] This trend has continued. The Bureau of Labor Statistics reported in May 1986, for example, that 30.5 percent of the jobs added since January 1980 were in retail trade, and nearly 60 percent were in miscellaneous services. According to Morehouse and Dembo (1986:14, emphasis added), annual wages in retailing averaged $9,036, or about $2,000 less than the poverty level for a family of four, and only 44 percent of average earnings in manufacturing, *down from 63 percent of manufacturing wages in 1962*.

not be fixed readily on the Democratic party (if only because Republican presidents presided over some of this troubled period), or indeed on anyone in particular. Even business leaders seemed exempted from blame, given their claim that survival in the international markets compelled them to take a tough new stance toward labor. But that is only to say that the Democratic party's promise of economic improvement was increasingly hollow.

A parallel corporate political mobilization prompted Edsall to describe it as "one of the most remarkable campaigns in the pursuit of political power in recent history."[70] The lobbying capacity of business, always formidable, became far more coordinated and proficient, achieving "the virtual dominance of the legislative process in the Congress" as the 1970s wore on.[71] Business won impressive victories under the Carter administration, foretelling the even larger steps that the ascendant business-Republican coalition would take after 1980. Corporate taxes, which had, in fact, been falling for some time, were cut again, along with capital gains taxes (which have since been raised), while Social Security taxes were raised. Labor's efforts at achieving modest reform through the Labor Law Reform Bill were defeated.[72] And business also organized to reduce government

[70] Edsall (1984:107 and chapter 3). See also Ferguson and Rogers (1986: chapter 3), who provide an account of the shift, and of the role of different business sectors in it.

[71] Edsall (1984:108). On the corporate political mobilization, see also Vogel (1983). Vogel thinks American business was reacting to the successes of the public interest movement in the decade from 1965 to 1975, and particularly to administrative and financial costs of government regulation. Accordingly, American corporate leaders themselves became political activists, investing themselves in "public affairs," mobilizing stockholders to make campaign contributions, engaging in political advertising, and vastly expanding their Washington-based lobbying operations.

[72] In Edsall's (1984:156) view, the unstinting efforts of big business to defeat this measure, which was a high priority for labor, signaled to union leaders more than anything else that the accord had broken down. He quotes A. H. Raskin on the matter: "What galled labor beyond measure, oddly enough, was not the treason of politicians who had taken labor's shilling at election time. It was the defection to the anti-union camp of a raft of chief executives from the Fortune 500—men whom the unions had come to think of as almost as allies. As many labor leaders see it, that crucial battle marked the end of a thirty-year *entente cordiale.*"

regulation, including environmental regulation, and to increase military spending, which began to rise sharply in the closing years of the Carter administration. Meanwhile, the real value of the minimum wage, which directly affects about 14 million workers whose earnings are pegged at or near the legal minimum, fell about 25 percent after 1978.[73] Finally, business pressed for reduced social program spending, by funding research and propaganda efforts to discredit social welfare programs and by lobbying to cut program funds. Business mobilized, in other words, to take back much of what labor, blacks, and the poor—the old working class and the new—had won from the New Deal coalition in the previous half century. During the closing years of the Carter administration, a Democratic president and a good many Democratic congressmen more or less went along. After 1981, under a Republican president, Democrats in the Congress simply gave way in the face of an even larger business offensive. In sum, as the economy faltered and the business-labor accord collapsed, the Democratic party forfeited its claim to be the party whose macroeconomic policies would ensure steady growth. Worse, under the combined pressures of slow growth, rising prices, and a mobilized business class, the party reneged on the political terms of the business-labor accord.[74] And as the Democratic party steadily gave ground to the political demands of business, working-class allegiance to the party faltered.

[73] The National Council on Employment Policy reports that in 1984 about 8 million workers received wages at or below the minimum wage of $3.35 an hour, and according to Sar Levitan, another 6 million received wages just above the minimum (*New York Times,* June 8, 1986).

[74] See Kelley (1986) for strong evidence that New Deal issues remained as salient as ever to the voters in 1980 and 1984, but confidence in the Democratic party's ability to deliver on these "bread-and-butter" issues had dropped sharply.

Demobilization

The extent of working-class voter defections and volatility not-withstanding, we think the more serious but less noticed difficulty for the New Deal coalition outside of the South was the decline of voter turnout, especially among the bottom third of the population, where Democratic preferences were overwhelming. Indeed, while partisan identification was shifting to the Republicans among the somewhat better off, among the bottom third of the population, Democratic preferences were actually increasing, as shown in table 5.5. But the changing ranks of the worse off were not being enlisted in the electorate. This is the most fundamental long-term issue.

TABLE 5.5 CHANGES IN DEMOCRATIC AND REPUBLICAN VOTER ALLEGIANCE AMONG DIFFERENT INCOME GROUPS

Income Group	1952–1958	1960–1968	1970–1978	1976–1980
Bottom third	64–36	66–34	69–31	71–29
Middle third	63–37	65–35	64–36	63–37
Top third	56–44	58–42	53–47	53–47

Source: Edsall (1984: table 1.4). The first percentage in each column indicates Democratic allegiance, and the second, Republican allegiance.

Postwar turnout peaked in the 1950s. Then it began to slide. Between 1952 and 1980, the national rate of voting dropped 9 points, from 64 percent to 55 percent, and the rate in the North and West dropped 14 points, from 71 percent to 57 percent (table 5.6). One reason for the decline was the enlarged proportion of young people in the electorate, particularly after the voting age was lowered to eighteen years before the 1972 election. Most analysts think that about one-fifth to one-quarter of the turnout decline is due to the incorporation of this huge youth cohort,[75] leaving most of the decline to be explained.

TABLE 5.6 PRESIDENTIAL TURNOUT PERCENTAGES, 1948–1980

	South	*Non-South*	*National*
1948	25	62	53
1952	38	71	64
1956	37	70	62
1960	41	73	65
1964	46	69	63
1968	52	66	62
1972	46	61	57
1976	49	58	56
1980	50	57	55

Source: Burnham (1981c:100, table 1). Based on total of all citizens legally eligible to vote, aliens excluded.

Lower-class groups, which are the strongest Democratic partisans, showed the greatest turnout declines (table 5.7).[76] Between 1964 and 1980, for example, voting by those with eight years of education or less was down by 16.4 percentage points. The unemployed voted less by 16.8 percentage points. Regional differences are striking: almost all of the national decline was centered in the North and West, where voting fell off by 13.6 percentage points, with whites falling 12.3 percentage points and blacks falling 19.2 points. Intensified competition for voters in the South after the passage of the voting rights legislation of the 1960s kept the South from joining the downward national trend:

[75] Cavanaugh (1981); Wolfinger and Rosenstone (1980:58); Boyd (1981). However, even low rates of voting among the young should not be taken for granted. We remind the reader of our critique of such social-psychological explanations in chapter 4.

[76] For a brief period, the combination of rising protest and national Democratic response did increase turnout among blacks in the North, although the increase was modest compared with that among southern blacks. Between the 1952–60 and the 1964–80 periods, black voter turnout outside the South rose by 8 percentage points. See Kleppner (1982:22).

black turnout rose by 4.2 percentage points, offsetting a slight drop of 2.1 points among whites.

TABLE 5.7 PERCENTAGE CLAIMING TO HAVE VOTED
IN 1964 AND 1980

	1964	1980	Net Change
National	69.3	59.2	− 10.1
White	70.7	60.9	− 9.8
Black	58.5	50.5	− 8.0
Male	71.9	59.1	− 12.8
Female	67.0	59.4	− 7.6
Employed	73.0	61.8	− 11.2
Unemployed	58.0	41.2	− 16.8
Not in labor force	65.0	57.0	− 8.0
0 to 8 elementary	59.0	42.6	− 16.4
High school			
1 to 3 years	65.4	45.6	− 19.8
4 years	76.1	58.9	− 17.2
College			
1 to 3 years	82.1	67.2	− 14.9
4 years +	87.5	79.9	− 7.6
North and West	74.6	61.0	− 13.6
White	74.7	62.4	− 12.3
Black	72.0	52.8	− 19.2
South	56.7	55.6	− 1.1
White	59.5	57.4	− 2.1
Black	44.0	48.2	+ 4.2

Source: Census Bureau/CPS Series P-20. In 1964, 8.6 percent more people claimed to have voted than did, and the inflation in 1980 was 7.6 percent (Series P-20, no. 405, table H).

Various measures of class reveal how skewed the electorate has become in recent decades. In 1972, for example, turnout among white male laborers with a grade-school education was 41 percent, but 86.6 percent of those in managerial occupations with a college degree voted. The same skew appeared in 1976:

among white males, 6 percent of the propertied middle classes reported never having voted, compared with 13.5 percent of white-collar and salaried workers, 20.2 percent of craftsmen and service workers, and 30.4 percent of lower- and working-class occupations.[77] Burnham remarks that "while race differences are most often commented about in discussions of turnout in America, in fact class differences are greater" for every income level.[78]

The strong correlation between declining turnout and the falling rates of registration in the past two decades among lower-strata groups suggests that the absence of Democratic party attempts to enroll new voters is important. Overall, registration fell 7.4 percentage points between 1968 and 1980 (table 5.8).[79] The largest declines were by education and unemployment status. Registration fell among those with less than a high school education by 13.9 percentage points. Registration among the unemployed was down by 10 points. The decline was greater in the North and West (− 8.6 points) than in the South (− 4.4 points). Black registration fell by 11.2 points in the North and West, and by 2.3 points in the South.

As we emphasized earlier in this chapter, the problem of low turnout among the strata who were potentially the strongest Democratic partisans existed from the beginning of the New Deal realignment. In 1934 and 1936, the potential reservoir of support in the South remained untouched, and the remobilization in the North was far from complete. Then, as the 1930s drew to a close, the combined power of resurgent business interests and the southern congressional wing ensured there would not be many new initiatives oriented toward the poor and working class. Moreover, with the ebbing of the protest movements

---

[77] Burnham (1979:114–15).
[78] Ibid. (114 and 137, fn. 11).
[79] The national registration level is shown in table 5.8 as having fallen to 66.9 percent in 1980, but the actual figure was about 60 to 62 percent. Appendix A contains an analysis of the reasons why voter registration figures are inflated.

of the decade, the task of reaching and activating the poor and working class and helping them surmount registration obstacles came to fall entirely on the unions and local big-city Democratic organizations. For different reasons, each proved to be unable or unwilling to reach out to the pool of nonvoters.

TABLE 5.8 PERCENTAGE CLAIMING TO BE REGISTERED,
1968 AND 1980

	1968	1980	Net Change
National	74.3	66.9	− 7.4
White	75.4	68.4	− 7.0
Black	66.2	60.0	− 6.2
Male	76.0	66.6	− 9.4
Female	72.8	67.1	− 5.7
Employed	76.6	68.7	− 7.9
Unemployed	60.3	50.3	− 10.0
Not in labor force	71.3	65.8	− 5.5
0 to 8 elementary	64.6	53.0	− 11.6
High school			
1 to 3 years	68.5	54.6	− 13.9
4 years	77.7	66.4	− 11.3
College			
1 to 3 years	82.9	74.4	− 8.5
4 years +	87.0	84.3	− 2.7
North and West	76.5	67.9	− 8.6
White	77.2	69.3	− 7.9
Black	71.8	60.6	− 11.2
South	69.2	64.8	− 4.4
White	70.8	66.2	− 4.6
Black	61.6	59.3	− 2.3

Source: Census Bureau/CPS Series P-20. We estimate that overall registration claims are inflated by 7 to 10 percent, although the inflation by particular subgroups may be more, or less. See appendix A for a discussion of the biases in registration data.

The point is often made that the capacity of the unions to mobilize their members and ensure their allegiance to the Democratic party diminished after World War II. One explanation attributes this long-term decline of Democratic voting among union members to the increasing prosperity of the rank and file. The New Deal coalition is thus said to be the victim of its own achievements. Having successfully propounded policies that brought prosperity, mass homeownership, and even suburbia to many of the have-nots of the 1930s, their interests and, inevitably, their partisan preferences changed. Galston's comments typify this view:

> The New Deal brought together Americans of low and modest income against the coterie of the wealthy that FDR ringingly labelled "economic royalists." Until well after the Second World War, this coalition of disadvantage was a clear majority. But in the next two generations, real incomes rose sharply. Homeownership soared. Tens of millions of Americans moved into the middle class, and their children did even better.[80]

There may be truth in the notion that prosperity, as well as aging and mortality, changed the politics of unionized workers. But this diagnosis misses the heart of the problem. Whether or not the unions' grip on those who were moving up in the class structure was loosening, it was the failure of the unions to reach the cohorts of new workers, especially minority and women workers employed in the new industries in the Sunbelt and in the rapidly expanding service sector, that made for the larger problem. In short, the recomposition of the working class was proceeding, but the recomposition of the unions lagged behind.

In part, the diminishing ability of the unions to organize

---

[80] Galston (1985:17). Edsall (1984:189–90) makes a geographic variant of this mobility argument, namely, that the population has increased in the more conservative southern, southwestern, and western regions of the country.

new cohorts of workers (public sector workers being an important exception), and to reach and enlist new voters, resulted from the increasingly comfortable and oligarchical character of union leadership, as well as from white male union members' resistance to the inclusion of new groups. But the stasis that overtook the unions was also ensured by the steady retreat of a Democrat-controlled national government from the support of labor. As normal politics was restored after the 1930s, accommodations by the party leadership to business interests, as well as to the southern congressional delegation, became the rule. During the 1930s, most American business, including most heavy industry, had virtually declared war on the New Deal and its labor and social welfare policies.[81] The advent of World War II moderated that antagonism. The tremendous increase in production and profits spurred by war demand, and the large concessions ceded industry by the War Labor Board, encouraged more accommodative relations between heavy industry and the Democratic party (symbolized by the appearance in Washington of the "dollar-a-year" corporate executives who joined the top command of the war economy).[82] With this *rapprochement,* the party's prounion tilt was reversed. In the mid-1940s, the National Labor Relations Board established under the Wagner Act was reconstituted to eliminate its prolabor members.[83] The Smith-Connally Act in 1943 and the Taft-Hartley Act in 1947 legislated as national policy many of the antilabor policies that had been enacted by the

[81] Ferguson and Rogers (1986:47–48) make the point that a small but powerful sector of the business community in fact supported the New Deal during the 1930s. These were the firms that were capital-intensive—and so not especially averse to the prolabor policies of the New Deal—internationalist, and imbued with the norms of scientific advance. They cite General Electric, IBM, Pan Am, and R. J. Reynolds; oil companies such as Standard Oil of New Jersey, Standard Oil of California, Cities Service, and Shell; and major commercial and investment banks, including Bank of America, Chase National Bank, Brown Brothers Harriman, Goldman Sachs, Lehman Brothers, and Dillon Read. See also Ferguson (1983 and 1984).

[82] On this point, see Davis (1986:75) and Ginsberg and Shefter (1985:2).

[83] See Millis and Brown (1950).

states.[84] Smith-Connally authorized the federal takeover of struck industries and banned direct political contributions by unions. Taft-Hartley outlawed secondary boycotts, and required anti-Communist oaths of union officials. Most important in the long run, section 14(b) of Taft-Hartley legitimated state right-to-work laws, which hampered efforts to organize the South, where new manufacturing was locating. A less sympathetic National Labor Relations Board also made it more difficult for new organizing drives to use the protections that the board ostensibly provided. Southern and business opposition, together with the union fratricide precipitated by the Cold War anti-Communist campaign, combined to shatter the CIO's "Operation Dixie," a much-heralded postwar campaign to organize the South. Finally, while the unions served as partisan mobilizing vehicles, they were not political machines. They had difficulty reaching and holding even their own members in the electorate and in Democratic columns unless the party offered strong rhetorical and programmatic appeals. And even apart from labor policy, the national Democratic leadership made little effort after World War II to improve or expand the programmatic initiatives of the 1930s. American workers never got a government health care program, for example, and other social welfare programs languished, falling far behind the initiatives of the European democracies.

The significance of weak party appeals and hamstrung unions has to be understood in the context of the restrictive registration apparatus inherited from the system of 1896. In the absence of mobilizing efforts, turnout did not continue to rise

---

[84] Of the 219 Democratic congressmen who voted for Smith-Connally, 191 had been supported by the CIO's Political Action Committee. Moreover, Taft-Hartley was passed over Truman's veto by margins of 331 to 83 in the House and 68 to 25 in the Senate. In any case, Truman's largely symbolic gesture of the veto freed him to use the legislation against strikes twelve times in the first year after its passage. See Green (1975:34); Yarnell (1974:22–25); Sitkoff (1974:92–97); Hartmann (1971:86–91); Martin (1976:540, 643, 660, 691).

after the 1930s, and eventually began to slide. The recomposition of the New Deal working class of the 1930s actually began in World War II, when millions of blacks and women joined the ranks of industrial workers. Davis reports a preelection survey of United Automobile Workers' locals in Detroit as early as 1944 showing that a bare 30 percent of the membership was registered to vote. And in the late 1950s, the director of the Committee on Political Education (COPE), the AF of L-CIO successor to the Political Action Committee (PAC), reported that less than 40 percent of members of affiliated unions were registered, while a survey by the Amalgamated Clothing Workers (with its larger proportions of women and minorities) found as few as 20 to 30 percent of their members registered.[85] But the full impact of a crippled unionism on electoral participation at the bottom began to tell in the 1970s, when the economy was changing more rapidly, and working-class recomposition was proceeding apace. As jobs in the old manufacturing industries shrank, as Sunbelt and service sector jobs expanded, and as a "contingent" work force of part-time, temporary, and home-workers grew, the reach of the unions into the working class narrowed. Moreover, the business campaign to slash wages and worsen working conditions in the 1970s was accompanied by the spread of union-busting efforts that harkened back to the era before the New Deal. Ferguson and Rogers report on the scope and intensity of the antiunion campaigns:

> The number of charges of employer violations of section 8(a)(3) of the Labor Management Relations Act, for example, which forbids employers to fire workers for engaging in union activity, doubled from 9,000 to 18,000 over the 1970–80 period. The number of workers awarded reinstatement or back pay by the NLRB rose from 10,000 to 25,000. By 1980, the number of illegal discharges for

[85] Davis (1986:84, 98n). See also Lens (1959:298).

union activity had risen to about 5 percent of the total
number of pro-union votes in representation elections before the Board. Put otherwise, by that time American workers faced a 1 in 20 chance of being fired for merely favoring
unionization.[86]

Not surprisingly under these conditions, unions began to lose a
majority of collective-bargaining elections, and the losses were
concentrated in the biggest firms.[87] The unionized share of the
work force continued to drop, from 25.7 percent to 20.9 percent
over the decade, as new organizing drives failed and as existing
members were lost through decertification elections.[88] However
limited their effectiveness, the unions had been one of the main
mobilizing mechanisms of the New Deal coalition. As their connections to the working class diminished, so did voter turnout.[89]

[86] Ferguson and Rogers (1986:84). Freeman provides similar indicators (1986:14–16).

[87] Edsall (1984:153).

[88] Ferguson and Rogers (1986:85).

[89] There is a broad parallel between the troubles besetting the Democratic party and the
problems afflicting Western European working-class parties based primarily on unionized
workers in heavy industries, which are also losing support. The causes are to be found in the
economic transformation of advanced industrial societies. In these postindustrial or service
economies, the old mass production industries are declining, their work forces shrinking,
and so are the trade unions that depend on these industries and that undergird the labor or
socialist parties. At the same time, radical changes in the structure of work, including smaller
production sites and increased reliance on "contingent" workers, make it unlikely that older
forms of labor organization can be reconstructed in the new economy.

The old labor party formations have so far been unable to cope with these shifts. Thus
the dramatic setback suffered by the Italian Communist party in the last election reflects the
fact that Italy has been losing industrial jobs for a decade, and as it has, the metalworkers'
and heavy-industry unions on which that party always depended have also shrunk. England
is a dramatic case. The Labour party's recent poor showing partly reflects the fact that since
1979, union membership has fallen from 12 million to 9 million, and the unionized share
of the work force has fallen from 51 percent to 37 percent. Of course, the party continues to
do well in the industrial North, but that region is turning into a backwater. In the South,
where high-tech industries are flourishing, the Labour party was devastated in the last
election. Similar difficulties afflict both the Socialist and Communist parties in France, and
the Social Democrats in West Germany. And although the Democratic party in the United
States is in many ways a distinctive formation, reflecting both the constriction of electoral
participation and the large role of the South in national party politics, it too is afflicted by the
shrinkage of its traditional constituencies and the atrophying of constituency organizations as
a result of economic transformation and class recomposition.

There was no vehicle to compensate for the growing incapacity of the unions. The other major agency of voter mobilization in the New Deal coalition was the big-city Democratic organization. In principle, the local parties functioned to reach potential voters, including the waves of newcomers who have successively populated American cities. In the post–World War II period, this task of integration was immense. The big-city parties were confronted with the vast in-migration of blacks displaced from the South, and Hispanics displaced from Mexico and Puerto Rico, at the very time that millions of older urban residents were leaving the central cities for the suburbs. The enormous turnover in population was bound to cause political repercussions, simply because large shifts in population always threaten to undermine established patterns of political organization.

In the past, the machines used their control over municipal government resources to minimize the disturbances associated with population shifts, enlisting successive generations of new voters and holding old voters with favors or friendship or intimidation. These clientelist exchanges muted both class and ethnic conflict in the polyglot and changing cities. However, as a result of municipal reform campaigns, the resources of city government came to be controlled by bureaucracies that were at least somewhat insulated from direct control by partisan leaders.[90]

Bureaucratization meant that the jobs and services that had earlier been used to cultivate allegiance among newcomers were no longer easily dispensed to new groups. The resources of the city agencies had become fenced in by civil service regulations, and later by union contract provisions. It was not that the bureaucratization of the goods, services, and honors controlled by city governments had depoliticized municipal administrations. Rather, bureaucratization provided a set of devices by which groups who already benefited from municipal largess could pro-

---

[90] Discussions of the bureaucratization of city politics can be found in Lowi (1968); Piven (1974a and 1984); and Shefter (1977).

tect their stakes, and thus impeded the use of municipal resources to integrate newcomers.

Moreover, the very fact of bureaucratization worsened the potential for conflict, which was in any case intense, between the older ethnics and the new minorities. Who got what in the more bureaucratic politics of the cities was no longer a matter of morseled and private exchanges between party organizations and their constituencies, as it had been in the clientelist system. Political allocations were now matters of public policy, and the process of allocation was therefore exposed to intense intergroup competition and animosity.[91]

The first main response of the national Democratic party to the political problems generated by population shifts in the cities was the urban renewal program. In its inception, the program provided something for everyone, including allocations for public housing that could reasonably have been oriented to the newcomers. But in fact urban renewal was implemented in ways that suited the interests of big-city mayors trying to ward off the disturbances associated with the new constituencies, and the interests of downtown businessmen with whom the mayors were allied. Very little public housing was built, but federal subsidies were used to acquire land in "blighted" central city areas that was subsequently resold to private developers for commercial and high-priced residential development. Downtown businessmen and mayors could unite around a program that would return better-off customers and taxpayers to the urban core. At the same time, urban renewal, which came to be known as "black removal," would remove the newcomers whose enlarging presence threatened to accelerate white flight and cause deepening fissures in local political organizations. There was even reason to hope that the destruction of the housing and neighborhoods of the minorities would retard the inflow of new migrants. However,

---

[91] An analysis of this competitive process and its bearing on the evolution of the urban fiscal crisis that developed in the late 1960s can be found in Piven (1974a).

given the powerful forces that were combining to generate the population shifts that were transforming the cities, urban renewal was not equal to its task of halting the recomposition of the urban electorate. Indeed, in the end, renewal exacerbated the political problems of the Democratic party, and especially of the national party.[92] On the one hand, it did not reverse the migration flows that were paralyzing the big-city political organizations. On the other hand, renewal itself became another source of grievance to the black and Hispanic populations who were being displaced, and this during the very period that urban black voters were becoming activated and volatile.

The political repercussions of these events could be seen in the election of 1956, for blacks either defected from the Democratic party, or sat out the election. Defections tended to be related to the civil rights turmoil in the South. As Moon remarked at the time, "The closer the Negro lived to the resurgent terror, the sharper was his defection from the dominant party. . . . In 1952 [Stevenson] carried the Atlanta Negro precincts by better than 2 to 1, but four years later he received less than 15 percent of the vote in those same precincts."[93] Overall, Stevenson's share of the black vote in 1956 was only 60 percent, down sharply from the 80 percent he received in 1952.

The problem in the North was different, and it revealed the conflicts that were paralyzing the ability of the local parties to enlist the newcomers:

There was a sharp decline in balloting [in 1956] in many Negro districts throughout the country, but particularly in Northern industrial centers from which, in previous years, the Democrats received huge majorities. This, despite an

[92] On urban renewal and the Democratic party, see Friedland (1983) and Mollenkopf (1983).

[93] Moon (1957:221).

increased Negro population in most of these cities. . . . In Philadelphia, 27,000 fewer votes were cast than in 1952 for a loss of 14.7 percent. Voting in Negro wards of Kansas City, Mo., was off a fifth for a decline of 5,900 in the number of ballots cast. The percentage loss was even higher in Boston where the vote was down 28.5. The Negro vote declined 19 percent in Atlantic City; 15.6 in Toledo; 15.4 in Pittsburgh; 12 in Chicago; 9.3 in Brooklyn; 9.1 in Youngstown, Ohio; 6.4 in Cleveland; and 5.9 in Harlem.[94]

If 1956 was not enough to signal the significance of trouble in the big-city organizations to the national party, Kennedy's narrow victory in 1960—a victory that could not have been won without the huge northern urban black pluralities—underscored the point. Despite low levels of registration, the numbers of blacks in the cities were growing, so that the total votes they contributed mattered increasingly in determining the outcome of presidential races in the industrial states:

It had been Kennedy's great strength in the great Northern cities to which Southern Negroes had migrated that produced hairline victories for the Democrats in the eight states experts consider crucial to success in any election—New York, Illinois, Pennsylvania, Michigan, Maryland, Missouri, Minnesota, and New Jersey. All but one—Missouri —went to Eisenhower in 1956. All eight went for Kennedy in 1960, on the strength of the big-city vote. The Republican National Committee, using Philadelphia as a laboratory, made a precinct-by-precinct study of why this happened. The study revealed, among other things, that

[94] Ibid. (228). Overall, turnout in the 1956 election was down from 72.1 percent in 1952 to 69.8 percent in 1956, according to Burnham (1981a:100, table 1).

their candidate won only 18 percent of the Negro vote, leaving 82 percent for Kennedy.[95]

In a word, while local Democratic political leaders protected their incumbency by excluding the newcomers, the political fortunes of the national Democratic party, especially its presidential wing, hinged on turning them out to vote. With southern support depleting, the northern cities were all the more crucial to winning and holding national power. What had emerged was a profound conflict of interests over the black vote: it was a source of jeopardy for local Democratic incumbents, and a source of strength for the presidential wing of the party. From the perspective of national Democratic leaders, something had to be done to firm up black support, especially since the national party was still trying to avoid action on civil rights.

What emerged, at first gropingly under the Kennedy administration, and then in rapid-fire order under the Johnson administration, was a series of federal service programs for the "inner city," a euphemism for the ghetto neighborhoods that the programs were designed to reach. The tactics recalled those of the old political machine. Local agencies were created, many of them in storefronts. They were staffed by professionals who offered residents help in finding jobs, in obtaining welfare, or in securing other public services. Neighborhood leaders were sought out and hired as "community workers" to draw large numbers of people into the new programs, and in that way to spread the federal largess. It made little difference whether the funds were appropriated under delinquency-prevention, mental-health, antipoverty, or model-cities legislation; in the ghettos and barrios, the programs looked very much alike.

In short, the national administration was revivifying the traditional strategy of urban politics: offering jobs and services

---

[95] Fuller (1962:113).

to build party loyalty.[96] But it was not altogether as simple as that. To field these programs, the federal government had to take a unique initiative. It had to establish a direct relationship between the national government and the ghettos, bypassing both state and local governments. That state governments were ignored by national Democratic administrations hardly required explanation. A number of northern states were controlled by Republicans, and in the South the controlling Democrats could hardly be expected to cooperate in new programs for blacks. But many of the big northern cities, traditional Democratic strongholds, also were bypassed, at least in the early years of the Great Society, a clear mark of the concern felt by national leaders over the rising number of blacks and Hispanics in the cities, and the failure of urban political organizations to incorporate them.

This was not the first time that shifting political alignments in the United States prompted federal action to undercut established relationships among levels of government. Federal civil rights legislation, for example, restructured the political order of the Old South despite the resistance of southern state and local governments. The New Deal Democratic administration had also sometimes bypassed recalcitrant state governments in order to channel grants-in-aid directly to the party's urban strongholds. But in the sixties, it was these very Democratic strongholds that had become recalcitrant. Federal officials viewed city government as an obstacle to be gotten around if the new funds were to reach blacks and Hispanics. Therefore, the money was given to a host of intermediaries, including new agencies created in the ghettos (75 percent of the antipoverty programs were conducted by private agencies, according to the Advisory Commission on Intergovernmental Relations). And even when funds were funneled into regular city agencies, specific guidelines were imposed on their use.

[96] For a fuller analysis of the Great Society programs as political strategy, and the effort to change the relationships between levels of government in the federal system that the strategy entailed, see Piven (1974b and 1974c).

Little of this was mapped out in advance, but neither was it random. Federal officials were feeling their way, step by step, casting about for a means of dealing with political problems in the cities. When controversies flared, the federal government generally retreated, especially in cities where white ethnic political organizations were still firmly entrenched. Some of the controversy over the Great Society programs grew out of the feature of the programs that bypassed local government, for local officials were hardly happy to have the substantial patronage and publicity of the new programs escape their control. They became outraged, however, when the new agencies then began to use federal funds to put pressure on regular municipal agencies in an effort to redirect benefits to the ghettos. Community workers and legal services attorneys were hired to badger housing inspectors and to pry loose welfare payments. Later, the new federally funded agencies even began to organize the poor to picket welfare departments or to boycott school systems.[97] Local political leaders depended on the distribution of these services to traditional white constituents in order to maintain their coalitions. That they reacted with indignation to federal efforts to reorganize city politics is hardly startling.

Just as disturbing to big-city politicians, "nonpartisan" voter registration drives were launched in the ghettos under the first of the programs, inaugurated in 1962 under the Juvenile Delinquency and Youth Control Act. More black voters meant larger pluralities for the national Democratic party, but they presented local white incumbent politicians with a new and threatening constituency. To such local leaders, voter registration in the ghettos seemed an incredible way to deal with juvenile delinquency or mental illness or poverty, and they were quick to say so. But as a device to promote a modest shift in the political

---

[97] For example, these programs were the crucial stimulant to the formation of the welfare rights protests in the late 1960s. For a history and analysis of the Great Society origins of the National Welfare Rights Organization, see Piven and Cloward (1977: chapter 5).

balance between voting constituencies, it was not incredible at all.

Most revealing for our argument, local politicians prevailed in the contest over voter registration. The flagship of the Great Society was the Economic Opportunity Act of 1964, and it inaugurated a series of programs for the ghettos, including legal services, community action, job training, and Headstart. In short order, however, a coalition of big-city mayors and their congressional allies secured legislative language explicitly prohibiting voter registration activities in federal poverty programs (and also ceding greater control over the programs to local officials). As a result, the "war on poverty" programs did virtually everything and anything. But one thing they did not and could not do was voter registration. Fearful of local political challenges, Democratic and Republican mayors alike lobbied Congress for explicit prohibitions on voter registration activities by antipoverty agencies. Instead of serving as mobilizing vehicles for the national party, in short, the local parties kept the gates closed, and they used the apparatus of voter registration to do it. Nor did things much change once the turmoil of the 1960s subsided. Local Democratic organizations continued to resist the conflict and uncertainty associated with new voters.

The Democratic apparatus to sustain voter participation was not working. The unions did little to enroll new black and Hispanic voters, or the poor women who were entering the work force. Nor did the local Democratic parties. Instead, local party officials who presided over registration used their control to maintain a narrow and reliable electoral constituency, a pattern that was brought to light in the course of the voter registration campaigns that broke out in the 1980–84 period (which are described in chapter 6). Even black mayors, once they were securely in office, used restrictive procedures to maintain a reliable electorate.

It is true that during the 1960s, civil rights protest and litigation resulted in the elimination of poll taxes, literacy tests, and residency requirements exceeding thirty days before elections. In this sense, aspects of the disenfranchising apparatus of 1896 were toppled; the formal right to register was won, conditioned only on people being citizens, of age, domiciled, and free of felony convictions, although it is worth keeping in mind how recent these reforms were. As late as 1970, fourteen states *outside* the South were conducting literacy tests.

But the administrative barriers remained, and the state and local parties resisted reducing or abolishing them. There was still only one registration office in many counties, and it might be open only during working hours, thus creating an income test because of travel costs, as well as an education test, since it was not easy to discover the location of many boards of elections. Few boards were willing to establish satellite registration centers in poor neighborhoods. (In order to vote, by contrast, it was not necessary to travel halfway across a county to a courthouse, or downtown in a big city; one went to a school or firehouse on election day.) Similarly, registration offices were rarely open nights or weekends, so people had to take time off from work (another income test).

The widely heralded reforms of the registration process during the last fifteen years have had little impact on these barriers. Registration by mail, which is now permitted in twenty-three states, covering roughly 60 percent of the population, has not raised registration levels appreciably because election officials refuse to make the forms widely available where people live or work. Arranging to obtain a form is not simple. Even finding the telephone number of an election office in the typical directory can be difficult, since the names by which elections boards go are bewildering. For example, in Travis County, Texas (which includes Austin), registration is handled by the Travis County Tax Collector. And then there is the problem of getting through to a telephone number that is often busy, especially as an election draws near. Some states also require forms to be notarized before they are mailed back to elections officials.

Moreover, many elections officials still fend off unwanted voters who appear before them, especially poor and minority applicants (officials have been known to complain that these registrants "dirty up" their ledgers because "they don't care about voting" and will end up having to be purged). For their part, poor people generally try to avoid public officials, whom they mistrust, except when the press of necessity forces them to seek government services. In addition, the registration forms themselves are booby-traps. In New York City, the board of elections routinely discards forms that are completed in pencil, or signed only on one side, or signed with a middle initial on one side but not the other, or with Mr. or Mrs. on one side only. For the less well educated and the less confident, the application process can be humiliating.

The tendency is to think that these administrative barriers are primarily southern, and aimed at excluding blacks. But the system of exclusion is national in scope, and is aimed at lower-class and working-class people generally. Of the dozen or so major voter registration suits taken in the last several years against obstructive elections officials who refuse to deputize volunteers associated with voter registration campaigns, half were filed in the northeastern and midwestern industrial working-class states of Massachusetts, Connecticut, Pennsylvania, Ohio, Indiana, and Michigan.

Finally, even when registration obstacles are overcome, they reassert themselves. As many as half of all households change residence between presidential elections.[98] If people move to new jurisdictions, they must reregister, and those moving within the same jurisdiction must report a change of address, a requirement tantamount to repeating the registration process.

---

[98] Squire, Wolfinger, and Glass (1987) found that one-third of the 1980 National Election Study sample had lived at their current addresses for less than two years.

Many people are turned away on election day because they are unaware of this rule.[99] The composition of the electorate also changes constantly, as some voters die and potential voters come of age. For these reasons, administrative procedures constantly reproduce the upwardly skewed electorate. Contemporary voter registration obstacles thus function as de facto equivalents of the poll tax, literacy test, and other class- and race-oriented restrictions on the suffrage of an earlier era.

In sum, the New Deal electoral coalition splintered in the postwar years, in part because it was constructed on the foundations inherited from the system of 1896. Eventually, part of those foundations began to give way. Party competition was restored in much of the country, and restrictions on the franchise were weakened. There will never again be a national Democratic party system predicated on the one-party oligarchy that governed the feudal political economy of the Old South. Nor will there ever again be a Democratic party politics predicated on the industrial political economy of the North. But the party apparatus constructed within the persisting constraints of the system of 1896 remains fixed: it is unable to stop the hemorrhaging of its old constituencies, and it is both ill placed and unwilling to enlist a new electorate from the enlarging reservoir of nonvoters in the recomposing working class.

[99] In Texas, to give one example, Travis County (Austin) elections officials received six thousand telephone calls on election day in November 1986 from irate voters who had been barred from voting. Ninety percent were from people who had changed their address.

Chapter 6

The Reagan Era:
Competition for New Voters

Between 1980 and 1984, competition for new voters flared up. By measure of the money spent, the number of people engaged in helping to register others, the variety of innovative registration approaches employed, and the number of people registered, this effort to expand electoral participation was unprecedented in American history. For the first time in more than two decades, the levels of registration and voting rose.

In a fundamental sense, this competition for new voters reflected the breakdown of the southern system of disenfranchisement; large numbers of people who had been nonvoters, both black and white, became available for mobilization. This volatile development obviously had large implications for the future of electoral politics in the South, as it did in the large northern states to which millions of blacks had migrated. During this same period, furthermore, growing numbers of Hispanics in many parts of the country also became a potential untapped electoral force.

However, the mass voter registration drives of the 1980–84 period did not quite reflect the classical idea that electoral participation expands through party competition for new voters.

Although the national Republican party joined the race for new voters, the national Democratic party did not. Instead, drives were mounted by activists who were trying to gain influence over the policy orientations of the parties by changing the makeup of their coalitions. At one end of the political spectrum, New Right and Christian Right activists mobilized more evangelical whites to participate in the Republican party; on the other, New Politics activists focused on enlisting more minorities and women in the Democratic party. In this chapter, we sketch the main outlines of these events, and we consider whether competition for new voters through registration drives has longer-term significance.

THE CONTENDERS

The recent voter drives were a renewal, on a much larger scale, of the competition for new voters that had erupted in the period of the civil rights struggle. Organizations associated with the civil rights struggle itself, such as the NAACP and the southern-based Voter Education Project, initiated such efforts. In 1976, partly in response to the decrease in black registration that began in the early 1970s, the National Coalition for Black Voter Participation was formed, with a voter registration arm called Operation Big Vote. The purpose was to coordinate drives among existing black organizations, and to stimulate additional drives throughout the country. Similarly, the low rates of registration among Mexican-Americans resulted in the formation, in 1974, of the Southwest Voter Education Project, and it has since had considerable success registering Hispanics in Texas and throughout the Southwest.

On the other side, southern white clergy became actively involved in voter registration in order to buttress conservative influence within the Republican party, and to support Reagan's candidacy in 1980 and his reelection in 1984.[1] Key religious organizations of the Christian Right, especially Moral Majority and Religious Roundtable, began to urge evangelical clergy to become politically active.[2] By 1980, this effort took form in voter registration drives.[3] However, the evidence suggests that the Christian Right mobilization did not involve many clergy from the major denominations,[4] but only "gained a firm hold among independent churches, minor denominations, and the ranks of dissidents within mainline denominations."[5] These "independent" churches—which included mainly Bible Churches and Assemblies of God—have strong traditions of local autonomy and pastoral authority. Their congregations tend to be less educated, of somewhat lower socioeconomic position, and are more likely to reside in rural areas and small towns than mem-

---

[1] It is not clear that evangelicals and fundamentalists exhibit cohesive values or distinctive voting patterns. See the Epilogue for a further discussion.

[2] Scholars are debating the question of why some white conservative religious leaders came to favor secular political action over miraculous conversion as the key to social reform. For example, some define the movement as a protest against modernity (Lipset and Raab, 1981); others as the efforts of a traditionally devalued group to exploit new opportunities provided by the economic revitalization of the South to enhance its status (Simpson, 1983); and still others as an example of "resource mobilization" in which religious networks are activated (Liebman, 1983a:61).

[3] Right-wing Republican organizers take credit for this development, claiming that it was their idea to enlist conservative white voters through religious networks, and that they provided the necessary technical assistance to enable participating clergy to begin the effort. Those who claim to have initiated this effort include Richard Viguerie, the direct-mail fundraiser, Paul Weyrich of the Committee for Survival of a Free Congress, the late Terry Dolan of the National Conservative Political Action Committee, and E. E. McAteer and Howard Phillips of the Conservative Caucus. However, analysts of the Christian Right electoral mobilization dispute these claims. In their view, Christian Right leaders possessed all the necessary resources to mount this venture on their own. See, for example, Liebman (1983b).

[4] One reason may be that many parishioners do not approve of mixing politics and religion. On the basis of survey data from the Dallas–Fort Worth area—which has often been called "the buckle of the Southern Bible Belt"—Shupe and Stacey (1983:114) found little support among lay people for religious involvement in politics. Furthermore, they conclude that Christian Right leaders "seriously overestimate the amount of agreement among sympathizers on the issues they hold dear. Divisions and inconsistencies seem to be the rule rather than the exception."

[5] Liebman (1983a:50).

bers of the denominationally affiliated churches, such as the largest of the southern denominations, the Baptists. It was mainly these nonestablishment churches that heeded the call to register their members.[6]

Opinion polls and other data showed that rates of registration were lower among evangelicals than nonevangelicals,[7] and that 30 percent of all nonvoters attended church services at least three times a week.[8] Using data gathered in the late 1970s, Lipset and Raab estimate that the evangelical core is comprised of 20 to 25 percent of the adult population, or roughly 30 million adults, as defined by the belief in the literal meaning of the Bible and the divinity of Jesus, by the acceptance of Jesus as one's personal savior ("born again"), and by the importance of proselytizing. However, blacks make up 25 percent of this core, and they are obviously not a Christian Right constituency. Another 10 percent are Catholics. Two of three are females. About 25 percent of the core group resides in the Midwest, and half in the South.[9] Moral Majority claimed that

[6] Guth (1983:126) and Liebman (1983a). Guth (1983:129) also claims that the increasing educational level and "professionalization" of the Southern Baptist clergy will diminish the number of conservative militants. In addition, "the continuing and rapid urbanization and upward mobility of Southern Baptists, and the organizational rationalization of their churches, will reduce the number of churches with favorable climates for Christian Right activities."

[7] Sawyer and Kaiser (1981).

[8] Moser (1980).

[9] Lipset and Raab (1981). There has even been speculation that the rise of the Christian Right presages a fourth "religious awakening," a movement for cultural revitalization like earlier ones that swept over the United States since the mid-eighteenth century (see McLoughlin, 1978). Hammond draws on Tocqueville's conclusion about nineteenth-century American religious awakenings that cultural reform results only when these movements successfully promote the widespread formation of civic associations through which religious ideas about social policy can then be promoted. Referring to the present period, Hammond (1983:218) says that the social characteristics of the evangelicals—low occupational prestige, low income and educational levels, and rural and small town residence—are not those that promote the formation of civic associations, so there is no reason to think "that an awakening is in the making." Our own sense is that the present-day religious revival is likely to remain considerably less than an awakening, and will turn out to represent an essentially regional reaction to the traumas associated with urbanization and the nationalization of the southern economy and politics.

cooperating churches registered 4 million to 8 million of these white evangelicals in the pre-1980 election period. A Harris poll credited them with registering between 1 million and 2 million.[10]

Several other developments helped stimulate voter registration campaigns after 1980. The deep recession of 1982 produced an upsurge in voting by blacks, blue-collar workers, and the unemployed in the midterm elections. A spontaneous electoral mobilization seemed to be under way. In response to the highest unemployment since the Great Depression, midterm turnout rose for the first time in two decades, reaching 64 million, or 10 million more than in 1978, and swelling the Democratic House vote by 6 million. The additional voters were mainly blacks and the unemployed, and turnout was up most in the Midwest and South. The sharp increase in blue-collar workers helped replace retiring GOP governors with Democrats in Michigan, Ohio, and Wisconsin, and Republican incumbents were ousted in a number of economically hard-hit congressional districts, contributing to the Democrats' modest victory of twenty-six additional House seats. "The question [for 1984] and the rest of the decade," the *Congressional Quarterly* editorialized at the time, "is whether this upsurge in the 'have-not' vote will continue. Both parties are making plans for 1984 on the assumption that it is here to stay, a result of the arguments and emotions of the Reagan era."[11]

Virtually every major political strategist predicted that overall turnout would rise sharply in 1984, especially among "marginal groups"—the poor and minorities, as well as among women. It was, to cite the *Congressional Quarterly* once more, a time of "potentially historic significance" for the Democratic party:

---

[10] Harris poll release, November 4, 1980.
[11] *Congressional Quarterly* (July 23, 1983:1503).

They have a large pool of potential voters to target. Following the 1982 elections, the Census Bureau reported that 7.2
million blacks, 5.4 million unemployed, and nearly 12.5
million blue-collar workers of all races were not registered
to vote. There are an estimated 2.5 million unregistered
Hispanic citizens. [On the other hand], with the possible
exception of fundamentalist Christians, [the Republican
party] has no new, reliably Republican voting bloc to mobilize. The likely GOP voters, for the most part, have
already been voting. [12]

Christian Right leaders naturally worried that Reagan's
prospects for victory in 1984 were endangered—for example,
Gary Jarmin, legislative director of Christian Voice, circulated
his view widely among religious leaders that they would have to
register 2 million fundamentalists in 1984 "just to stay even"
with the Democratic party. [13] Consequently, a number of these
leaders, including representatives of Moral Majority and Christian Voice, coalesced to launch a national umbrella organization,
the American Coalition for Traditional Values. Its main goal was
to register 2 million fundamentalists in twenty-five states.

At the other end of the political spectrum, the possibility
that a ground swell was running among the have-nots stimulated
greater efforts among activists who were oriented toward building electoral influence among what they defined as the "natural"
constituencies of the Democratic party—primarily the poor, minorities, and women. In addition to the minority voter registration efforts mentioned earlier, new organizations were formed
and existing groups turned to registration drives. The Citizen
Action network, which grew out of the shift by some civil rights
and welfare rights organizers at the end of the 1960s toward

[12] Ibid. (1504 and 1507).
[13] This quote comes from the archives of the Committee for the Study of the American
Electorate. David Michael Smith (1985) assembled data from a variety of sources on the
registration campaigns mounted by the Christian Right and by the Republican party.

white working-class and lower-middle-class constituencies, was active in about ten states. ACORN, in accord with its traditional commitments, focused more on poorer and minority communities in the slums and ghettos of New York, Detroit, St. Louis, and Bridgeport, for example. The Midwest Voter Education Project was created in 1982 to reach Hispanics who had migrated to the Midwest, and the National Puerto Rican/Hispanic Voter Participation Project was formed in 1983. Other nonpartisan voter registration organizations were established in the same period. The Women's Vote Project was organized to stimulate and coordinate drives by a wide range of women's groups. Project Vote, the Human SERVE Campaign, and the Churches' Voter Registration Project (which was financed by a consortium of northern Protestant denominations, although on nowhere near the scale of the evangelical effort) worked to register the unemployed and welfare and food-stamp recipients. Public Interest Research Groups (PIRGs) and the United States Student Association targeted college students. And some peace and environmental groups joined in registration drives. The funding for these efforts came mainly from liberal foundations broadly associated with the causes of the New Politics. Foundation contributions reached $7 million, and a few millions more were added by private donors.

Finally, predictions by Republican analysts that as many as 10 million additional voters might go to the polls in 1984, a majority of them Democrats, jolted the Republican party into mounting a registration campaign. "What Reagan is in the process of doing," James Reston said at the time, "is to scare the voters and wake up the dropouts, and encourage them to register and vote. This, no doubt, is a contribution to democracy and the Democrats, but not necessarily what the President had in mind for the Republican Party."[14] James Kilpatrick, the right-wing columnist, issued the obvious warning:

[14] *New York Times*, January 4, 1984.

Make no mistake. Democratic leaders will go after votes from blacks, Hispanics, welfare recipients and disenchanted women for one unimpeachable reason. That is where the votes are. If the Republicans fail to mount a massive effort to register likely new Republican voters, the Republicans will take a drubbing in 1984. A Republican registration drive must concentrate on middle-income whites and Hispanics, conservative women and young people, and non-union families.[15]

Unnerved by these forecasts, Reagan-Bush campaign officials announced in January 1984 that the increased registration of Democratic voters presaged a close race, thus making a concerted drive for at least 2 million new Republican voters a prerequisite to Reagan's reelection. The press subsequently reported that $10 million to $25 million was raised for this effort.

In spite of both the Republican and Christian Right drives, the Democratic National Committee (DNC) did little except issue press releases announcing multi-million-dollar registration campaigns that never materialized, in part because available funds were consumed in the primary fights. But the larger reason was that Mondale in fact decided against a registration strategy, despite a 250-page study written by his aides concluding that "the only way Mondale can win is by pitching his appeal to the white working class and minorities, not the middle class."[16] Mike Ford, Mondale's field director, asserted that a Mondale victory "is nearly impossible with the current electorate. . . . We must consider dramatic and perhaps high-risk strategies," and he urgently recommended that $12 million be spent to register 5 million to 6 million new black, Hispanic, and union voters.[17] But these recommendations were ignored in favor of a

[15] *Staten Island Advance*, December 6, 1983.
[16] Marable (1986).
[17] *Newsweek*, Election extra, November/December 1984, p. 81.

campaign oriented toward existing registrants. Overall, the DNC and the Mondale campaign distributed perhaps $2 million to state and local Democratic parties, which was used to get-out-the-vote among those already registered rather than to register new voters. Ironically, one party galvanized itself to cancel out an electoral mobilization that the other party never attempted.

VOTER REGISTRATION STRATEGIES

In the course of the campaign, door-knocking as a voter registration strategy virtually became extinct. In its stead, computers coupled with phone banks were employed to pinpoint unregistered voters. Or people were reached through local institutions such as community organizations, churches, and community agencies, and in the waiting rooms of unemployment and welfare agencies. Some political officials even began to instruct state, county, and municipal employees to offer to register their clients to vote.

Hi-Tech Registration

At first, Republican strategists expressed anxiety that there might be relatively few unregistered voters with Republican sympathies, raising a tactical problem of how to identify and reach them. Helen Cameron, head of the Reagan-Bush registration effort, complained that even in heavily Republican areas, telephone surveys found only 10 to 18 percent of the unregistered were Reagan supporters.[18] Traditional registration methods,

---

[18] Edsall and Johnson (July 7, 1984). Republican drives also confronted a further problem. In a postelection study in Los Angeles County, Cain and McCue (1984, 1985) found that Republican registration drives in high socioeconomic areas were subject to a law of diminishing returns because people from such areas had a high probability of registering anyway. The more Republicans registered by drives, the fewer Republicans who registered themselves. By contrast, campaigns to register lower-income and minority people were much more likely to reach those who would not have registered themselves (1985:12).

such as setting up tables in shopping malls, could thus boomerang, producing more Democratic than Republican registrants.
Republican pollster Lance Terrance had already warned that the
downward tilt of the unregistered pool meant that "for every new
voter the Republicans pick up, the Democrats pick up two." [19]
And Democratic strategists crowed that while the Republicans
were registering the "needles," Democrats were registering the
"haystack." [20]

But with the huge amounts of money available to them,
Republican organizers could turn to modern technology to solve
the problem of finding the needles. Computer data tapes were
bought from the Census Bureau, credit bureaus, motor vehicle
bureaus, financial magazines, upscale mail-order houses, and
boards of registrars. Beginning with aggregate lists of as many
as a million names in a particular city or locality, technicians
then merged and purged these lists until, for example, they could
pinpoint twenty thousand unregistered people living in affluent
neighborhoods, owning late-model cars, and subscribing to financial magazines who were then called by paid phone bank
staffers and volunteers to see whether they agreed that Reagan
was doing a good job. If they agreed, canvassers either stopped
by or sent registration cards to them. [21] By August 1984, Republican strategists claimed to have recruited fifty-five thousand volunteers and to have made 2.5 million phone calls. Costs in some
states ran as high as $5.00 to $7.00 per registrant. High-tech
pinpointing, Edsall and Johnson remarked, has become "a 1984
version of the American political machine." [22]

Although twenty-five states were initially designated for Republican drives, the main campaigns were actually mounted in
Illinois, Texas, California, and Florida. Registration gains by

[19] *Congressional Quarterly* (July 23, 1983:1503).
[20] Salmans (July 6, 1984).
[21] See Salmore and Salmore (1985:188) for a further description of the Republican computer
strategy.
[22] Edsall and Johnson (April 22, 1984).

blacks and Latinos in Illinois were offset by campaigns in the Illinois suburbs, often with the slogan, "Are you registered to vote? Chicago is."[23] Retirees and the affluent were targeted in Florida. Higher-income whites were the focus in Texas and California. Although Puerto Ricans and Mexican-Americans tend to vote Democratic two-to-one, the Republican National Hispanic Assembly, or Viva '84, was formed to enlist upwardly mobile and middle-income Hispanics in the Southwest, and Cubans in Florida.

Churches and Voter Registration

In 1984, the Christian Right strategy included mass mailings to clergy (including instructional materials to churches in three hundred cities), urging them to undertake local registration campaigns—for example, by forming "good government" committees in their churches, and by arranging to have church members deputized as voter registrars.[24] Some three hundred training sessions were held in roughly two hundred cities with clergy and lay persons. And Senator Paul Laxalt, representing the Republican party, wrote a letter to thousands of fundamentalist ministers in August 1984 asking that they help register Republican voters in their congregations.[25] Finally, some leading evangelists in the "electronic church" also urged their audiences to register.

Generally, the Christian Right concentrated its efforts in states with large fundamentalist populations and critical contests, mainly in the South. In North Carolina, the American Coalition may have been the decisive factor in the reelection victory of Senator Jesse Helms over Governor James Hunt. Although

---

[23] Herbes (October 16, 1984).

[24] In some jurisdictions, these efforts ran afoul of restrictions prohibiting registration on Sundays. In Florida, for example, right-to-life groups are presently lobbying the legislature to abolish these restrictions.

[25] For a general summary of these actions, see Smith (1985).

large drives were under way among blacks in North Carolina, the religious Right succeeded in reaching many more "Christian whites." Over 77,000 blacks registered between January and May 1984, for example, but more than 144,000 whites also registered during this period, and the fundamentalists have been credited with registering 100,000 of them.[26] Generally speaking, the religious Right's registration campaign (together with the Republican campaign) overwhelmed black registration increases in the South. In five southern states surveyed by the *Washington Post*, more than three times as many whites as blacks registered.[27] The electoral mobilization of the Christian Right is thus a serious effort, and an important part of the Republican party's attempt to build a Republican South.

Canvassing in Welfare State Waiting Rooms

The nonpartisan drives employed a range of voter registration strategies. A common method was to identify and make small grants to existing grass-roots organizations, or to emerging ones, which appeared to have the capacity to enlist new voters in poorer, minority, and working-class neighborhoods. This method, which was widely used by organizations such as the Southwest Voter Education Project, Citizen Action, Operation Big Vote, and ACORN, also had as its purpose the building of ongoing neighborhood organizations.

Another method that emerged in this period was to enroll people waiting on food-stamp lines, at surplus cheese distribution centers, and in unemployment and welfare waiting rooms. Sanford Newman of Project Vote was a leader in developing this strategy. The advantages of this approach over traditional methods of door-to-door registration were obvious. Canvassers often

---

[26] Johnson and Edsall (September 30, 1984) and Herbes (October 26, 1984).
[27] Cited in Osborne (February 25, 1985).

felt unsafe in poorer neighborhoods, the people who lived there often felt unsafe opening their doors to strangers, and the one-to-one transaction itself was time-consuming. Registering people in agencies was not only safer, it was far more efficient than door-knocking because there was a large overlap between unregistered voters and the beneficiaries of social welfare programs who were crowded into waiting rooms. Project Vote volunteers thus registered more than 500,000 people in advance of the 1984 election. As the overall campaign expanded between 1982 and 1984, this method was widely used by other organizations focusing on the poor and minorities. For example, the Human SERVE Campaign recruited hundreds of volunteers, who registered 320,000 people in welfare and employment offices in the large industrial states, about 150,000 of them in New York City. (In a related effort, Human SERVE also undertook an institutional reform program, to be described in the next chapter, which involved lobbying governors and mayors, and the executives of nonprofit health and welfare agencies, to establish voter registration services in a broad range of social agencies.)

Many of these nonpartisan organizing activities had roots in the protest movements of the 1960s, and they sometimes acquired a spirit reminiscent of that period. ACORN mounted direct action and civil disobedience campaigns against obstructive voter registration officials in Bridgeport and St. Louis who refused to deputize volunteer registrars. In Cincinnati, a female Project Vote organizer who was canvassing in a welfare waiting room was arrested and strip-searched, setting off a furor. In an action jointly initiated by Connecticut Planned Parenthood, Citizen Action, and Human SERVE, a federal judge cited the Voting Rights Act for authority when he ordered Waterbury, Connecticut, election officials to deputize volunteers. The NAACP mounted an "Overground Railroad" march under the banner "Bury Voter Apathy," which began in Richmond on August 20 and ended in New York City on Labor Day, and reported that some thirty-five thousand people were registered in urban black neighborhoods along the way. Ninety-one students joined a "Freedom Summer '84 Voter Registration Campaign," jointly sponsored by the United States Student Association and Human SERVE, and organized ten-week drives in unemployment and welfare offices in sixty-three cities in twenty-three states. USSA recruited sixty students, whose $1,500 stipends were funded by foundations, and Human SERVE persuaded graduate schools of social work to recruit and finance the other thirty-one. These same schools, together with local organizations such as YWCAs, Planned Parenthood agencies, churches, grassroots community groups, NAACP chapters, unions, and cooperating voter registration campaigns provided the student coordinators with free offices and telephones. The Freedom Summer coordinators organized grass-roots coalitions, or staffed existing ones, recruited thousands of volunteers to canvass in social welfare waiting rooms, generated widespread local publicity celebrating the twentieth anniversary of Mississippi Freedom Summer while drawing the media's spotlight to persisting voter registration barriers. By the end of the campaign, they had signed up 230,000 people,[28] often inventing flamboyant tactics, as when they called themselves "freedom riders" and registered thousands of people on the Transit Authority buses serving the poorer districts of Houston.

There was even an attempt at a general mobilization of activists to conduct voter registration. Human SERVE appealed to religious, environmental, peace, and other cause-oriented organizations to participate in an "October 4 National Day of Voter Registration" by spending the day registering people in unemployment offices, welfare centers, food-stamp offices, hospital outpatient rooms, public housing projects, and at transportation stops serving poorer neighborhoods. Although some eighty-odd

---

[28] This figure resulted from a careful audit of the weekly reports prepared by the student coordinators, whose estimates of the numbers registered were then halved.

national organizations signed on, and although about 225,000 people were registered nationally, the plan was not announced until early July, leaving too little time to organize on a national scale. It was mainly in New York that the potential of such a concerted effort was actually tested. There PIRG organizers and students took the lead and, together with human service volunteers, the Gray Panthers, and peace organizations (such as the Women's International League for Peace and Freedom, the Committee in Solidarity with the People of El Salvador, Mobilization for Survival, Freeze Vote '84, and Women's Action for Nuclear Disarmament), they completed sixty-two thousand cards in a single day, causing the head of the elections board to complain in the *New York Times* about registration "fanatics." On the same day, social work faculty and students from the University of Indiana/Purdue, together with local human service workers, joined with the Indianapolis Citizen Action chapter to bus four thousand low-income and minority people to the elections office. When the doors closed at midnight, the thousand or so who were still unregistered jammed in, forcing the office to process applications until 4:00 A.M., and producing a spate of front-page publicity about Indiana's archaic registration laws.[29]

OPPOSITION BY BOARDS OF ELECTIONS

One of the most important achievements of these campaigns is that they activated and exposed the historic pattern of govern-

---

[29] The National Elections Commission, in its report of April 1986, was prompted by the October 4 National Day of Voter Registration event to conclude that Congress ought to establish a National Registration Day (although Congress is not likely to do so). The commission said that "there would be great merit in the Congress's designating a weekday in late September or early October in all even-numbered years to be National Registration Day. On National Registration Day, each state and locality should work within its laws and traditions to increase opportunities for voter registration to the extent possible—at the court house, city hall, polling places, schools, and work place. With imagination and dedication, this day of voter registration can become second only to election day as a symbol of practical democracy, public education, and involvement."

mental obstruction of voter registration. Local boards respond to volunteer voter registration campaigns by throwing up all sorts of obstacles, typically arguing that it is their responsibility to maintain the "quality" of the electorate, to guard against fraud, and so forth. The simple fact is that these local officials are closely connected to local politicians who want the security of a stable and reliable electorate and who therefore resist new and unpredictable voters. Elections officials also have their jobs to protect, and they show the usual reluctance of bureaucrats to take on additional work or to entertain novel developments. County boards of elections preside over what is in effect the disenfranchising apparatus of the American electoral system.

It is worth noting that, for all of the volumes written by political analysts on electoral arrangements and on the question of why people don't vote, there has been virtually no attention paid to these state and county voter registration apparatuses. There are no studies of the political environment of these agencies, or of the political influences that determine their procedures. Nor are there studies of the relationship between specific registration practices and who does and does not vote.

Obstructive board practices are not limited to the South, nor do they just limit electoral participation among minorities. The system of exclusion is national in scope, and it is in the working class as a whole that voting numbers are kept down. In a number of postcard registration states, most of which are northern, boards of elections often try to frustrate registration campaigns by keeping few forms in supply. Or they demand that registration organizations pay for printing additional forms. Or they limit the number of forms given out to ten or twenty-five at a time, with the result that volunteer registrars spend as much time traveling as registering. Regulations governing mail registration in a number of states also frustrate campaigns. West Virginia, for example, requires that every registrant appear before a notary public, and that presented a well-nigh insuperable logistical problem for large-scale campaign efforts.

In states without mail registration, many boards refuse to deputize campaign volunteers. They typically justify these refusals with the familiar adage that if people aren't interested enough to travel to an office where voter registration is available (which might be halfway across a county), or sophisticated enough to figure out where the local office is, they don't deserve to vote. Local boards often fail to deputize campaign volunteers even when state laws contain language to the effect that they may deputize as many volunteers as are necessary to ensure that all citizens have the opportunity to vote. The time and resources required to mount campaigns under these conditions are formidable. Steve Kest of ACORN made that point when he complained that there was no time for political work in Bridgeport, Connecticut, because the organizing staff spent months raising money to bus seven thousand people from public housing projects to the elections office, which had refused to deputize organizers and volunteers.

Restrictive local boards created something of a farce in Connecticut, where there was no deputization except in Hartford, and to a limited extent in New Haven (and there only under an earlier court order).[30] Human SERVE had urged the governor both to issue an executive order establishing registration in state agencies and to pressure the local boards to deputize state workers (as well as volunteers from community groups). He decided instead to direct his department heads to submit plans showing how they would make it easy for volunteers to canvass for new registrants in waiting rooms (e.g., by making tables available, etc.). Every department sent in detailed plans, some of them enthusiastically. But he did not press town election officials to liberalize deputization practices. Consequently, agency administrators throughout Connecticut waited over the summer of 1984 for volunteer registrars who never appeared

---

[30] After years of concerted lobbying by a coalition of groups, Connecticut enacted a postcard registration bill in the early summer of 1987.

because they could not get deputized. The farce was repeated in Massachusetts, where most boards of elections refused to deputize volunteers. After considerable pressure from a voting rights coalition, Governor Dukakis agreed to permit voter registration services in public agency waiting rooms, but the local boards of elections declined either to deputize volunteers or to send their own employees to staff tables, and the governor put no pressure on them to cooperate. In Boston, Mayor Flynn, stung by accurate public criticisms that deputization practices were as bad in Boston as in Mississippi, agreed to allow board employees to go to a range of human service sites, such as hospitals, where volunteers then located potential registrants and directed them to the official registrar, who generally could be found sitting in an out-of-the-way corner reading a magazine. As the volunteer effort built up, the monthly reports of the Boston elections board showed a rapid rise in registration: April, 243; May, 545; June, 1,339; July, 2,253.[31]

Boards that do deputize often do so selectively; they will deputize members of the League of Women Voters or Moral Majority, but not members of the NAACP, of ACORN, or of human service agencies. Moreover, volunteer deputies are sometimes told that some sites are off limits—such as welfare and unemployment offices, or public housing projects. The Richmond, Virginia, board revoked the deputy status of NAACP volunteers canvassing on federal surplus cheese distribution lines; a Catholic registrar in New Haven refused to permit volunteers to canvass at family planning offices. In Massachusetts, elections officials are presumably required by state law to dispatch their own employees to sites of "principal activity" at a designated time if petitioned by ten registered voters. However, the Worcester and New Bedford town clerks simply denied that

---

[31] This concession notwithstanding, Mayor Flynn appears to have no intention of easing deputization practices; the structure of the existing electorate that put him in office suits his interests.

welfare centers, unemployment offices, and community health facilities where low-income minority people congregate are places of principal activity.

A number of boards that are willing to deputize volunteers so hobble them with restrictions—"Pick up the forms after 9:00 A.M., and return them by 4:45 P.M. Late forms will be voided" —that volunteers give up in frustration. In Indianapolis, volunteers are given twenty-five forms at a time. To make matters worse, after the forms are completed and returned, Indianapolis officials require the volunteers to repeat the entire process by which they were initially deputized: they must again secure permission from representatives of one of the political parties, again secure the permission of the county registrar, and again undergo training, after which they again receive only twenty or twenty-five cards.

These are only some of the typical problems in non-mail-registration states; a complete inventory of obstructions would fill a small book. So there is something to be said for legislation permitting registration by postcard. By itself, as we noted earlier, postcard registration does not appreciably raise registration levels because no provision is made to distribute the forms widely. It nevertheless reduces the ability of boards of elections to control access to registration. Anyone, or at least any registered voter, can usually get at least some forms to register others.

Campaign organizers responded to these obstructions in a variety of ways. The older voter registration organizations tended to treat board procedures as a more or less fixed feature of the political environment, and they tried to work within the structure of procedures, or to negotiate limited exceptions to them. But newer campaign organizations—not having yet been worn down by struggles with the elections clerks—reacted with outrage. Not only were the boards unwilling to mount outreach efforts themselves, but they were also preventing others from doing so.

Consequently, the newer voter registration campaign organizations came to define board procedures as illegitimate, and to call for court challenges. A coalition of legal organizations was formed to launch a barrage of suits against elections boards in various states. The participating organizations include the American Civil Liberties Union, the NAACP Legal Defense and Educational Fund, the Lawyers' Committee for Civil Rights Under Law, the Lawyers' Guild, representatives from the major nonpartisan voter registration organizations and from other groups participating in voter registration, such as the Public Interest Research Group and the Planned Parenthood Federation of America. The coalition, which was at first chaired by Hulbert James of Human SERVE, is now chaired by Lani Guinier of the NAACP Legal Defense and Educational Fund. A substantial number of suits have been filed challenging board practices, especially restrictions on deputization.[32]

How Many Were Registered?

Despite these obstructions, the major contenders claimed to have registered more than 7 million people, as noted in table 6.1. Indeed, the 1980–84 election cycle was the first since 1960 in which the level of registration rose, and it rose rather sharply. The Census Bureau/CPS reported a net increase of 11.1 million registrants (105 million to 116.1 million). This translates into a 2.5 percentage point rise in the national level of registration between 1980 and 1984, or from about 60–61 percent to 63–64 percent.[33] If it is assumed that the registration rate of 60 percent in 1980 would have been the same in 1984 *in the absence of organized drives,* and given a net voting-age population in-

---

[32] The main legal theories underpinning these suits, and the responses of the courts to them, are described in appendix D.

[33] We estimate that the level of registration in 1980 was about 60–61 percent. See appendix A for technical problems in calculating registration levels.

crease of 9.5 million,[34] the registration rolls would have risen by a net of 5.7 million. But since the actual net registration increase was 11.1 million, a net excess of 5.4 million remains that can be credited to organized drives. This figure is consistent with the claims of the large drives that more than 7 million in absolute numbers were registered.[35] The actual numbers registered will always be larger than the net increase because some of those reached would have registered or reregistered on their own, or they were already registered but just wanted to be certain of it by registering again, and so forth. In this respect, organized drives are inefficient. They necessarily register many people who need not have been, with the result that their *net* contribution to the registration rolls is necessarily less than the absolute number they register. In sum, and considering both this source of inefficiency and that the net voting-age population increase consists of young people who register less, a net increase of 5.4 million registrants is a substantial achievement.[36]

[34] The Census Bureau/CPS reports a lower rate of increase of 1.4 percentage points. When we queried the Census Bureau/CPS about this, they indicated that the 1980 "civilian noninstitutional" voting-age population (VAP) figure used by the Current Population Survey had been underestimated by about 4 million, and it was not corrected until 1984 (after the 1980 decennial census results were known). Consequently, the 1980–84 "civilian noninstitutional" VAP increase is shown to be almost 4 million more than the "resident" VAP increase employed by the population division of the bureau, as the accompanying table shows. In other words, if the Current Population Survey had used the proper voting-age population increase of 9.5 million, it would have reported a 2.5 percentage point rise in the registration rate, rather than 1.4 points.

DISCREPANT CENSUS BUREAU ESTIMATES OF THE 1980–1984
VOTING-AGE POPULATION INCREASE (MILLIONS)

Census Bureau VAP Definition	1980 VAP	1984 VAP	1980–84 VAP Net Increase
Resident VAP	164.5	174	9.5
Civilian VAP	157.1	170	12.9

[35] Again, we do not know the additional number registered by a variety of other groups, such as unions and miscellaneous community groups. Nor can we estimate the impact of Jesse Jackson's candidacy on black registration, or on white registration in reaction.

[36] The Committee for the Study of the American Electorate (1984:2) also conducted a study that showed that "states in which there was intense voter registration activity tended to have significantly increased registration rates, while those in which there was little or no registration activity tended to have stable or even a declining percentage of voter registration."

TABLE 6.1 REGISTRATION CLAIMS

Partisan campaigns		
Republican party		2,000,000
Christian Right		1,500,000
Nonpartisan campaigns		
Churches' Voter Registration Project		223,000
Citizen Leadership Foundation		565,000
League of Women Voters		17,000
Midwest Voter Education Project		163,000
National Coalition for Black Voter Participation		359,800
National Student Campaign for Voter Registration		311,000
Project Vote		529,000
Southwest Voter Education Project		432,000
Human SERVE		
Registered by volunteers	320,000	
Registered by community agency staff	275,000	
Registered by public agency staff	75,000	
Human SERVE subtotal		670,000
Freedom Summer '84		230,000
October 4 National Day of Voter Registration		225,000
Total		7,224,800

Survey data corroborate this conclusion. Peter D. Hart Research Associates conducted a poll following the election of a national sample of 883 first-time-ever registrants (reregistrants were excluded), 850 of whom were interviewed for twenty minutes by telephone, and 33 of whom received personal interviews because they had no phones. Only 33 percent of the respondents reported that they had been registered by organized drives. However, we requested a breakdown of the places where people registered, which showed that a third of the people claiming to have registered on their own were in fact recruited at tables staffed by volunteer registrars in churches, in social agency waiting rooms, and at other locations such as supermarkets. They were not wrong to have thought that they registered themselves; after all, even if a campaign organization had set up a table, it was still the prospective registrant's decision to take advantage of the proffered opportunity. With this correction, 55 percent of the Hart respondents were registered as part of group activities.[37] This interpretation is consistent with a study in Los Angeles that verified from election board records that over 60 percent of new registrants had been enlisted by organized drives.[38]

WHO WAS REGISTERED

The largest proportional registration increases (table 6.2) occurred among minorities: 6.3 percent among blacks, and 3.8 percent among those of Hispanic origin. The rate increased by 4 points among the unemployed, but employed persons showed virtually no increase. Women showed a rise of 2.2 points, compared with a rise of only 0.7 points among men. By education, all groups showed rises, except those with four years of college or more. And the proportional rise in the South of 2.1 percent was larger than the 1.1 percent increase in the North. These data are consistent with the overall way in which registration campaign resources were deployed.

TURNOUT AMONG CAMPAIGN REGISTRANTS

Despite a 2.5 percentage point registration increase between 1980 and 1984, turnout increased by only 0.7 percent. Various

[37] In the meanwhile, the Committee for the Study of the American Electorate, which had commissioned the Hart survey, inaccurately reported to the press that only 33 percent of new registrants had been enlisted by organized drives. See the committee's undated report included in the citations at the close of this book.

[38] Cain and McCue (1984, 1985). Groups conducting registration drives in Los Angeles were required to record the name of their organization on all completed registration forms, and the names were computerized by elections officials, thus providing a valid basis for distinguishing between people who registered on their own and those who were registered by organizations.

TABLE 6.2 PERCENTAGE CLAIMING TO BE REGISTERED IN
1980 AND 1984

	1980	1984	Net Changes 1980–1984
National	66.9	68.3	+ 1.4
White	68.4	69.6	+ 1.2
Black	60.0	66.3	+ 6.3
Hispanic origin	36.3	40.1	+ 3.8
Male	66.6	67.3	+ 0.7
Female	67.1	69.3	+ 2.2
Employed	68.7	69.4	+ 0.7
Unemployed	50.3	54.3	+ 4.0
Not in labor force	65.8	68.1	+ 2.3
0 to 8 elementary	53.0	53.4	+ 0.4
High school			
1 to 3 years	54.6	54.9	+ 0.3
4 years	66.4	67.3	+ 0.9
College			
1 to 3 years	74.4	75.7	+ 1.3
4 years +	84.3	83.8	− 0.5
North and West	67.9	69.0	+ 1.1
White	69.3	70.5	+ 1.2
Black	60.6	67.2	+ 6.6
South	64.8	66.9	+ 2.1
White	66.2	67.8	+ 1.6
Black	59.3	65.6	+ 6.3

Source: Census Bureau/CPS Series P-20. We estimate that overall registration claims are inflated by 7 to 10 percent, although the inflation by particular subgroups may be more, or less. See appendix A for a discussion of the biases in registration data.

explanations have been given for the relatively lower turnout increase—such as opinion surveys showing that Reagan's victory was a foregone conclusion, and television network projections on election night of a Reagan victory long before the polls had closed in much of the country. In any event, turnout held up as well or better among "marginal" groups as among other groups (table 6.3). Although employed persons reduced their voting slightly (−0.2 points), voting by the unemployed rose (+2.8 points), as did voting by those who were not in the labor force (+1.9 points). Voting by males dropped marginally (−0.1), but females turned out in greater numbers (+1.4). Finally, whites showed a small increase (+0.5 points), but blacks showed

TABLE 6.3 PERCENTAGE CLAIMING TO HAVE VOTED 1980 AND 1984

	1980	*1984*	*Net Change*
National	59.2	59.9	+ 0.7
White	60.9	61.4	+ 0.5
Black	50.5	55.8	+ 5.3
Hispanic origin	29.9	32.6	+ 2.7
Male	59.1	59.0	− 0.1
Female	59.4	60.8	+ 1.4
Employed	61.8	61.6	− 0.2
Unemployed	41.2	44.0	+ 2.8
Not in labor force	57.0	58.9	+ 1.9
0 to 8 elementary	42.6	42.9	+ 0.3
High school			
1 to 3 years	45.6	44.4	− 1.2
4 years	58.9	58.7	− 0.2
College			
1 to 3 years	67.2	67.5	+ 0.3
4 years +	79.9	79.1	− 0.8
North and West	61.0	61.6	+ 0.6
White	62.4	63.0	+ 0.6
Black	52.8	58.9	+ 6.1
South	55.6	56.8	+ 1.2
White	57.4	58.1	+ 0.7
Black	48.2	53.2	+ 5.0

Source: Census Bureau/CPS Series P-20. In 1980, 7.6 percent more people claimed to have voted than did, and the inflation in 1984 was 9.9 percent (Series P-20, no. 405, table H).

a substantial increase (+5.3 points), with the black increase in the North and West slightly higher (+6.1 points) than in the South (+5.0 points). The changes by educational level show no pattern.

Regarding voting by campaign registrants themselves, the Churches' Voter Registration Project polled a sample of their registrants, 89 percent of whom claimed to have voted—96 percent of those with family incomes over $20,000, and 81 percent of those under $10,000.[39] The Hart survey was able to avoid such inflated claims because it verified voting by checking election board records, and found that the "overall turnout . . . [of first-time-ever registrants] . . . closely approximated the turnout of registered voters." The figure was 77 percent; as might be expected, those who registered on their own voted at a slightly higher rate than those who were registered by campaigns.[40] And a follow-up check of elections records in Los Angeles County found that 75 percent of all new registrants had voted (again, self-registrants voted slightly more), and that 80 percent of new Republican registrants voted compared with 69 percent of new Democratic registrants.[41]

PARTISANSHIP

No comprehensive data are available showing how campaign registrants voted, but reasonable inferences can nevertheless be drawn. The Republican effort emphasized upscale whites and Hispanics. The Christian Right also registered whites, but they were probably middle-class and lower-middle class, and largely southern. As for the nonpartisan organizations, perhaps as many as half of their registrants were also white and at least somewhat

[39] Livingston (April 1985).
[40] Committee for the Study of the American Electorate (undated:13–14).
[41] Cain and McCue (1985:15; see also 1984).

better off, although they were mainly northern. In other words, the wide impression that the nonpartisan drives were oriented just toward poorer and minority people is inaccurate. For example, women's organizations frequently canvassed at sites such as suburban shopping malls as part of a gender-gap strategy. The campus-based drives also registered substantial numbers of northern middle-class whites. The Citizen Action registrants were mixed. One-third of those registered by the Churches' Project had incomes above $20,000. Social agencies, such as family planning clinics and YWCAs, also registered a mixed constituency. Only a few organizations, such as ACORN, Project Vote, and Human SERVE, specifically targeted groups at the bottom. In a word, the overall effect of the 1982–84 drives was to expand the active electorate without reducing its upward class skew; it was a class stalemate.[42]

Given the broad spectrum of groups targeted by the registration drives, it is not surprising that 61 percent of the Hart survey respondents reported having voted for Reagan (although allowance should be made for people's tendency in postelection surveys to overreport voting for the winner). By contrast, 64 percent of a sample registered by the Churches' Project (who were generally of lower income) said they had voted for Mondale: 54 percent of those with family incomes above $20,000, and 74 percent with incomes below $10,000. These respondents also said that the most important issues determining their voting preference were education, jobs, and "how poor people are treated"; the least important were "military spending, abortion, and school prayer."

Based on the data presented in this chapter, it is fair to conclude that the New Politics effort failed to alter the class skew of the

---

[42] Cain and McCue reached a similar conclusion based on their study of registration drives in Los Angeles County. As many Republican as Democratic registrants were signed up. In the end, they say, it was probably "a wash" (1985:17).

active American electorate by enlarging participation among the poor and minorities. Its efforts were counteracted by the combined resources of the Republican party and the Christian Right. Similar stalemates could easily occur in future election cycles. Unless the Christian Right becomes immobilized by the deep cleavages in its leadership ranks, or by the recent sex and financial scandals that have both undermined its perceived legitimacy and shrunk the funds available to electronic churchmen, the religious networks can continue to enlist new middle-class voters. And the Republican party has staggering sums at its disposal to register higher-income people. Taken together, the Christian Right and the Republican party can offset the numbers registered among poorer and minority groups by nonpartisan campaign organizations. The 20 million unregistered people above the median income constitute a reservoir that can be drawn upon for years to cancel out those who may be registered from the more than 40 million below the median. The political arithmetic is as simple as that. For those oriented toward creating a more representative electorate, the future of registration campaigning could shape up as a treadmill. Put another way, campaigns based on private resources will always be biased; they will always reproduce a class-skewed electorate because money will always flow disproportionately to organizations devoted to registering better-off people.

The very notion of relying on private resources to reach potential voters is unique to the United States, as we said in chapter 1. In other major democracies, government assumes the affirmative obligation to register voters. This is the only way to guarantee that all citizens will be registered. The experience of the recent voter registration campaigns thus forces attention to the question of whether government can be made to assume the same obligation in the United States. Some of the organizing work undertaken in the 1982–84 period addresses that question and is the subject of the next chapter.

Chapter 7

Prospects for Voter Registration Reform

In 1982, we developed an analysis of the way we thought registration reform might be accomplished in the United States, and formed an organization to try to carry through these ideas. We proposed to try to enlist public and nonprofit agencies to register their clients to vote. The potential reach of this approach is enormous. People would be able to register at unemployment and welfare offices, motor vehicle bureaus and departments of taxation, hospitals and public health centers, day-care centers and family planning clinics, senior citizen centers and agencies for the disabled, settlement houses and family service agencies, libraries and municipal recreation programs, and public housing projects and agricultural extension offices. Everyone has some dealings with public and nonprofit agencies of one kind or another, and poorer and minority people, who are less likely to be registered, are more likely to have contact with health, housing, welfare, and unemployment agencies. If citizens could register in the course of using these services, *access* to voter registration would become nearly universal.

Human SERVE was formed in 1983 to implement this

strategy.[1] It undertook a lobbying effort to persuade executives (governors, county executives, and mayors), and legislatures (state, county, and municipal) to make voter registration services available at government offices serving the public. It also tried to persuade nonprofit health and welfare agencies to offer similar services. Finally, Human SERVE worked with a coalition of legal defense organizations to try to establish through the courts that public officials are obligated to offer registration services in public agencies.

This chapter sets out the political reasoning that led us to think this particular approach might succeed and summarizes the accomplishments so far. As will become clear, this strategy is premised on the oft-noted fragmentation of the American state structure. It tries to take advantage of the decentralization of public authority, of the dispersion of power among the branches of government, and of the existence of networks of private health and welfare agencies. We think this strategy is viable precisely because all branches of government at all levels of government have the authority to make voter registration available in public agencies. If registration services cannot be won at one level, or by one branch, they can sometimes be won at another level or by another branch, or they can be implemented by the voluntary sector.

We emphasize that registration reform at the state and local levels is not an alternative to the enactment by Congress of a system of comprehensive national registration reform along European lines. Rather, *reform at the state and local level is itself a precondition for eventually winning reform at the national level.* If registration services were available in public and nonprofit agencies throughout much of the country, registration levels would gradually rise. Once the electorate was enlarged, much of the political resistance that currently frustrates national reform ef-

---

[1] Human SERVE is an acronym for Human Service Employees' Registration and Voter Education Campaign.

forts would dissipate. And we think an analysis of the conditions that made the passage of the Voting Rights Act possible provides reason for thinking this is so.

ELECTORAL VOLATILITY AND REFORM: THE VOTING RIGHTS ACT COMPARISONS

Before turning to the similarities between the contemporary situation and the Voting Rights Act period, we should note a large difference. There will be more resistance by the political parties to national voter registration reform because it threatens to change the national party system. The immediate impact of the Voting Rights Act, by contrast, was regional. Republicans in particular will resist national reform, and that is a major shift from the voting rights era when they had nothing to lose, and much to gain, from allowing southern blacks to be enfranchised. Virtually all Republican members of the U.S. Senate were located in the North, and Republican moderates could obtain some political advantage among blacks and white liberals by supporting civil rights. More important, the Republican party was a direct beneficiary of the Democratic party's troubles in the South. Republican strategists—such as Kevin P. Phillips—saw in the fragmenting of the Democratic southern wing the beginnings of a regional (and even national) realignment that, by the late 1960s, they could claim was actually taking place. Consequently, the Republicans broke ranks with their conservative southern Democratic coalition partners in the Congress and seized the initiative. The Civil Rights Act of 1957 was enacted largely because of unanimous support among Senate Republicans who also gave the same unanimous support to a civil rights act in 1960. In 1964, at the height of the voting rights conflict in the South, 27 of 31 Senate Republicans voted to override a filibuster by southern Democrats that stood in the way of the Civil Rights Act of 1964. And again in 1965, all Republican senators except one opted to support the Voting Rights Act. The virtual unanimity in Republican ranks made voting rights legislation a certainty.

But if the Republican party benefited from sectional reform, it would clearly not benefit from national reform. The danger is too great that it could lead to a new Democratic majority coalition. The emerging Republican majority that Phillips predicted in 1969 rested on the (unstated) assumption that lower-stratum people would remain dependable nonvoters. By 1975, as the idea of national voter registration began to be discussed seriously in liberal circles, Phillips (writing this time with Blackman) warned of its dangers: *"It has the potential for altering the American party system by changing the coalitions of groups which now make up each of the major political parties."*[2] Indeed, by 1983, Phillips felt that a Republican realignment might be aborted even without registration reform. Under the title *Post-Conservative America*, he declared that the latent voting power of poorer and minority people was the single most important force that could potentially deter realignment, and that the economic hardship inflicted by a conservative economic program could well make that force manifest at the polls:

> The American electorate is disproportionately white and prosperous. Blacks constitute 11 percent of the national population, but cast only 7 percent of the total ballots in 1980. Hispanic turnout rates are even lower. One can reasonably suggest that the economic bottom third of the country cast only 20–25 percent of the total vote, while the top third cast perhaps 40–45 percent. This is a much greater imbalance than exists in any other major Western industrial nation, and could easily begin to change as the effects of . . . a conservative-dominated zero-sum economics [in which upper-strata groups prosper at the expense of lower-

[2] Phillips and Blackman (1975:3–4, emphasis in original).

strata groups] become fully felt. To protect transfer payments and government spending programs, low-income and minority turnout has the potential to surge. These voters could come to the polls to protest conservative economic policies tailored to redistribute income toward *upper* rather than *lower* income groups. *Of all the trends that will affect the 1980s, this could be the most important.*[3]

Business will also use its influence in the parties to resist reform. This, too, differs from the civil rights period when northern capital had no reason to oppose political modernization in the South. With the plantation economy in decline, the links between northern businessmen and the plantation system were dissolving. Meanwhile, northern capital was financing the industrialization of the South, and looked benignly on the prospect of managing the control and allocation of labor through market relations rather than caste relations. For that reason, the Republican party could act out of purely partisan motives in supporting southern voting rights reform.

Business is not likely to stand aloof in this period, however. National registration reform would incorporate poor whites and minorities more fully, and the Democratic party would experience intensified pressures to intervene in social and economic life on behalf of these new constituents. In the 1960s, a period of rapid economic growth, business tolerated new demands on the state from the have-nots. In the present period of economic instability and transition, business interests are not likely to be tolerant. Business groups are already in the midst of a campaign to scale back programs that protect and advance the interests of poor and working people. The disarray of the Democratic party and the sharp fall in voting by lower-stratum people during the past two decades facilitated this campaign. A reconstituted Democratic party would risk new demands on the state and new

---

[3] Phillips (1982:103, our emphasis).

threats to the business program. In short, the fear of a national realignment favoring the Democrats, together with business opposition to any reform that would promote an electoral mobilization among lower-income people, are good reasons to expect that the national Republican party will resist liberalization of the registration system.

Many national Democratic party leaders will also oppose reform. In order to implement a conservative economic program, the business community has shifted its contributions away from the Democratic party, which is still tied to labor and lower-income constituencies, and toward the Republican party. That has had the ironic effect of making the national Democratic leadership particularly sensitive to business concerns. After the 1980 defeat, the Democratic National Committee exerted itself to court business:

> Through the new Democratic Business Council and the Democratic Congressional Campaign Committee, party leaders offered business figures more "access" to and say in party affairs—in exchange, of course, for more financial support. Individual candidates were strongly urged to tone down their "anti-business rhetoric" (they hardly needed the instruction), wealthy business executives were urged to run for office, and Democratic fundraisers were encouraged to participate directly in candidate selection.[4]

Electoral expansion poses other serious long-term threats to blocs in the Democratic party. Large numbers of new voters from the lower strata, with distinctive grievances and aspirations, would provoke conflicts over public policy, jeopardizing both business support and support among traditional electoral constituencies. Moreover, developments of the last two decades ensure that new voters will be more politicized and more likely

---

[4] Cohen and Rogers (forthcoming:38).

therefore to generate conflict. These are some of the longer-term costs of an electoral mobilization that the Democratic party leadership has not been willing to pay.

Politicans are not always oriented to such distant horizons. A surge of new voters from the bottom could also be troublesome, even fatal, to the short-term election interests of political incumbents. President Carter, in explaining why his election-day registration bill failed in 1977, said:

> In spite of a strong and well organized campaign [to enact this bill], we were unsuccessful. The conservatives, Democrats and Republicans, almost to a person opposed this legislation. I was taken aback that many of the liberal and moderate members of the Congress also opposed any increase in voter registration. . . . The key [source of resistance was] "incumbency." Incumbent members of the Congress don't want to see additional unpredictable voters registered. I'm speaking in generalities and there were obviously some exceptions. But I tell you that what I say is true. The more senior and more influential members of the Congress have very safe districts. To have a 25 or 30 percent increase of unpredictable new voters is something they don't relish. . . . I would suggest to you that this is the single most important obstacle to increasing participation on election day.[5]

Despite these differences in the balance of interests, an important similarity with the conditions that led to the Voting Rights Act provides hope for registration reform. Now, Democratic congressional incumbents oppose reform for fear that new and unpredictable voters would upset their reelection chances, and would have potentially disruptive consequences for national party

[5] Harvard/ABC News Symposium (1984:18).

coalitions and funding. *But if registration levels were to rise substantially among poorer and minority people in many states, congressional incumbents would no longer have much reason to resist enacting comprehensive reform; they would be ratifying what had already largely occurred.* Given greatly increased registration levels, the main effect of subsequent national legislation would be to bring recalcitrant states in line, and to simplify the process of sustaining high levels of registration over time.

Furthermore, if rising registration levels among poorer and minority people caused defections among traditional Democratic constituencies, the resulting balance of interests in the party might actually produce more pressure for national reform. Comprehensive reform could then be seen as the means to compensate for shrinking support among older constituencies by enlisting new voters. Put more generally, we think that the conditions favoring reform are the entry of new groups into the electorate against a background of defections among existing constituencies. It was such political dynamics that led to the passage of the Voting Rights Act.

A crucial precondition for the enactment of the Voting Rights Act was rising levels of southern black registration coupled with southern white defections to the Republican party. Agitation for black civil rights, together with the new middle class thrust up by industrial modernization in the postwar period, eventually fragmented the southern wing of the Democratic party. Independent electors, third-party movements, and presidential Republicanism created a rising tide of defections that eventually undermined the Democratic party's historic dominance in the South. As these dealigning processes accelerated, one could virtually hear the ripping of the Democratic party's North-South coalitional seam.

National Democratic party leaders vacillated, unsure of their political course—whether to resist rising black demands and keep trying to prop up the tottering Southern Democracy, or to impose political modernization on the South. The rise of black registration tipped matters in favor of reform, for the policy of accommodating the white South no longer clearly produced a net gain at the polls for the national party. Southern whites were defecting in any case, and the system of 1896 was no longer capable of keeping blacks from the polls. As the proportions of black registrants steadily increased—reaching 35 percent in March 1965 [6]—national Democratic leaders changed course by supporting the Voting Rights Act as a means of replacing southern white defectors with new black voters, thus beginning the process of rebuilding the southern wing. In this sense, the Voting Rights Act both ratified a change that was already occurring and accelerated it.

The fragmentation of the southern wing of the Democratic party has since become generalized, as have efforts by national Democratic leaders to conciliate the defectors. But will the erosion of traditional Democratic bases eventually prompt Democratic leaders to turn elsewhere for support by seeking the full enfranchisement of poor whites, blacks, and Hispanics? The prospects for such a shift are not bright. However, if the Voting Rights Act parallel is apt, such a shift might be brought about by raising the levels of registration among these groups.

STATE STRUCTURE AND OPENINGS
FOR VOTER REGISTRATION

Today no protest movement is feeding the registration rolls as during the civil rights period. Instead, we think state, county, and municipal government, and the nonprofit sector, can become

---

[6] Kleppner (1982:116). According to the *Voter Education Project News* (November 15, 1964, and November 1969), registered blacks had come to represent 11 percent of registered southerners in 1962, and 14 percent in 1964.

the vehicles for mass enlistment by making registration services available in an array of agencies serving the public. Because of the growth of state functions, especially in the field of social welfare, and the resulting overlap between unregistered populations and the clientele of social welfare programs, government can readily reach and enlist nonvoters through an agency-based strategy.

The question is whether it is possible to draw state and local government into this process on a large scale. One reason for thinking it might be is that the Democratic party is not monolithic. Some key Democratic politicians have an incentive to register the have-nots. A number of Democratic governors, for example, won office on the upsurge of voting among the poor and minorities in 1982 in states such as Texas, Ohio, New Mexico, and New York. The minority mayors who won office in the 1983 municipal elections also benefited from new voters. More generally, the cities are suffering badly from domestic program cuts. Augmenting the city voting base would help urban interests strengthen their lobbying presence at the national level.[7] Furthermore, social service spending cuts give the public employee unions and national human service associations representing the millions of workers who staff public and nonprofit agencies of the welfare state a similar interest in mobilizing the people whom their members serve. In addition, public and nonprofit social service agency staff are mostly women, many are members of minorities, and they mainly serve poor and minority women and children. Agency registration means that women would register women voters, and minority people would register minority voters. Human service workers who identify with the women's and civil rights movements might discover that this

---

[7] According to the Census Bureau/CPS report for 1984, rates of registration among renters who tend to be concentrated in cities are 25 percentage points lower than among those who live in owner-occupied housing—53 percent versus 79 percent in 1984—suggesting that access to registration services in municipal agencies could produce millions of new voters.

is the only practical way to enlist lower-income women and minorities on a large scale.[8]

A further condition favoring this strategy is that the fragmented character of the American state structure allows an agency-based registration strategy to be tailored to take advantage of the numerous openings provided by the different levels of government, the overlapping powers of different branches, and the vast network of nonprofit health and social service providers. Legislative action provides one such route to reform—not just action by state legislatures, but by county boards of supervisors and city councils as well. And if legislatures refuse to act, the versatility of an agency-based approach is that the executive branches at the state, county, and municipal levels are also empowered to order registration services. Despite general constitutional provisions in many states reserving control over registration procedures to state legislatures, the courts in New York and Ohio have declared (as we will presently describe) that governors do not infringe on legislative prerogatives by ordering state agencies to establish registration services. The freedom of governors to circumvent legislative resistance is an important development, since legislative coalitions in support of registration reform are often as hard to assemble at the state as at the national level. Similarly, county executives and mayors can provide registration services in county and municipal agencies. Big-city mayors could, by themselves, produce millions of new registrants among poorer and minority people. A mayoralty approach even seems feasible in the South, where most legislatures and governors would not want access to registration widened. Some large southern cities have black or progressive white mayors, and they can arrange for registration services in munic-

---

[8] This point was demonstrated during the 1984 campaigns. Volunteers associated with women's groups generally recruited new voters at middle-class locations, such as shopping malls. To the extent that lower-income women were registered—and many were—it was mainly by other campaign organizations that sent their volunteers to unemployment, welfare, and food-stamp agencies.

ipal health and welfare agencies. Agency-based registration might also result from suits taken against state governments over restrictive registration practices. Popular referenda are still another means by which agency-based registration can be achieved. Finally, the huge nonprofit health and welfare sector might undertake voter registration. Roughly 125,000 nonprofit agencies provide direct services nationally. They, too, could register millions. These are the several ways, then, in which a decentralized and fragmented governmental structure may facilitate efforts to widen access to registration.

Agency registration has precedents. Libraries distribute voter registration forms in a number of places, and social agencies such as settlement houses and YWCAs have from time to time offered to register people as a public service. When Human SERVE formed in 1983, there were five states that allowed people to register to vote at motor vehicle bureaus (Maine, Ohio, Michigan, Arizona, and Oregon). These "motor voter" programs clearly demonstrated the effectiveness of agency registration. The Michigan legislature enacted the first program in 1975, with impressive results. The secretary of state reported 266,273 new registrations and 505,888 address changes, for a total of 772,161 voter registration transactions in 1984 alone.[9] This probably explains why the level of registration in Michigan reached 74 percent in 1984, measurably higher than the 65 percent in Pennsylvania and 64 percent in New York,[10] comparable industrial states. Motor voter programs also demonstrate that agency registration is administratively simple and cheap. Michigan's secretary of state estimates that it costs $0.17 per registrant or reregistrant, and there is no reason why costs should be greater in unemployment or welfare programs.

[9] Booklet published by the Office of the Secretary of State, Michigan, entitled *A New Approach to Voter Registration*.

[10] These are Census Bureau/CPS figures, and they are inflated by roughly 9 percent because of overreporting by sample respondents. See appendix A for a discussion of biases in registration data.

Equally important, the public seems to approve of making it more convenient to register, as two referenda on motor voter programs showed. Arizona's motor voter referendum passed in November 1982 by 51 percent, following a string of failed attempts to win reform measures in the legislature, and despite full-page ads in local newspapers warning that this measure would open the door to fraud. More than a quarter of a million people were registered to vote during the next three years, and the Arizona secretary of state reported that the state registration level, which had fallen by 9 percentage points between 1972 and 1980,[11] then jumped by 9 points (from 57 percent to 66 percent) between 1980 and 1984. Later, in November 1984, 61 percent of Colorado's voters approved a motor voter initiative. This action also followed a series of failed efforts to secure legislative action. Colorado had no postcard registration, no deputization, registration was only permitted at county elections offices between the hours of nine and five; people could be purged for missing a single election; and the state's registration level ranked thirty-fifth in the nation. The League of Women Voters, Colorado Common Cause, and the Colorado Public Interest Research Group organized a coalition of thirty groups to sponsor the initiative.[12] In the first year after the program was begun, 175,000 people were registered to vote: 82 percent, or 144,000, were new registrants, and they represented 11 percent of Colorado's already registered voters. By 1990, according to estimates by state officials, this program will have reached 2.2 million adults in the course of license transactions, plus a substantial number of people who obtain nondriver IDs from motor vehicle bureaus.

[11] The decline was in fact greater, since the figures supplied by the secretary of state included increasing proportions of "deadwood" registrants, thus offsetting part of the real fall in registration levels during this period. The way deadwood registrants inflate official registration levels is discussed in appendix C.

[12] Among other groups, the coalition included the AF of L-CIO, Black Women for Political Action, Gray Panthers, Sierra Club, Rocky Mountain Farmers' Union, League of United Latin American Citizens, Colorado Education Association, and the Jefferson County Board of Realtors.

However, motor voter programs by themselves have a serious limitation. They expand the electorate without overcoming its upward class skew, a feature that may explain why both Republicans and Democrats sometimes support them. In 1983, only 47 percent of the 36 million adults in households with incomes under $10,000 held driver's licenses. But 93 percent of the 31 million adults in households with incomes over $40,000 had licenses.[13] Poorer and minority people, especially women, are least reached. The solution is obvious. If one public agency provides registration services, why not others, including day-care, welfare, food-stamp, Medicaid recertification, and unemployment centers? And why not in nonprofit health and welfare agencies as well? If public agencies generally were to include voter registration questions on their regular applications, any citizen filling out a government form would automatically be registered, or address changes would be recorded for voting purposes. Agency-based voter registration could thus become the American version of the European system of automatic registration.

TARGETING THE NONPROFIT SECTOR

Human SERVE began advancing agency-based registration among nonprofit agencies in early 1983. The organizing approach was both top-down and bottom-up. Human SERVE promoted endorsements and publicity by national human service organizations while simultaneously urging their local affiliates to establish registration services. The message was simple: to defend social programs, it was necessary to widen access to voter registration in the United States, and nonprofit health and welfare agencies were a principal means. Almost immediately, a number of national organizations authorized their presidents or executive directors to join Human SERVE's board of directors.

---

[13] The source is the Federal Highway Administration, Washington, D.C.

Early sponsoring organizations included the Council on Social Work Education, the National Association of Social Workers, the American Public Health Association, the Affiliated Leadership League of and for the Blind of America, the American Orthopsychiatric Association, the National Board of the YWCA, the Children's Foundation, and Wider Opportunities for Women.

In succeeding months, more national social welfare organizations endorsed the strategy: the American Association of Citizens with Disabilities, the American Humane Association, the American Nurses' Association, the Community Services Division of the AF of L-CIO, the National Family Planning and Reproductive Health Association, the National Abortion Federation, and the National Medical Student Association, as well as the National Organization for Women and the American Federation of State, County, and Municipal Employees. Most of these organizations publicized agency-based voter registration in newsletters and mailings, and some, including the American Public Health Association, Planned Parenthood Federation of America, and the National Board of the YWCA, assigned national staff to spur local affiliates to implement voter registration.

The legitimacy of these efforts was enhanced when the National Association of Secretaries of State issued a report in the late fall of 1983 urging "voluntary agency staff members to conduct voter registration," as well as "state, county and municipal employees whose work brings them into frequent contact with the public." [14] Later, other organizations of public officials also endorsed the effort: the National League of Cities, the National Conference of Black State Legislators, the United States Conference of Mayors. The Conference on Alternative State and Local Policies, which reaches the more progressive state and local officials, also invested staff time in helping to promote the strategy.

[14] National Association of Secretaries of State (undated:4).

Meanwhile, Human SERVE's field staff expanded to cover thirteen states,[15] and these organizers concentrated on enlisting local voluntary social and health agencies to begin offering voter registration services, especially those affiliated with the national organizations that had endorsed the drive. At the local level, schools of social work were often helpful, serving as supplementary organizing centers by encouraging their students to press for the development of voter registration services in the agencies where they interned several days a week, and by calling meetings of agency executives in their communities to promote the campaign.

Because the voluntary sector is so sprawling, there is no good way of knowing how many agencies picked up the idea. National newsletters reached thousands of agencies, but we do not know how many participated in the campaign. They did not report to Human SERVE, nor could Human SERVE maintain a census of participants. As a guess, perhaps fifteen hundred agencies registered about 500,000 people. We could actually verify that some five hundred agencies across the country had registered 275,000 people. (We have generally discounted by half the totals that were reported to us, since there is always a tendency to inflate results.)

Three national human service organizations attempted to monitor their affiliates: Planned Parenthood registered 30,000; the National Board of the YWCA registered another 100,000; and 25,000 were registered by the National Abortion Federa-

---

[15] In addition to its national office staff in the 1984 period, Human SERVE hired field organizers in New York, New Jersey, Massachusetts, Pennsylvania, Florida, Ohio, Michigan, Texas, California, and Oregon; it contributed toward the costs of a Citizen Action organizer already working with local groups in Illinois who agreed to help mobilize voluntary agencies and to persuade Mayor Washington to issue an executive order; and it reimbursed the expenses of volunteer organizers in Connecticut, Tennessee, and West Virginia. The headquarters staff in New York City dealt with funders and the media, spoke before human service audiences across the country, worked with the national social welfare associations and public officials, organized a litigation campaign against obstructive boards of elections, prepared publicity materials for use in the field, and coordinated the work of field organizers.

tion, women's health clinics, and day-care programs. As these data suggest, agencies serving women were probably the most active.

A number of faculty and students in graduate and undergraduate social work programs also registered a good many people; they either worked at such sites as federal surplus cheese distribution centers, or students registered clients in the social agencies where they interned. On one Saturday morning in March 1984, for example, twelve social work student volunteers worked with the minister of Harlem's Antioch Baptist Church, who was distributing surplus cheese, and registered 1,875 people in four hours, a feat to which the *New York Daily News* devoted a full-page article. Social work students staged similar mass registrations in such places as San Diego, Chattanooga, and Normal, Illinois; each produced 5,000 or more new registrants.

In some places, disability agencies were active. The New York Jewish Guild for the Blind registered its entire client population. The Federation of Jewish Philanthrophies in New York City asked all affiliates to develop registration programs, but the numbers registered are not known. Also in New York City, the United Hospital Fund urged its affiliates to participate, and thirty-five hospitals throughout the city had some kind of registration program. In some places, human service workers held meetings and rallies to promote registration. At one 1984 rally in Minneapolis, representatives of 125 agencies from throughout the state announced they were participating and that 19,500 people had been registered in the Minneappolis–St. Paul area.

Overall, however, the results were modest. Nonprofit agencies have the capacity to register millions, but few agencies integrated registration services into their regular programs and most abandoned their efforts once the 1984 election was over. Some human service workers claimed to be concerned that beneficiaries might feel coerced to register as a condition of receiving service, or said they wondered if registering people might be considered a "political" activity and therefore "unprofessional." Many are also ambivalent about their clients as political allies, despite the obvious relationship between the pattern of electoral participation and social service spending.

Fear of political repercussions was probably the major deterrent to registration efforts, however. Agency directors were afraid to antagonize their boards of directors or local political leaders who dispense grants and contracts. Even public endorsements were not always easy to get. The National Association of Community Health Centers decided not to provoke the Reagan administration, which had opposed funding community health center programs. The same was true of the Community Action Foundation, which represents local community action agencies; in this case, as we noted in chapter 5, a federal statute prohibits antipoverty agencies from using federal money to conduct voter registration. Human SERVE also failed to gain an official endorsement from the United Way of America because national officials wanted to protect their tens of millions of dollars in corporate contributions. Few local United Way executives could be persuaded even to tell the local agencies that voter registration was a legitimate public service.[16]

Risks of political reprisals seemed greatest where Republicans were in control. Agency directors were quick to say so in Republican-controlled counties on Long Island, for example. Although registration services were strictly nonpartisan, it was widely agreed that poorer and minority people would vote disproportionately Democratic. More interesting, and revealing, was the jeopardy nonprofit agencies felt in some Democrat-controlled jurisdictions, particularly where incumbent political leaders were at odds with the minority community. Many New York City nonprofit agencies with minority constituencies that relied on Koch administration subsidies shied away from partic-

---

[16] A notable exception was a letter from Horace Morris of the Greater New York Fund/ United Way, and a former Urban League executive, to four hundred affiliated agencies endorsing the strategy. As a result, Human SERVE got dozens of inquiries from New York agencies about how to get voter registration started.

ipation for fear of appearing to take sides in the tense relationship between the mayor and minority political leaders. For obvious reasons, few voluntary agencies in the South felt free to participate.

These fears were exacerbated in the spring and summer of 1984. By then, six governors had ordered that voter registration services be established in the local offices of state agencies, and a political controversy broke out, fueled by legal challenges from state Republican parties and Reagan administration threats to cut off grants-in-aid. Under the circumstances, many nonprofit agency directors took a wait-and-see attitude.

TARGETING PUBLIC OFFICIALS

Human SERVE initially singled out Democratic governors who had been elected because of the upsurge of voting by the unemployed and minorities in the 1982 elections: Anaya in New Mexico, Celeste in Ohio, Cuomo in New York, and White in Texas. The thought was that this would make them responsive to the idea of expanding the low-income end of the electorate. Between March and September 1984, Human SERVE did succeed in obtaining these four gubernatorial executive orders, and two others.[17] The governors of Texas, Ohio, New York, and Montana[18] directed that voter registration services be established

[17] The New Mexico order was stimulated by national news articles describing the Human SERVE strategy. Joseph Goldberg, a former professor of social welfare who headed the state Department of Human Resources under the newly elected Hispanic governor, contacted Human SERVE and was given technical assistance. The gubernatorial order in Ohio was promoted by Secretary of State Sherrod Brown, who has been a vigorous advocate of agency-based voter registration. Again, he read national news stories, and contacted Human SERVE. Norman Adler and Victor Gotbaum of District Council 37-AFSCME were crucial in persuading Governor Cuomo to issue an order, as were political leaders Ruth Messinger, Carl McCall, and Herman Badillo. The Texas order was won by a coalition of human service organizations, labor unions, and local political leaders brought together by the Human SERVE state organizer. The state AF of L-CIO was especially helpful.

[18] The gubernatorial order in Montana was prompted by news articles about the actions being taken by governors in other states.

in all state agencies, and the governors of New Mexico and West Virginia [19] ordered that voter registration be established in state human service agencies. (In addition, the governor of Minnesota issued a letter to department heads saying he favored agency registration, but left it to them to act, which none did. [20])

These early gubernatorial executive orders generated a good deal of political controversy, since no one knew for sure how this new method of registration would affect the 1984 election. Consequently, politicians (mainly Republicans, but also some Democrats) attempted to block the orders. Indeed, the Michigan state legislature moved to prevent agency registration even though there was little reason to think it was going to happen. Michigan's governor was fighting off a tax revolt in the spring of 1984, and Human SERVE had no hope that he would issue an executive order. Instead, the Michigan Human SERVE organizer persuaded the secretary of state and the commissioners of five state departments to circulate a letter endorsing (but not ordering) voter registration services in public agencies. This largely symbolic gesture provoked majorities in both houses of the legislature (including decisive numbers of Democrats) to pass an amendment to an appropriations bill in March 1984 prohibiting these departments from offering voter registration, and expressly enjoining them from cooperating in any way with Human SERVE.

As a practical matter, the Michigan legislature need not have bothered. The elections clerks throughout the state would have frustrated any attempt to get voter registration activities

[19] The West Virginia order was issued by the head of the state Department of Human Resources, Leon Ginsburg, who was also president of the American Public Welfare Association, with which Human SERVE worked closely. Although APWA did not endorse the strategy, Edward Weaver, the executive director, featured this method of registration in newsletters, and issued a "guidance memorandum" explaining to local public welfare directors how they could implement voter registration services without runnning afoul of federal auditors on the grounds that grant-in-aid funds were being used for unauthorized purposes.

[20] This permissive letter resulted from the efforts of local activists who formed a Minnesota Human SERVE chapter. This same coalition went on in 1987 to secure passage of an agency registration bill in the legislature.

started in public agencies, as they had already frustrated Human SERVE's efforts to have voluntary agency staff deputized. In Detroit, for example, applicants for deputy registrar status were required to attend a two-hour training session to learn how to fill out forms (which are, it should be added, the most complicated in the country). They were also required to repeat the training process and to be redeputized each time registration was closed, as it always was during December and January, and before primaries or general elections, including school elections. This meant that to offer registration services, social agencies had to arrange for staff members to be retrained about six times each year. Some social agency staff went through the process several times, but were worn down by it. The situation elsewhere in the state was complicated for other reasons. Michigan has fifteen hundred boards of elections (25 percent of the total in the United States), and anyone deputized by a particular board was only allowed to register people who resided in the same tiny jurisdiction. Consequently, social agencies had to send staff to be deputized in all of the jurisdictions from which they drew clients. Needless to say, few agencies went to the trouble.

The Michigan controversy was an omen of others to come. When New Mexico's Governor Anaya authorized registration services in state welfare offices as the first step in a plan to extend registration services to a wide range of public agencies, the reactions were explosive. Republicans, Democrats, and most editorialists and political cartoonists in the state charged that the program was nothing more than a ploy to register poor Hispanics. Subsequently, the attorney general, a member of a wing of the Democratic party not particularly sympathetic to the new Hispanic governor, declared that the order violated article 2, section 8 of the state constitution, which says, "All elections shall be free and open and no power, civil or military, shall at any time interfere to prevent the free exercise of the right of suffrage." As the controversy boiled up, the governor simply rescinded his order.

The Separation of Powers Controversy

The main result of the controversies in this period was to clear away some of the legal obstacles thrown in the way of agency-based registration. One concerned separation of powers—whether governors have the authority to intervene in registration arrangements without legislative consent. Within seventy-two hours of the announcement of a broad executive order in New York State, the state Republican party persuaded a state Supreme Court (New Yorks' lowest court) to issue an order restraining Governor Cuomo from proceeding. The court accepted both the claim that the governor had invaded the legislature's constitutionally granted power over voter registration, and that the Republican party would be "irreparably harmed" because state employees would try to bias new registrants toward the Democratic party. Upon appeal, however, the courts rejected the "presumption that state agencies will act improperly," and lifted the restraining order.[21] The Appellate Division unanimously rejected the charge that the governor had infringed on legislative prerogatives, as did the New York State Court of Appeals (the highest court). They held that the legislature, in enacting postcard legislation some years earlier, had intended that registration forms be widely accessible, and that the governor was doing nothing more than carrying out that intent.[22] However, the Republican party also won: it succeeded in persuading the courts that state employees should be prohibited from asking citizens whether they wished to register, or from answering questions,

[21] By then, of course, the Republicans had effectively succeeded in delaying implementation until after the presidential election, just as Cuomo had delayed issuing the original order until after the state Democratic presidential primary in June in which Jesse Jackson was running.

[22] Arthur Eisenberg of the New York Civil Liberties Union made this argument in an *amicus* brief on behalf of a range of voting rights organizations.

or from assisting in completing forms, or from collecting completed forms; the agencies were forbidden by the courts to do more than make the forms available on tables in waiting rooms.

A similar suit was filed against Governor Celeste in Ohio, although with a more favorable outcome. The court began by noting "a disturbing discrepancy between the number of Ohio citizens eligible to vote and those registered to do so," and went on to declare that "it is a situation mandating action." In turn, the court found that the governor's action to make registration services available in agencies "is within the powers and duties of the Governor," and that the executive order is "constitutional and valid." Executive orders have since been issued in a number of additional states, none of which have been challenged.

Restrictions on the Use of Federal Funds

The Reagan administration also attempted to head off the governors by declaring that federal grants-in-aid legislation did not authorize state employees whose salaries were partly paid by federal funds to engage in voter registration activities, and by alleging that these state employees would be improperly engaging in partisan activities if they assisted citizens in registering to vote. The trouble began in Texas, where the director of the state employment commission balked at implementing Governor White's March 1984 executive order, and wrote instead to the United States Department of Labor asking whether it would be proper for federally funded state personnel to pass out voter registration forms. (This problem does not arise in state-funded agencies like motor vehicle bureaus; it arises in agencies, such as welfare and unemployment, which are funded in some part by federal grants.) The Labor Department not unexpectedly replied that it would be improper, and immediately distributed a similar opinion to all state employment directors.[23] The department conceded that it would not object if registration forms were placed on tables, since the only federal funds involved were for the rental of a few square feet of space under the tables. But it would object if employees were permitted to ask unemployment applicants whether they were registered or to answer questions about how to fill out the forms. The "passive" rather than "staff active" approach, as administrators refer to it, was (and continues to be) the typical method of implementation.

But the Reagan administration did not let it go at that. On September 27, 1984, Donald Devine, director of the Office of Personnel Management, wrote Governors Celeste, Cuomo, and White:

> It has come to our attention that your state is using its employees to ask individuals if they are registered to vote. . . . If they express some interest in registering, state employees are used to help the individual to become registered. The concern has been raised as to whether this use of state personnel interferes with or affects the results of the election this November 1984.

The OPM letter went on to imply that governors were forcing state personnel to influence people to register as Democrats, thus violating the 1970 Intergovernmental Personnel Act (i.e., the Hatch Act), which prohibits state employees involved in administering federal grants from pursuing "partisan political purposes and . . . from using their official authority for the purpose of interfering with or affecting the result of an election." The letter ended by demanding that the governors forward all

[23] The federal government was, at the same time, establishing another type of registration program that involved Texas employees. The Department of Labor and the Selective Service System were encouraging federally funded state job training officials to act as "uncompensated registrars" for Selective Service, so that applicants for job training could register for the draft.

materials pertaining to their registration programs, and hinted that federal grants-in-aid might be in jeopardy.

The OPM letter created an opportunity for political theatrics that no one involved let pass. Within a few days, the Republican-dominated Senate tried to deflect possible criticism that the Republican party was attempting to discourage people from registering and voting by approving a "sense of the Congress" resolution to the effect that "voter registration drives should be encouraged by government at all levels; and voter registration drives conducted by state government on a nonpartisan basis do not violate the provisions of the Intergovernmental Personnel Act." Meanwhile, Governor Celeste called Devine's action "blackmail"; Governor Cuomo complained of "a transparently political attempt to curtail the access of United States citizens to the ballot box, not only here in New York but in other states as well"; and Governor White convened a press conference in a state agency waiting room and distributed voter registration cards, declaring that he was going to begin a vigorous program to implement his executive order throughout all state agencies (which, as it happens, he never did). All three governors rejected the allegation that state employees were being compelled to engage in partisan activities—Celeste and White because voters in Ohio and Texas do not register by party, and Cuomo because New York's program was not "staff active." As a result of the Republican lawsuit, New York State employees were doing nothing more than making registration forms available on tables in waiting rooms.

In response to this controversy, hearings were held by the House Subcommittee on Government Operations, chaired by Barney Frank (D-Mass.), which ended with a bipartisan conclusion that Devine had made "selective application and misuse" of the Intergovernmental Personnel Act with the intent, in the chairman's words, to "intimidate three Democratic governors of large states from continuing to encourage voter registration in the critical two week period before the books closed for the presidential election."[24] Devine was subsequently denied reconfirmation by the Senate, in part because of this affair, and also because of the opinion in Congress that he had politicized the Office of Personnel Management. Then, in September 1985, the Reagan administration retreated altogether and wrote the governors: "We conclude that no substantial evidence of a pattern of misuse of state employees in violation of federal statutes has been found. This constitutes our final judgement in the matter and no further action is planned."

These controversies nevertheless had a chilling effect in the 1984 period. For example, in Florida, where the legislature had authorized state-agency voter registration in 1984, officials declined to implement the program, giving as their reason fear of federal reprisals. More important, governors continue to avoid the threat of confrontations with federal auditors over the use of federal grants-in-aid by requiring that their agencies do nothing more than place stacks of registration forms on tables in agency waiting rooms, and refusing to allow staff to distribute them along with routine agency forms, or to answer questions, or to collect and deposit completed forms with elections officials.[25]

Since the gubernatorial executive orders came late in the presidential campaign and were immediately embroiled in controversy, relatively few people were in fact registered by this method in 1984. Nor, for that matter, has this strategy's potential been more than barely tapped in the years since. Indifferent implementation has been a serious problem. Here is a general overview of the situation to date.

[24] Press release, April 18, 1985.
[25] Despite the fireworks, there is a very simple solution to this problem. States can reimburse the federal government for that portion of federally subsidized staff time devoted to registration activities. Using the $0.17 cost per registration in the Michigan motor vehicle offices as a guide, a state could register 500,000 people at a cost of less than $100,000. Even if there were legislative opposition to appropriating such modest sums, most public executives have some discretionary funds. But none of the governors have been sufficiently committed to voter registration to adopt this solution.

In New York, the court injunction was lifted during a two-week period in September 1984. Tables with registration forms were immediately made available in unemployment offices throughout the state. Approximately twenty-five hundred post-card registration forms were completed and deposited in drop-in boxes, and another seventeen thousand forms were taken home (but we do not know how many were completed and mailed back to local boards of elections). After the courts approved Governor Cuomo's executive order in 1985, it was implemented in nine state agencies with 389 local offices in fifty-six counties. During the first six months of operation, 41,533 voter registration forms were completed, over half of them in unemployment offices, and 8,763 in motor vehicle offices (which have so far claimed to be too busy to implement the program fully). Eight additional state agencies with seventy-seven local offices were subsequently added. In his 1987 State of the Union address, the governor reported that state agencies had facilitated the registration of up to 150,000 voters" in 1986, and he announced plans to establish a Task Force on Voter Registration, whose charge would include developing plans to send registration forms to citizens routinely via state agency mailings, such as the mailing of motor vehicle registration renewals and tax forms. As for the accuracy of these numbers, Human SERVE surveyed rough samples of state motor vehicle and unemployment offices on three occasions. A fall 1985 survey of fifteen state office sites showed that registration forms were available in nine of them, but in only seven were they displayed conspicuously. Of twenty-three sites surveyed in the spring of 1986, forms were available in six, and were displayed conspicuously in five. In the fall of 1986, twelve agencies were surveyed, eight had forms, and they were in plain sight in seven of them.

In Ohio, when new statewide forms (returnable to the secretary of state's office rather than directly to local elections boards) were made available during August and September before the 1984 election in state liquor stores, lottery outlets, and unemployment offices, the secretary of state reported that fifty-nine thousand completed forms had been received.

The Texas story was dismal. The Department of Human Services took two limited steps. In the pre-1984 election period, a desktop box containing voter registration forms was sent to each of the 450 branch offices, and a flier was mailed to welfare, food-stamp, and Medicaid recipients urging them to register (but without mentioning that forms were available in local welfare centers). The only action we know of since the election is that eighty thousand forms were provided to state agencies before the May 1986 primaries, but it is unclear what the agencies did with them.[26] Similarly, there was no effective implementation in either Montana or West Virginia.

Several gubernatorial orders have been issued since the election. Governor Evans of Idaho acted, but an executive order by a Democratic governor is not likely to be effectively implemented in a state that consistently votes Republican, and where the elections clerks have sole authority over who is deputized (thirty-one of the forty-four clerks are elected Republicans). Another order, issued by Governor Kunin of Vermont, covered motor vehicle offices and community colleges, with results that are not yet known.

Interesting, though, is the fact that Governor Bellmon of Oklahoma, a Republican and a former United States senator, issued an order in February 1987 that may result in new voters. It directs state agencies to work with the appropriate county election authorities to make voter registration services available to the public. An official task force, to be headed by the secretary of the state elections board, will be appointed to complete a

---

[26] White lost his reelection bid in 1986 by 225,000 votes out of 3.4 million cast. It is interesting to speculate whether active agency registration would have turned the election. The Texas Employment Commission dealt with 958,000 different clients in 1986, 47 percent of them minorities, and fewer than half of them registered. The Department of Human Services saw 450,000 different adult heads-of-household in its food-stamp program, a large majority of them minorities.

detailed plan for implementation. To facilitate that process, both of the Democrat-controlled houses enacted a bill permitting deputy registrars, including state employees, to register people from adjacent counties. Under previous rules, deputy registrars could only register people in the same county in which they were deputized. Bipartisan collaboration is apparently possible in Oklahoma because the governor is popular among poorer and minority voters, and some key Democrats in the state legislature have been experiencing erosion of their support (a senior black legislator recently lost his seat).

As for legislative action, we noted earlier that there was no implementation in Florida.[27] The comprehensive state agency registration bill enacted in Washington State in 1984 also produced little effect; it exempted agencies if they considered themselves overworked, and most have climbed through that loophole.[28] On the bright side, the legislator who introduced a bill in the Maryland legislature in 1984 mandating motor voter registration was persuaded by a voting rights coalition organized by Maryland Planned Parenthood to include other state agencies as well.[29] The bill, passed in April 1985, provided that space, posters, and newly devised statewide registration forms be made available in the departments of human services, health, mental

---

[27] In this case, the authorization was an amendment to another bill. The legislative maneuvering was handled by a staff member who had worked for both the Florida chapter of the National Association of Social Workers and Florida IMPACT, a voter registration organization. Human SERVE subsidized his salary. Ethel Gilman, head of the Florida NASW, was active in promoting voter registration.

[28] A legislative staff member on the Democratic side read about this method of registration in the national press, and wrote up a bill. The Republican secretary of state, Ralph Munro, supported it, and the legislature acted without much knowing what it was approving. Governor John Spellman, a Republican, signed the bill, but did nothing to implement it, except that the secretary of state's office distributed voter registration posters to be placed in all state offices with forms. A Democrat, Booth Gardner, is now governor, but his staff take the attitude that having gotten elected, it is best not to risk "upsetting the applecart." Efforts are now being made to have the state Democratic party take a hand in trying to secure implementation.

[29] The key organizer of the coalition was Steve Riviles, public affairs director of Planned Parenthood of Maryland.

hygiene, and motor vehicle bureaus. It is now possible to register in more than 240 state offices. Maryland's secretary of the state elections board reported that 25,472 people were registered during the first ten months after registration services were established in state agencies in 1986, representing 18 percent of all registration forms filed in the state during this period.

In May 1987, the Minnesota legislature enacted a model bill. It requires that state employees in all agencies doing business with the public ask people whether they are registered, and provide them with needed assistance. Moreover, the legislation also requires that "nonprofit corporations that contract with the state . . . shall provide voter registration services for employees and the public"—an extremely important precedent.[30] The bill also requires that Community Action Program agencies, which are prohibited by federal laws from engaging in voter registration, shall nevertheless provide registration services. (Some representatives of the CAP agencies actively supported this provision, in part because of their anger at being prohibited from registering young men to vote even as they were required to register them for the draft.) Republican opponents tried to limit the bill to motor vehicle agencies. The measure was signed by Governor Rudy Perpich, and Secretary of State Joan Growe is publicly committed to implementing it.

At the same time, the Iowa legislature was considering a motor voter bill,[31] but Secretary of State Elaine Baxter, after consultations with Human SERVE, testified that citizens who

---

[30] The Minnesota coalition that obtained this legislation grew out of the Human SERVE chapter that was formed in the 1984 period. It included Minnesota PIRG, AFSCME, the state association of community action agencies, the AF of L-CIO, representatives of some voluntary agencies, the League of Women Voters, and Common Cause. Paul Wellstone, a Minnesota political activist who is a member of the Democratic National Committee, was a leading influence. The lobbying effort itself was led by Sheryl Graeve, chief lobbyist for the Minnesota PIRG. Democrat Paul Ogren managed the bill in the House, and the Senate assistant majority leader, Democrat William Luther, shepherded it through that chamber. The farm revolt in the 1986 elections made this legislation possible by returning control of the House to the Democrats.

[31] The bill was introduced by House member Rod Halvorson (D-Fort Dodge).

did not own or drive cars, including many lower-income Iowans, might be denied the opportunity to register unless state offices with which they came in contact also provided registration forms and assistance. The provisions of the final bill, which was enacted by wide margins and with substantial bipartisan support on May 9 and signed into law on June 8 by Terry Branstad, the Republican governor, mandated that registration services also be established in such agencies as the departments of human services and employment services and the Civil Rights Commission, and that employees shall routinely inquire whether people wish to register and assist them in doing so. Elsewhere, reform bills that include provisions for agency-based registration services have been introduced in the legislatures of California, Texas, Nevada, Illinois, New Jersey, Arkansas, Connecticut, Massachusetts, and Pennsylvania.

Beginning in 1985, Human SERVE began to focus on big-city mayors, particularly minority mayors.[32] Mayor Harold Washington's September 1986 order went into effect in Chicago about two weeks before the registration deadline for the mayoralty primary expired on January 19, 1987.[33] City agency tallies

---

[32] During the 1984 presidential campaign, a number of county boards of supervisors or county executives, and a few mayors, directed that registration be offered in various agencies. Some of these counties contained large central cities, such as Travis County (Austin), Texas; Essex County (Newark), New Jersey; Cuyahoga County (Cleveland), Ohio. Directives limited to human service agencies were issued in Contra Costa County, California; Orange (Tallahassee) and Dade (Miami) counties in Florida; Middlesex County, New Jersey; and Multnomah County (Portland), Oregon. Overall, we doubt that much registration actually went on. However, some counties remain active: for example, California's Alameda County offices registered 1,191 people between September 16, 1986, and April 7, 1987, and Contra Costa County has also been active.

The municipal orders during the 1984 campaign included New Brunswick and Camden, and eight Ohio cities—Akron, Canton, Cleveland, Columbus, Dayton, Mansfield, Shelby, and Steubenville. It is unlikely that more than a few thousand were registered, and only a few city departments have remained active.

[33] Mayor Washington's order was actually issued in September, but implementation was delayed by Illinois's stringent deputization procedures. A bill enacted by the legislature that became effective in 1984 permitted representatives of qualifying "civic" organizations to be deputized to register voters. Consequently, before municipal employees could be trained, deputized, and supplied with forms by the Cook County and Chicago election authorities,

show that roughly one thousand persons a day were registered, mainly in multiservice centers serving low-income clients, for a total of ten thousand. On February 17, 1987, mayor Tom Bradley of Los Angeles issued a letter to department heads to begin planning for voter registration programs, and announcing the formation of the City Voter Assistance Program that will require "City employees who deal with the members of the public in the course of conducting City business to . . . ask those individuals if they would like assistance in registering to vote." Voter registration cards are now available in 350 locations in fifty city departments. Registration services at fifty sites within ten departments began in San Antonio in August 1987 as the result of joint action by the city council and the city's Hispanic mayor, Henry Cisneros. Alabama's association of thirty-three black mayors has endorsed the principle of agency-based registration; about a dozen of the mayors have said publicly that they will implement it (Hobson City is now doing so), and the association plans to press the governor to issue an executive order.

Progress has also been good among nonminority mayors. In Texas, more than nine thousand forms were distributed in municipal health clinics and courts in the city of Houston during the first six weeks of a program that began in the summer of 1987. And the "Coordinator of Voter Registration" for the Harris County Hospital District, which includes the city of Houston, reports that eligibility workers—who certify 250,000 people annually for medical care—distributed twelve thousand voter registration forms between February and August 1987. The city of Austin distributed six thousand forms through city libraries, utility customer service offices, and neighborhood recreation centers between January and June 1987.

Meanwhile, Mayor Edward Koch, having won reelection handily in New York City in 1985 with substantial black and

---

they had to be certified as members of an appropriate civic organization or of the city's municipal union. The problem of released time for training of deputies who were city workers also had to be settled before the program could be carried out.

Hispanic support, has also issued an order covering a wide range of agencies, the most significant of which is the welfare department. The program is supposed to begin in spring 1987 and will be launched with public service announcements. More than eight hundred municipal employees in twenty-six departments have been trained to distribute registration forms and assist in their completion. In addition, U.S. Senators Moynihan and D'Amato have agreed that Mayor Koch may use their franking privilege to mail postpaid registration forms (and a copy of the U.S. Constitution) to 2 million unregistered voters in the city of New York.

Progress is being made in New Jersey. An executive order was issued by the mayor of Trenton, forty municipal staff members have been trained, and the director of human services is entering a question on intake forms asking whether applicants are registered to vote. Prospects also appear excellent for the implementation of an executive order in Jersey City (where a supportive city council resolution was also enacted). Finally, the Newark City Council enacted a resolution, and the mayor appears to be favorably inclined toward going forward with a voter registration program.

San Francisco (which is both a city and a county) now has forms available at one hundred locations, and employees have been instructed to ask clients whether they wish to register. Finally, the Minneapolis City Council, with the mayor's support, passed a resolution in late July, and plans for implementation are apparently under way.

Finally, agency-based registration may result from lawsuits taken against election officials who limit deputization as well as the times and places of registration. An agency-based remedy is now being demanded in consent decree negotiations in Arkansas by the NAACP Legal Defense and Educational Fund, and in Pennsylvania by Project Vote. And a sweeping victory has been won against restrictive registration procedures in Mississippi under section 2 of the Voting Rights Act in a case prepared by the Lawyers' Committee for Civil Rights Under Law and the NAACP Legal Defense Fund. Following a trial, a federal court in November 1987 struck down Mississippi's "dual registration" law (which requires people to register separately for municipal elections, and again for county, state, and federal elections). The court also held that laws governing times and places of registration were unduly restrictive, and allowed Mississippi's governor and legislature 120 days to develop a plan for expanded access to registration, although in the meantime the court ordered that all municipal clerks be deputized, including clerks in municipalities with populations of under five hundred, where many blacks are located. In the negotiations with state officials, plaintiffs will probably demand that the legislature enact mail registration and that government employees throughout the state be deputized. According to Frank R. Parker of the Lawyers' Committee, "This case is extremely significant as the first court decision invalidating statewide restrictions on when and where citizens may register to vote. The case constitutes an important precedent for challenging time and place restrictions in states throughout the country." Other southern states are prime candidates for such legal challenges, but so too are states such as Massachusetts, Indiana, and Illinois.

One further case has large strategic implications for the spread of agency-based registration, for it suggests the possibility that states can be sued for not rigorously implementing their own elections codes. These codes often contain general language about the responsibility of government to encourage full democratic participation. Thus the California Election Code states:

> It is the intent of the Legislature that voter registration be maintained at the highest possible level. . . . It is the intent of the Legislature that the election board of each county, in order to promote and encourage voter registrations, shall establish a sufficient number of registration places throughout the county, and outside of the county courthouse, for

the convenience of persons desiring to register, to the end that registration may be maintained at a high level. . . . In furtherance of [this purpose], the governing board of any county, city, city and county, or other public agency, may authorize and assign any of its citizens or employees to become deputy registrars or voters and to register qualified citizens on any premises and facilities owned or controlled by such public agencies during the regular working hours of such officers or employees.

A related regulation also says that "each county shall provide for the solicitation of registration by personnel of state agencies." However, it had never been implemented. Consequently, Human SERVE collaborated with the southern California chapter of ACLU to prepare a case against the county of Los Angeles,[34] with chapters of Common Cause, the Southwest Voter Education Project, and the Southern Christian Leadership Conference joining as plaintiffs. (The League of Women Voters subsequently filed an *amicus curiae* brief in support.)

In July 1986, the Los Angeles Superior Court issued a preliminary injunction ordering the county to instruct twenty thousand health and welfare workers to begin soliciting voter registration, and suggested that they engage in the following "brief dialogue with their clients":

(i) "Are you registered to vote?";

(ii) "If you would like to register, I can provide you with a voter registration card";

(iii) "Please fill out and sign the card, and I will forward

[34] The suit was prepared by the southern California chapter of ACLU. Prior to filing, the California Human SERVE organizer arranged for Edmund Edelman, one of the members of the Los Angeles County Board of Supervisors, to submit a motion to instruct county election officials "to work with all departments whose employees have daily contact with the public . . . to develop a voter registration program." This motion was rejected by a 3 to 2 vote of the board of supervisors, thus laying the basis for the suit.

it to the County Registrar, or you can mail it in yourself";

(iv) "The decision to register or not to register is yours. It
will not affect your receipt of County services in any
way." [35]

In a straight party-line vote, the three Republican members
of the five-member Los Angeles County Board of Supervisors
voted to appeal the decision (one of them called agency registration "socialism"). The three-judge panel of the court of appeals
upheld the lower court in June 1987 and affirmed the obligation
under law of county election officials to reach out to unregistered
voters, including by deputizing county workers. Indeed, the
appeals court explicitly declared that the lower court had acted
properly because "the use of county employees as deputy registrars will significantly increase the number of registered voters
who are poor and non-white" in accord with the intent of the
legislature. The county board of supervisors has voted to take a
final appeal. Whatever the outcome, this case opens a range of
new legal possibilities for the reason, as we said earlier, that
most election codes contain general language about government's obligation to enroll its citizens for maximum democratic participation. There is even the possibility of taking
suits to force the implementation of agency-based executive
orders and laws.

SUMMING UP

How should we evaluate this effort to open the voter registration
system to lower-income people? It certainly did not result in a

---

[35] The court also directed that "those County employees who are deputized pursuant to this
injunction shall not engage in any partisan political activity in discharging their duty as
Deputy Registrars."

brush fire of reform. But neither was it simply stymied. Agency-based registration clearly holds considerable promise. Motor voter programs continue to spread, whether by referendum, legislation, or executive order.[36] However, the prospects for registration programs in public agencies serving the poor and minorities are less certain. As for voluntary agencies, it remains to be seen whether they will be readier to act now that the controversies over the legality of agency registration have been more or less settled.

One other point should be considered in appraising the viability of this strategy. Whatever Human SERVE has so far accomplished was done by a small staff organization with virtually no political resources. The fact that there were successes at all suggests that there are indeed political openings at the state and local level. If influential organizations with stakes in voting rights were to join in bringing pressure to bear on state and local governments, much larger advances could be made.

We close with a reiteration of our earlier assertion that state and local reform is the key to eventual comprehensive national reform. At this time, a bill providing for broadened access to registration is in the drafting process,[37] and a national coalition is forming to mobilize support once the bill is introduced to the Congress.[38] The bill has these main features: day-of-election reg-

---

[36] Nevada, where Governor Richard H. Bryan, a Democrat, signed a motor voter bill on June 26, 1987, is the latest example. In one of the first counties to implement the bill, three thousand people were registered in four weeks. Liberal Democrats in the state legislature—together with lobbyists for Common Cause, the League of Women Voters, and the AF of L-CIO—had been pressing for a mail-in bill, which was successfully opposed by both conservative Democrats and Republicans. The motor voter bill represented a compromise because, according to close observers in the state, conservative Democrats did not think it would bring disproportionate numbers of the poor and minorities into the electorate and Republicans did not think it would alter the partisan balance in the state.

[37] The bill will be introduced in the Senate by Alan Cranston (D-Calif.), the Senate majority whip, and he is reaching out for bipartisan sponsorship. A companion bill will be introduced in the House, where mail-in and day-of-election registration bills had been introduced regularly in previous sessions by John Conyers (D-Mich.)

[38] Currently, the coalition consists mainly of voter registration and public interest organizations such as ACORN, the Churches' Voter Registration Project, the U.S. Public Interest

istration,[39] mandatory state mail-in registration, and, at Human SERVE's urging, a requirement that both federal agencies and federally assisted state, local, and voluntary agencies dealing directly with the public offer registration services. The latter section of the bill contains this language:

> Notwithstanding any other provision of law, all Federal agencies and all State, county, municipal and non-profit agencies receiving grant-in-aid monies and serving the public directly shall, during the entire year, offer non-partisan voter registration services including distributing voter registration forms, answering questions, assisting in completing forms and . . . forwarding completed registration forms to the proper local election officials.

The bill's different provisions are each oriented toward widening access to registration. Measures providing for registration in agencies, or on election day (or, for that matter, national canvasses), each use a different method to expand the times and places people are allowed to register. If people could register in the course of using services in agencies as diverse as welfare, Social Security, nutrition, employment, agriculture, education, and day care, the United States would have universalized access to the electoral system. In effect, it would have created a func-

---

Research Group, the NAACP Legal Defense and Educational Fund, the Lawyers' Committee for Civil Rights Under Law, Citizen Action, the Advocacy Institute, People for the American Way, and Human SERVE. The ACLU has also been actively involved in drafting and building support.

[39] This measure has gained some legitimacy from recent endorsements by commissions studying low voter turnout. The Harvard/ABC News Symposium, *Voting for Democracy*, urged Congresss and state legislatures to reform registration procedures, "including, but not limited to, election-day registration" (1984:17). And the bipartisan Commission on National Elections, co-chaired by Melvin R. Laird and Robert S. Strauss, concluded that "more than any other single action, taking steps to make possible voter registration on election day would increase the number of Americans who vote for president and vice-president" (*Final Report of the Commission on National Elections*, 1986:46).

tional equivalent of election-day registration, or of the European automatic and canvass systems.

The virtue of the bill is that it will keep the issue of the relationship between registration barriers and low voter turnout before the public. But like similar efforts in the past, the bill will confront broad opposition. To lessen resistance over time, such national legislative reform proposals need to be undergirded by efforts at the state and local levels to drive up the registration rolls. Agency-based registration may make that possible.[40]

[40] Formal support for this method of voter registration reform is growing among national organizations of public officials. The National Association of Secretaries of State released a report in July 1987 declaring that "public agencies that have frequent contact with the general public provide effective and efficient locations for voter registration. Agency administrators and workers can easily incorporate nonpartisan voter registration services into the routine job activities of each office." The Council of State Governments adopted the Minnesota model for agency-based voter registration for inclusion in its 1988 annual volume. The League of United Latin American Citizens' national convention in July 1987 adopted a resolution "strongly supporting the establishment of voter registration services in federal, state, and local government agencies including human services, health, employment security, and drivers' license bureaus." The Election '88 Task Force of the National League of Cities is distributing kits for municipal officials interested in establishing voter registration services in municipal agencies. The National Conference of Black Mayors, as its annual meeting in April 1987, unanimously urged its members to make municipal agencies voter registration sites. And the Democratic National Committee's voting task force issued a report in October 1987 stating that "voter turnout can be dramatically increased when local and state election and government officials take steps to actively promote voter participation through the agencies of government."

Epilogue

New Constituencies,
New Politics

At the close of the nineteenth century, the nation had reached a turning point. Enlarging state intervention in economic relations had become inevitable, given the requirements of a developing industrial capitalism. But what form that intervention would take, who would benefit, and who would bear the costs were not dictated by economic forces. Business mobilized on an unprecedented scale, overwhelming Populist demands and the protests of the new industrial workers, so that farm families and the working class paid the price for the transition to industrialism. The partial disenfranchisement of the northern working class and the more or less complete disenfranchisement of southern blacks and poor whites were crucial to this outcome. By reproducing in the twentieth century the class restrictions on the suffrage of a predemocratic age, economic elites ensured that they would encounter little political resistance as they moved to shape government policies in their interests.

The persistence of these disenfranchising measures has without doubt been the most remarkable feature of twentieth-century American electoral arrangements. It helps to explain why the United States followed a political path so different from Western Europe. There the consolidation of the industrial working class was coterminous with the winning of the suffrage, and with the subsequent emergence of labor-based political parties to compete for influence on the state. Under these conditions, increasing economic concentration precipitated a political struggle over the terms of state intervention. Working-class parties were able to force substantial political accommodations, including the right to unionize, limitations on working hours, less hazardous working conditions, and substantial welfare state protections.

In the United States, the working class did not win important concessions until the tumultuous events of both the 1930s and the 1960s produced an expansion of the electorate and correlative changes in the party system and in domestic policy. Even so, American workers still lag behind the workers in European industrial nations, especially in respect to social welfare protections.

Much about the current political situation in the United States is reminiscent of the closing years of the nineteenth century. A rapidly changing economy has once again made shifts in state policy inevitable. Now, as a century ago, the question is how government will intervene and who will benefit. Business has again mobilized on a huge scale to influence electoral politics; it has once again realigned in support of the Republican party; and it is again pressing for a series of radical changes in public policy that would depress working-class living standards.

Business claims that existing labor policies and regulatory policies impede the capacity of the United States to adapt to the imperatives of international markets. This analysis is intended to persuade people of the narrow limits within which they can think and act politically. Invoking international market forces (especially cheap labor in the Third World) induces a sense of fatalism; there is presumably no option except to give way to business demands in the name of restoring competitiveness. But in fact, some industrial nations have forged different solutions. Sweden and Austria, for example, have so far managed to maintain low unemployment and high social benefits by enacting government policies oriented to improving competitiveness by promoting capital-intensive and high-wage economic restructuring while at the same time protecting the living conditions of workers during the transition. At the other extreme, England has responded to the same international pressures with policies that impose high unemployment, an increasingly polarized wage structure, and deteriorating social services. Whether the English approach to restructuring—and the relatively similar approach in the United States—will succeed over the longer run remains to be seen. Policies that sustain profits by driving down living standards may well be shortsighted and anarchic. In any case, what is clear is that this approach to the pressures of global economic change imposes the full costs of restoring competitiveness on the working class.

There is also the distinct possibility that, no matter what policies are adopted, the dominance of the world economy by Western industrial nations may finally be ending, with a consequent shift in the global distribution of wealth and a long-term decline in Western living standards relative to those in emerging industrial nations. If so, efforts to increase U.S. competitiveness will merely slow the drift toward relatively lower living standards. The resulting political issue is obvious enough. How should the inevitable costs of economic restructuring be allocated among the classes? And, if living standards cannot be maintained, how should the costs of economic decline be allocated? Who will be protected, and who will pay?

Once more, the political alignments that will determine our response to economic change are not foretold. Whether a majority coalition will be formed that might temper the current business program depends on two important conditions. One is the extent to which voting preferences among both southern and northern white workers will continue to be strongly influenced by racism; the other is the extent to which the ranks of the new working class are mobilized for electoral participation.

Much has been made of the realignment of southern whites,

at least in presidential elections. As southern blacks began moving into the electoral system and the Democratic party after World War II, many whites deserted to the Republican party, which has come to embody the legacy of the region's racism and conservatism.[1] Lower-stratum whites are now divided evenly between the parties in the Deep South, and favor the Democrats only by a slight margin in the Border States.[2]

The future of alignment of the South obviously depends upon the continuing ability of the Republican party to induce lower-stratum whites to coalesce with middle- and upper-class whites. A century ago, poor southern whites permitted themselves to be duped into giving up the franchise in order to ensure that blacks would be deprived of it. Now that they have the vote, the question is whether they can continue to be duped, this time by joining permanently in alliances with better-off whites to offset black electoral influence. However, racial animosity may not be adequate to the task of keeping southern whites aligned against their own interests. Phillips warns that "the social-issue constituency has a New Deal economic past,"[3] and the data show

[1] It is not only racial conflict that has caused Democratic defections. The Republican party has benefited from the intense traditionalism among southerners, as evident in the followings gained by the leaders of the religious Right, who focus on the social issues. However, the religious and family social policies demanded by the religious Right also represent a potential source of cleavage that could impede the formation of a stable Republican majority by alienating younger, upwardly mobile, and economically conservative elements in the North who are culturally permissive.

[2] The relevant poll data are shown below:

WHITE SOUTHERN PARTY IDENTIFICATION BY SOCIOECONOMIC STATUS, 1984
(PERCENTAGES)

	Democratic	Independent	Republican
Border States			
Middle-upper SES	54	9	38
Lower SES	61	6	33
Deep South States			
Middle-upper SES	41	9	50
Lower SES	42	18	40

Source: Petrocik (1987b: appendix table 4).

[3] Phillips (1983:xxii, 96–97).

that voters are volatile and shift their allegiances in response to economic conditions.[4] The possibility of change in southern electoral politics is suggested by the increased liberalism of southern Democratic congressmen who now depend on the support of blacks and moderate whites.[5]

Meanwhile, the decay of the industrial working class continues, and this fact has profound implications for the future of the American parties. The transition to postindustrialism is being ushered in with a vast proliferation of low-paid jobs that are being filled by minorities and women. Bluestone and Harrison report that the rate of growth in low-paying jobs in the United States during the period from 1979 to 1985 was twice as high as it had been from 1963 to 1979.[6] Many of these jobs are part-time or temporary, and pay few if any benefits, and most service workers are not unionized. Women and minorities are coming to constitute a new and unprotected service sector proletariat.

---

[4] Thus, some analysts of the religious Right claim that the voting patterns of evangelicals and fundamentalists may not be particularly distinctive. Lipset and Raab (1981:29) conclude that they tend to vote much the same as the general electorate—which is to say, they vote according to the state of the economy. In the same vein, Himmelstein (1983:38) concludes that "across-the-board political conservatism is characteristic of a relatively narrow range of evangelical opinion, located primarily among fundamentalist clergy and a few committed laymen. There is little evidence of a massive new commitment of evangelicals to the ranks of Republicans or ideological conservatives."

[5] One consequence of the rise of black voting in the South has been the weakening of the coalition between Republicans and southern Democrats that exercised a marked conservative influence in the Congress since the New Deal period. The *Congressional Quarterly* (1987:1700) reports that southern Democrats and Republicans joined in 30 percent of the votes in Congress in 1971, but that the percentage dropped to 16 percent in 1986, and to a mere 7.5 percent in 1987. In part, the breakup of the ruling congressional coalition reflects the takeover of previously conservative southern seats by Republicans, and of the emergence of Democrats in the remaining seats who tend to be more liberal because of black voting. But it also reflects the breakdown of the one-party South. Earlier, southern Democrats had no reason to fear that Republicans would try to unseat them; now, however, competition for seats is intense, and the incentives for cooperative action have been correspondingly reduced. Furthermore, southern Democrats can no longer count on the Republicans as a source of patronage and support, and that has made them more dependent on the national Democratic party, a fact which tends to modify their narrowly sectional outlook with more national perspectives. Because of the breakdown of the system of 1896 in the South, in short, the Congress is more aligned along partisan lines than at any time in the past half century.

[6] Bluestone and Harrison (1986).

At a comparable stage in their evolution as a class, industrial workers in the United States were partially disenfranchised. Service workers are also being disenfranchised by an oligarchic Democratic party apparatus riddled with race and gender conflict. Formed in the 1930s on an older white male industrial working-class base, the Democratic party has not reorganized to incorporate the women and minorities who make up the new working class being created by the shift to a service economy. In the meantime, the Republican party has made some gains among the old industrial working class, whose loyalty to the Democratic party has been strained by race and gender conflicts and by the failure of the party to protect their interests. The resulting division and paralysis among the Democratic party constituency organizations smooth the way for increasing business influence.

The usual strategy to overcome this paralysis is to call for new leaders and new programmatic initiatives. But neither can be wished into existence. At those junctures in our history when political leaders have mattered, when they have reached beyond party platitudes and self-interested business programs to arouse popular hopes, it was because they were confronted by new voters or by unrest among existing voters, and by protest movements that gave those voters voice and leverage. In any case, programmatic initiatives are likely to evolve gradually and experimentally. And it will matter crucially whether they are formulated and implemented in an electoral context that is supportive of the interests of lower-stratum people. A "New Politics," in short, requires new constituencies. Throughout this book, we have emphasized the dynamic interaction between the shape of the electorate and party organization. As new constituencies enter the electoral system, the parties adapt, and their adaptations then also affect turnout. By this reasoning, a substantial influx of new voters can be expected, over time, to exert pressure for new leaders and programmatic appeals that reflect their interests. Widening access to voter registration could thus be the key to orienting the Democratic party toward the new service proletariat.

Although the Democratic party remains immobilized, the possibilities for a new stage in the metapolitics of participation are large. Voter turnout is down to almost half, mainly as a result of falling participation by minorities and lower-stratum whites in the North. If substantial numbers of these nonvoters were enlisted, the potential for a major electoral convulsion is evident, a convulsion that might eventually result in a party system capable of articulating the issues that divide American society.

Whether a more representative electorate eventually would lead to parties reorganized by class will, of course, be debated. On one side of the argument, there is survey evidence suggesting that political attitudes are not strongly differentiated by class in American society. On the other side, however, there is the experience of other countries, which suggests that political attitudes are not formed simply as a reflection of an objective class position. Rather, political attitudes are crucially shaped by the socializing influences of political parties competing to assemble majorities.[7] In the United States, where many in the working class did not have the vote during the twentieth century, there was less reason for the political parties to play this role by projecting class appeals.

Finally, there is the evidence of the outlooks of elites. The history of conflicts over the franchise suggests that dominant groups are not confident of their capacity to manipulate the attitudes of the electorate or to subvert electoral decisions. Consequently, they have exerted themselves to forge and maintain electoral institutions that have kept the franchise limited to those who were at least somewhat better off. Elites are confirmed structuralists. If that were not so, they would have long since ac-

---

[7] See generally Przeworski (1977) on the role of parties in class formation. The same argument can, of course, be applied to the shaping of an electorate by gender.

quiesced to the universal registration of American citizens in the sure confidence that nothing would change.

Whether an enlarged electorate would transform American politics can only be known, finally, by obliterating the remaining obstacles to voting.

Appendix A

How Many People Are Registered to Vote?

There are three major sources of information on levels of voter registration in the United States. All are subject to biases that seriously inflate local, state, and national rates.

In 1984, the secretaries of state reported that 127 million people were registered in a voting-age population of 174 million, or 73 percent.[1] This estimate, based on figures supplied by boards of elections, was inflated because the local registration rolls contained the names of millions of people who had died, or who had moved and reregistered elsewhere so that they were counted twice in national totals. As a result, the official registration level exceeded the actual level by about 10 percentage points in 1984, as will be discussed in appendix C.

The National Election Study (NES) conducted after each presidential election by the University of Michigan's Survey Research Center is widely used in academic analyses of registration and turnout, partly because the survey includes questions about partisan identification and attitudes toward government policies. The NES is based on a very small sample (fewer than

[1] The voting-age population figure is based on the Census Bureau's "resident" definition, which includes both institutionalized populations and military personnel resident in the United States.

two thousand in 1984), and it is subject to *sampling bias* because lower-income people who register less are sharply underrepresented. This survey would also be subject to *normative bias* resulting from the reluctance of respondents to admit to not being registered or not having voted, except that the NES verifies these claims by checking the records at boards of elections. In 1984, 83 percent of the NES sample claimed to be registered, but only 74 percent could be verified.[2] Because of the upscale tilt of the NES sample, even this verified figure is grossly inflated. The probable magnitude of inflation is suggested by voting comparisons. In 1984, 74 percent of the NES respondents claimed to have voted, and 63 percent, or 11 percentage points fewer, were verified as having done so. Even so, national turnout in the 1984 election was only 53 percent, or about 10 percentage points less than the NES verified figure.

The Census Bureau's Current Population Survey (Census Bureau/CPS) is the least-biased source. It is based on interviews with large national samples following every presidential and midterm election (fifty-eight thousand households in 1984). There were 170 million persons of voting age in 1984,[3] and the Census Bureau/CPS reported that an estimated 116 million persons claimed to be registered, producing a national registration level of 68.3 percent. Correcting the voting-age population to eliminate aliens (of whom there were an estimated 7.3 million) produces a registration level of 71 percent.

However, the Census Bureau/CPS has not conducted studies to determine how many respondents claim to be registered when they are not. One possible indication of this normative bias is provided by inflated voting claims. In 1980 and 1984, the proportion of respondents who claimed to have voted exceeded the actual national turnout by 7.6 percent and 9.9 percent re-

[2] The comparable figures for 1980 were 79 percent claiming to be registered and 71 percent verified as registered.

[3] The Census/CPS uses the "civilian non-institutional" definition of the voting-age population, which, as the term implies, excludes institutionalized persons and military personnel.

spectively.[4] Lacking any other way to estimate the inflation of registration claims, we assume that it approximates the inflation of voting claims, which averaged about 9 percent in 1980 and 1984. Reducing the 71 percent figure noted above by this percentage yields a 1984 national registration level of about 65 percent.[5] There were also an estimated 9.5 million households in which the registration status of adults was listed as not known or unreported. The likelihood is that these adults were registered at somewhat less than the national average. At the most, then, the national level of registration in 1984 was probably in the 63 to 64 percent range.[6]

Numerous studies show that blacks are particularly likely to overreport being registered, probably in deference to the civil rights struggle to win the vote.[7] For example, validation studies based on the NES samples in 1964, 1976, 1978, 1980, and 1984 found that overreporting by blacks exceeded overreporting by whites in every case. Thus, 24 percent of blacks overreported in 1976, but only 14 percent of whites.[8]

Overreporting by blacks appears to be higher in the South. For example, in a recent study, Lichtman concluded that only 54 percent of Mississippi blacks were registered in 1984;[9] however, the Census Bureau/CPS reported that 86 percent of Mississippi blacks claimed to be registered. In Florida, Georgia, Kentucky, and North Carolina, blacks claimed to be registered at levels exceeding the official registration levels reported by the secretaries of state. (Generally speaking, the differences almost

---

[4] Current Population Reports, Series P-20, no. 405, table H.

[5] See ibid., table 1.

[6] By the same estimating process, our judgment of the 1980 registration level is that it was in the 60 to 61 percent range.

[7] Shingles (1981).

[8] Katosh and Traugott (1981:519). For other studies bearing on the same point, see Abramson, Aldrich, and Rohde (1981); Abramson and Claggett (1984); Clauson (1968); Katosh and Traugott (1979); and Sigelman (1982).

[9] Lichtman (1987).

always run the other way, since the official data reported by secretaries of state are subject to a large bias owing to incomplete purging of those who have died or moved.)

There is also reason to believe that southern whites overre-port more than is typical of whites elsewhere in the country. This suspicion is prompted by the wide discrepancy between voting claims and the actual level of voting in the South. There were twelve states in which the discrepancy between Census Bureau/CPS voting claims exceeded the actual 1984 turnout in those states by a 15 percent difference or more. Eleven were in the Census Bureau's definition of the South. Mississippi, for example, showed a 33 percent difference. If voting claims are so seriously inflated, registration claims are likely to be as well.[10]

---

[10] Alabama, 21 percent; Arkansas, 12 percent; Georgia, 23 percent; Louisiana, 18 percent; North Carolina, 18 percent; South Carolina, 19 percent; Tennessee, 17 percent; Kentucky, 16 percent; Oklahoma, 15 percent; and Texas, 17 percent. The nonsouthern state was New Mexico, 17 percent.

Appendix B

Do Registrants Vote?

People vote if they are registered. Nonvoting is almost entirely concentrated among those who are not registered. This is *prima facie* evidence of the deterrent impact of registration procedures on voting. In 1980, 89 percent of registered voters told the Census Bureau/CPS interviewers that they had in fact voted; 88 percent reported voting in 1984. In an overall review of the relationship of registration to voting between 1964 and 1980, the Census Bureau/CPS declared that "one clear-cut finding of the data is that once people register, they overwhelmingly go to the polls" in presidential elections.[1] Similarly, the National Election Study (NES) reported a verified turnout level by registrants of 84 percent in both 1980 and 1984.

Furthermore, registrants turn out in high proportions despite differences in race, income, and education. Here are comparisons between those at the *extremes* of education—eight or fewer years versus college/postgraduate—as reported by the Census Bureau/CPS for the 1984 election (these percentages are slightly inflated because some respondents falsely claim to be registered or to have voted):

[1] United States Bureau of the Census (February 1984).

- Of the highest educated, 83.8 percent are registered, but only 53.4 percent of the lowest educated, a spread of 30 percentage points.
- In 1984, 79.1 percent of the highest educated voted, but only 42.9 percent of the lowest educated, a spread of 36 points.
- The spread narrows to 14 points when *voting by registrants* is compared—94.4 percent of the highest educated and 80.3 percent of the lowest educated went to the polls.

Of course, these findings do not necessarily warrant the conclusion that more people would in fact register and vote if registration were made easier. However, the studies that bear directly on this matter suggest that they would. Peter D. Hart Research Associates conducted a post-1984 survey of a national sample of first-time-ever registrants (reregistrants were excluded from the sample), a majority of whom were enlisted by organized voter registration campaigns in the 1982–84 period, and who might not otherwise have registered on their own. When election board records were checked, 77 percent were found to have voted.[2] Moreover, a national voter registration organization—Project Vote—verified from election board records that from 65 percent to 70 percent of the people whom they had registered on the lines in food-stamp, unemployment, and welfare centers, as well as in poor neighborhoods, did in fact vote in 1984.[3] And a follow-up check of elections records in Los Angeles County found that 75 percent of all new registrants had voted; 60 percent had been registered by organized drives.[4]

It should also be noted that more people try to vote than are recorded as doing so. In every election, some people go to the

[2] Committee for the Study of the American Electorate (undated:13).
[3] Personal communication from Sanford Newman, executive director of Project Vote.
[4] Cain and McCue (1985:15; see also 1984).

polls whose efforts to vote do not always end by being counted. We omit from consideration those who go to the wrong polling place, or who get discouraged because of long waiting lines, or who cannot remain on the lines because of employment obligations, child-care problems, or other reasons that cast no reflection on the motivation to vote. The number of people who get to the right voting place and attempt to vote, but whose ballots are not counted or who are not permitted to vote in the first place, is itself considerable. In the official processing of paper ballots, some are mutilated or lost; others are invalidated because they were improperly completed. Votes are also invalidated because people do not understand how to operate the voting machines, or because the machines themselves do not function properly. In still other cases, people are properly registered but are turned away because their registration records are not at the polling place on election day. Wolfinger and Rosenstone estimated that 2 to 3 million votes may not get counted in presidential elections for such reasons as these.[5]

Declining levels of registration, rather than falling levels of voting by registrants, are the main cause of the decreasing turnout of the past two decades (although there was a turnout increase of slightly less than 1 percentage point between 1980 and 1984). The national registration level fell by 6 percentage points between 1968 and 1984, but the rate of voting by registrants fell by only 3 percentage points.

TABLE B.1 REGISTRATION, AND VOTING BY REGISTRANTS, 1968–1984
(PERCENTAGES)

	1984	1980	1976	1972	1968	*Net Change*
Census Bureau/CPS						
Voters registered	68.3	66.9	66.7	72.3	74.3	−6.0
Voting by registrants	88.0	89.0	89.0	87.0	91.0	−3.0

[5] Wolfinger and Rosenstone (1980:115–17).

Still, the myth persists that low turnout results from the failure of registered voters to go to the polls. To give one egregious example, a consortium of foundations commissioned an evaluation of the effectiveness of the nonpartisan voter registration campaign organizations that they had been supporting in the 1984 period. The research organization selected, called Interface, specializes in research on public education management, and it assembled a team of educators to conduct the evaluation. That alone might explain why the evaluators emphasized that nonvoting is an educational problem. It is clear from the body of the report, however, that the predisposing bias toward educational remedies was reinforced by the voter registration groups themselves. Everyone shared the premise that poor and minority people will not vote even if registered, and the evaluators concluded that the main task confronting the voter registration community is to develop "instructional, consciousness raising or other activities broadly grouped under the heading of voter education if *sustained* voter participation is to be achieved."[6]

The larger significance of this explanation of nonvoting is, of course, its impact on public debates about registration reform. Nothing so undercuts the justification for comprehensive national registration reform as the persisting idea that the cause of low voting is poor education and the like, rather than registration barriers.[7] Consistently, upon publication of the Interface report, the editorial writers at the *New York Times* readily picked up the message: the task now, they said, is to "lead eligible voters all the way" to the voting booth.

---

[6] New York Interface Development Project (1985:11 and 16; emphasis added).

[7] Opponents of liberalized voter registration procedures persistently dismiss the need for reform by alleging that low voting is a problem of civic education. Here is a statement by Frank K. Fahrenkopf, Jr., chair of the National Republican Committee: "[We need] an educational process—of the media, our schools, our service organizations, our political parties—attempting by educational process to instill these duties, so that our children will see us on election day and ask, 'Did you vote?' And if you say, 'No, I did not,' you know that you will be quickly reminded. . . . So education, I believe, is the basis of getting more turnout" (Harvard/ABC News Symposium, 1984:20).

Appendix C

Misleading the Public: The Abuse of Registration and Voting Statistics

The public obtains most of its information about registration and voting from the media, and the media rely mainly on the secretaries of state for information. What makes these data so attractive to the media is their timeliness. Reports from the secretaries of state are issued at election time, when voting is in the news. By contrast, Census Bureau/CPS findings are not available until several months following each national election, and National Election Study (NES) data are not available until much later.

However, the data from the secretaries of state are seriously biased and misleading because of incomplete purging. As a result, they convey two false impressions. *One is that far more people are registered to vote than actually are. The other is that many registrants do not vote.* By widely circulating these conclusions to the public, the media help perpetuate the popular belief that barriers to registration are no longer a problem in the United States, and that low voter turnout results instead from the poor motivation of registrants.

The source of bias is that local registration lists are clogged with the names of millions of "deadwood" registrants who have died or moved but who have not been purged from the local rolls. There is often no automatic method of notifying voter registrars about those who die or move, with the consequence that registrars continue to carry them on the rolls for extended periods of time. Just how long depends on state "purge" laws and practices. Roughly 2 million persons of voting age die each year, or 1 percent of the eligible electorate. One-third of the 1980 NES respondents reported that they had lived at the current addresses less than one year before the election;[1] even allowing that some adults in such households will not reregister and that others not previously registered will remain unregistered, the inflation of the voter registration rolls due to residential mobility is nevertheless very large. If the movers reregister, as most eventually will, many end by being counted twice in national totals simply because their names have not been purged from the rolls in the jurisdictions where they previously resided.

To estimate the size of this "deadwood" component of the official voter registration rolls, we located a county (Essex, New Jersey, which contains Newark) where the rolls are purged every year, not just every two, four, five, or ten years, as in most other jurisdictions. The method consists of dropping people who have not voted in four years, as well as conducting annual address verification by mail. The Essex County registration rolls contained 385,166 names in 1980. The following year-by-year purges occurred:

Total 1980 rolls	385,166
Number purged in: 1981	66,970
1982	42,360
1983	42,519
1984	40,595
Total purged 1980–1984	192,444
Ratio of those purged to 1980 rolls	50 percent

[1] Squire, Glass, and Wolfinger (1984:10).

In other words, *the volume of names that Essex County election officials thought did not properly belong on the rolls at one time or another during the 1980–84 election cycle represented 50 percent of their 1980 registration rolls.*

The problem of inefficient purging from registration rolls of people who die or move their places of residence is widely recognized in academic analysis of turnout.[2] In a recent paper by Squire, Glass, and Wolfinger, this instructive incident is recounted:

> The inadequacy of state records may be judged by a recent episode in Rhode Island which purges those people who have not voted for five years. In the fall of 1983, informational pamphlets on the impending statewide election were routinely mailed to the state's 530,000 registrants. Because these are mailed at the bulk rate, in the past all undelivered ones had been destroyed at the post office. But in 1983, the Secretary of State arranged for the post office to return undelivered pamphlets to her. More than 100,000 came back [about 20 percent].[3]

Based on detailed conversations with election officials in the secretary of state's offices of fifteen states, we judged that the minimum deadwood being carried on the rolls in any state was 10 percent, and in a few states it was upwards of 50 percent. The average for the country was probably between 15 and 20 percent.

When these bloated data are used in the numerator of the formula,

$$\% \text{ registered} = \frac{\text{Number on registration rolls}}{\text{Voting-age population}}$$

[2] See Erikson (1981:261), for example.
[3] Squire, Glass, and Wolfinger (1984:4).

the registration level is artificially inflated. And when they are used in the denominator of the formula,

$$\% \text{ of registrants who vote } = \frac{\text{Number of registrants who vote}}{\text{Number on registration rolls}}$$

the equally obvious consequence is to deflate the rate at which registered people actually go to the polls.

Furthermore, the volume of these deadwood registrants has been expanding steadily, so that *trends in official registration levels are being progressively inflated*, and *trends in rates of voting by registrants are being progressively deflated*. The reason is that "purging" laws and practices have continually been liberalized: nonvoters have been given longer and longer to reappear in a voting booth before being struck from the rolls. Some states do not purge unless the registrant fails to vote for ten years.[4]

Michigan is a case in point. According to the deputy in charge of the election division of the secretary of state's office, a law enacted in 1975 permits inactive registrants to remain on the rolls for ten years. Moreover, the fifteen hundred local boards of election to not conduct mail verification of addresses to detect either movers or the deceased. After ten years, letters are supposed to be sent to those who have failed to appear to vote, and they are given ten days to respond before being struck from the rolls. But because of the expense, few boards send letters to the entire inactive list. The result, according to the election division deputy, is that "a lot of dust accumulates, but it doesn't hurt

---

[4] Only nine states still allow people to be purged if they do not vote once every two years (although we do not know that they do in fact strike them from the rolls so quickly). Other states only purge (if they do so even then) after failure to vote in "two general elections," or in a "presidential election," or in a five-year period, or even within ten years. Eight states, containing more than 20 percent of the population, no longer have automatic purge rules at all; whether or not to purge is entirely discretionary with local officials, which probably means that the frequency of purging varies with the availability of funds for clerical staff, as well as with local political and partisan considerations (which often means that it is largely those from certain neighborhoods who are purged). The point is that there has been a steady inflation of the voter registration rolls over the past two decades.

anyone." Little wonder, then, that the secretary of state reported that 90.2 percent of age-eligible Michiganites were registered in 1984. Other states with similar demographic and industrial characteristics, but with shorter purge periods, reported much lower registration levels in 1984: Illinois, 76.9 percent; Massachusetts, 73.6 percent; New Jersey, 72.0 percent; Pennsylvania, 68.9 percent; California, 68.6 percent; and New York, 67.9 percent.[5] In some southern states, there are local jurisdictions that have not purged their rolls since the passage of the Voting Rights Act in 1965, which doubtless explains why the overall 1984 registration level was 81.5 percent in Alabama and 92.2 percent in Mississippi (where half the counties report registration levels that exceed their respective voting-age population.)[6]

A reasonable way to estimate the growth of deadwood registrants is to compare the secretary of state figures with the Census Bureau/CPS figures. Although some people report to the Census Bureau/CPS that they are registered when they are not, there is no reason to believe that the rate of misreporting has changed over the years. Consequently, enlarged discrepancies between these two sets of figures can probably be attributed to the growth of deadwood registrants on the official rolls. As table C.1 shows, discrepancies have been enlarging from election to election— from 3.4 million in 1968 (or 3.9 percent of the Census Bureau/ CPS total of self-reported registrants) to 11 million in 1984 (or 9.5 percent of self-reported registrants). Furthermore, if the Census Bureau/CPS figures were reduced by approximately 9 percent to correct the people's tendency to overreport being registered,[7] the discrepancies would be nearly twice as large—or more than 20 million deadwood registrants in 1984.

[5] Because of its motor-voter program, Michigan does in fact have a higher level of registration than most other states. The Census Bureau/CPS reported in 1984 that 74 percent of Michiganites claimed to be registered, compared, for example, with 65 percent in Pennsylvania and 64 percent in New York.

[6] Lichtman (1987).

[7] See appendix A for the conclusion that the Census Bureau/CPS estimates of registration are probably inflated by about 9 percent.

TABLE C.1 NUMBER OF REGISTERED VOTERS
(MILLIONS)

	1984	1980	1976	1972	1968	1964	1960
Secretaries of state	127.0	114.7	106.5	103.0	90.0	87.0	82.5
CPS self-report	116.1	105.0	97.8	98.5	86.6	NA	NA
Difference	10.9	9.7	8.7	4.5	3.4		

The obfuscations that result from using these data are shown in table C.2. The Census Bureau/CPS shows a sharp drop of 6.0 percentage points in the level of registration since 1968; because of the increasing proportions of deadwood registrants, however, the secretaries of state report that the drop has been only 1.8 points. Similarly opposed trends are shown for voting by registrants. The Census Bureau/CPS data show that the falloff in voting by registrants has been slight—from 91 percent in 1968 to 88 percent in 1984, or only 3 percentage points. By contrast, the secretary of state data show a large falloff from 81.0 percent to 72.6 percent, or 8.4 percentage points, the result of increas-

TABLE C.2 REGISTRATION, AND VOTING BY REGISTRANTS,
1964–1984
(PERCENTAGES)

	1984	1980	1976	1972	1968	Net Change
Census Bureau/CPS*						
Registered	68.3	66.9	66.7	72.3	74.3	−6.0
Voting by registrants	88.0	89.0	89.0	87.0	91.0	−3.0
Secretaries of State**						
Registered	73.0	69.8	71.0	73.0	74.8	−1.8
Voting by registrants	72.6	75.2	76.6	75.5	81.0	−8.4

* *Voting-age population base calculated according to the Census Bureau's "civilian non-institutional" definition.*
** *Voting-age population base calculated according to the Census Bureau's "resident" definition.*

ing numbers of deadwood registrants who of course do not vote.

None of this would be important were it not that these worthless data, and the confusion they generate, are widely disseminated, largely as a result of the efforts of a Washington-based organization called the Committee for the Study of the American Electorate, headed by Curtis Gans. Unlike other research organizations that define the academic community as their principal constituency and publish their findings in professional journals, Gans's committee defines its constituency as the media. Gans's value to the media is that he issues press releases updating registration levels just days before national elections (and summarizing turnout just days after elections). In order to provide this on-the-spot information to the press, Gans must necessarily rely on the data supplied by the secretaries of state. Consequently, the conclusions he reports to the press are subject to the errors discussed above. He continues to insist, for example, that because of the "dramatic and continuing decline of the percentage of registered voters who are casting their ballots, it is getting less and less certain that registration [and registration reform] is the key to higher turnout"; registered voters are "losing faith in the efficacy of the ballot"; and so forth.[8] Nowhere does he indicate that the data supplied by the secretaries of state on voting by registrants are sharply at variance with those provided by the Census Bureau and other research organizations, or that scholars and academic research institutes uniformly spurn these "official" data because they are so filled with deadwood registrants.[9] The

---

[8] Press release, November 9, 1984.

[9] One exception is Burnham's analysis of the 1984 election. Relying on reports issued by Gans that make no corrections for deadwood, Burnham wrongly claims (1985:215 and table 8-2) that "three quarters, more or less, of the adult citizenry are registered," and that nonvoting by registrants rose "very substantially" between 1980 and 1984 (2.4 percentage points, according to his estimate). The Census Bureau/CPS data show (after being suitably corrected for inflated claims, aliens, and nonreporting) that the level of registration in 1984 was only about 63 to 64 percent, or some 11 or 12 percentage points lower than the figure employed by Burnham, and that voting by registrants fell by only 1 percentage point between 1980 and 1984, rather than by 2.4 percentage points.

committee's reports thus reinforce the widely held impression that low voter turnout is simply a motivational problem and has little to do with registration barriers.

Finally, in recent years these official data have also been employed by state governments defending against legal challenges to registration procedures. Several major cases were recently lost in the lower courts because state officials successfully maintained that, given high levels of registration, the allegation that registration procedures impede voting is unwarranted.[10]

---

[10] These and other recent lawsuits are discussed in appendix D.

Appendix D

Current Litigation Challenging Voter Registration Procedures

by Cynthia A. Williams

Generally speaking, legal challenges to voter registration procedures seek to show that they impermissibly burden the right to vote, or that they are discriminatory. In developing these challenges, voting rights litigators have appealed to a well-articulated body of favorable precedent regarding the right to vote. In a landmark decision a century ago, the Supreme Court wrote:

> The very idea that one man may be compelled to hold his life, or the means of his living, or any material right essential to the enjoyment of life, at the mere will of another, seems to be intolerable in any country where freedom prevails, as being the essence of slavery itself. . . . The case of the political franchise of voting is one [illustration]. Though not regarded strictly as a natural right, but as a privilege merely conceded by society, according to its will, under certain conditions, nevertheless it is regarded as a fundamental political right, because preservative of all rights.[1]

Cynthia A. Williams was formerly associate national director of Human SERVE.

[1] *Yick Wo* vs. *Hopkins*, 118 U.S. 356, 370 (1886) (dicta). *Yick Wo* struck down city

However, this 1886 judicial opinion was substantially at odds with the legislative and administrative practices governing the franchise that developed in the late nineteenth and early twentieth centuries. Voter registration laws, literacy tests, poll taxes, extensive durational residence requirements, and grandfather clauses were enacted around the turn of the century to limit voting. As a result, blacks, low-income people, and immigrants were massively disenfranchised. For instance, in 1896, 164,088 white citizens and 130,344 black citizens were registered to vote in Louisiana. By 1904, after the enactment of voter registration procedures, 106,360 white citizens remained registered, compared with 1,718 blacks.[2]

The large-scale disenfranchisement of blacks did not begin to change until the civil rights movement of the late 1950s and early 1960s forced federal judicial and legislative action. The voting rights protests in the South highlighted discriminatory restrictions on black voter registration and won important precedents challenging such restrictions.[3] Moreover, the massive protests demanding desegregation and an end to discriminatory voter registration practices created the political pressures that led to the passage of the Civil Rights Act of 1964 and the Voting Rights Act of 1965.[4]

---

ordinances in San Francisco that gave the board of supervisors, at their discretion, the power to refuse permission to applicants to establish laundries. The ordinances were being used to discriminate against Chinese applicants.

[2] Comment, "Access to Voter Registration," 9 *Harvard Civil Rights–Civil Liberties Law Review*, 482, 484 (1974).

[3] See, e.g., *United States* vs. *Duke*, 332 F.2d 759 (5th Cir. 1964) (evidence of state action that resulted in one registered black voter in a county of 7,250 blacks of voting age was sufficient to establish *prima facie* case that registration officials had not "freely and fairly registered qualified" blacks); *Hamer* vs. *Campbell*, 358 F.2d 215 (5th Cir. 1966) (court found that a black woman had standing to bring class action where she was denied the right to register because of racial discrimination; was registered under federal court order; and then was denied the right to vote because she hadn't paid poll taxes for two years previously); *United States* vs. *Ramsey*, 353 F.2d 650 (5th Cir. 1965) (findings of fact regarding voter registration practices were sufficient to prove the pattern and practice of discrimination where three blacks out of five thousand were registered as of July 1961).

[4] Bachmann, "Lawyers, Law, and Social Change," 13 *New York University Review of Law and Social Change* 1, 19–20 (1984–85).

The Supreme Court responded by giving increased importance to the franchise,[5] upholding both nonracial challenges to limitations on voter registration and challenges to racially discriminatory procedures. Examples of the first category of decisions include *Reynolds* vs. *Sims*, in 1964, in which the Supreme Court recognized that any restrictions on voting must be given exacting scrutiny and characterized the right of suffrage as "a fundamental matter in a free and democratic" society.[6] The following year, in *Carrington* vs. *Rash*, the court held, for the first time, that state voter qualifications were subject to the equal protection clause.[7] Equally important, *Carrington* stated that "states may not casually deprive a class of individuals of the vote because of some remote administrative benefit to the State."[8] This has been interpreted to mean that "[if] less restrictive [administrative] alternatives were available, although more costly and difficult to administer, [they] were required by the equal protection clause."[9] *Kramer* vs. *Union School District* further expanded this precedent by explicitly stating the need to impose more stringent equal protection standards to disenfranchising legislation.[10]

---

[5] The Warren Court developed a two-tiered mode of analysis for determining the constitutionality of legislative classifications. One level of analysis asks if a classification is "rationally related" to a legitimate state interest. If so, it is found constitutional. Under this standard, legislation is very rarely overturned. This posture is traditionally associated with, *interalia*, review of fiscal and economic regulatory matters. Until 1964, this was the standard applied to voting rights issues. *Lassiter* vs. *Northampton Election Board*, 360 U.S. 45 (1959) (upholding state literacy requirements). The other mode of analysis is the "strict scrutiny" or "heightened scrutiny" test, under which a state must bear the burden of showing that there is a *compelling state interest* justifying a classification. Legislation is often declared invalid using heightened scrutiny. This standard is now used to evaluate classifications based on religion, race, age, and national origin, and those affecting fundamental rights such as freedom of speech. Although *Reynolds* vs. *Sims* did not explicitly adopt the "heightened scrutiny" test, it did presage that test's later articulation.

[6] 377 U.S. 533, 561–62 (1964).

[7] 380 U.S. 89 (1965).

[8] Ibid. at 96.

[9] *Castro* vs. *California*, 85 Cal. Rep. 20, 466 P.2d 244 (1970), striking down California's constitutional provision conditioning the right to vote upon an ability to read English.

[10] 395 U.S. 621 (1969).

Cases that put forward important principles protecting the right to vote from racially discriminatory procedures include *Harper* vs. *Virginia Board of Elections,* declaring Virginia's poll tax unconstitutional,[11] and *Louisiana* vs. *United States,* striking down Louisiana's literacy test.[12] In *Louisiana,* the Supreme Court stated that "[t]he cherished right of people in a country like ours to vote cannot be obliterated by the use of laws like this, which leave the voting fate of a citizen to the passing whim or impulse of an individual registrar."[13]

Moreover, the lower courts and the Supreme Court have applied the equal protection clause to registration barriers in a series of cases that challenged cutoffs of registration three to four months in advance of elections.[14] In *Ferguson* vs. *Williams,* the Northern District of Mississippi held that the four-month cutoff was unconstitutional.

> [T]he state may not, consistent with the Equal Protection Clause, justify a longer registration period by the use of part-time, ill-paid election officials, assisted only by limited staff, or by adhering to slow-moving election machinery adequate in other times. The state's plain duty, where it insists upon the maintenance of registration books, is to provide efficient and expeditious registration procedures that impose only the imperatively needed restriction.[15]

Yet attempts in 1984 to expand constitutional protection of voter registration were not, on the whole, successful. In order to understand why, a number of the legal theories developed in 1984 will be discussed, excerpts from some of the more note-

---

[11] 383 U.S. 663, 666 (1966).
[12] 380 U.S. 145 (1965).
[13] Ibid. at 163.
[14] For an earlier discussion of these theories, see Armand Derfner, "Three Legal Theories for Challenging Restrictive Registration Practices," April 2, 1984, unpublished.
[15] 330 F.Supp. 1012 (N.D. Miss, 1971), vacated, 405 U.S. 330 (1972), on remand, 343 F.Supp. 656 (N.D. Miss. 1972).

worthy opinions will be given,[16] and the future prospects of this litigation will be assessed.

LEGAL THEORIES

Lawsuits brought in 1984 challenging restrictions on access to voter registration tended to emphasize one of two theories: that these restrictions are a violation of the Voting Rights Act, as amended, or that they are a violation of the First and Fourteenth Amendments of the Constitution.[17]

Voting Rights Act Theory

The Voting Rights Act of 1965 was structured to severely limit the power of the states to control who can register and vote, and to interject federal supervision into this process.[18] Section Two of the Voting Rights Act, which applies nationwide, now provides that

> [no] voting qualification or prerequisite to vote or stan-
> dard, practice, or procedure shall be imposed or applied
> . . . in a manner which results in a denial or abridgement

---

[16] The briefs and cases emphasized in this analysis are not more significant than those relegated to the footnotes. They are selected simply because they provide more illuminating examples for audiences unfamiliar with legal materials.

[17] All of the cases were brought in federal court. In the federal court system, any claim or theory related to the litigation must be raised, or it is potentially precluded in later litigation. Thus, attorneys tend to raise all potential claims in any given lawsuit. Most of the litigation discussed both the Voting Rights Act and constitutional theories, but emphasized one or the other.

[18] Comment, "Access to Voter Registration," 9 *Harvard Civil Rights—Civil Liberties Law Review* 482, 487 (1974). For a comprehensive discussion of the use of the Voting Rights Act to address restrictions on voter registration, see Lapidus, "Eradicating Racial Discrimination in Voter Registration." 52 *Fordham Law Review* 93 (1983).

of the right of any citizen of the United States to vote on account of race or color.[19]

In 1982, strengthening amendments were passed, including a new standard for proving violations. It is no longer necessary to prove that an electoral procedure was *intended* to be discriminatory, merely that it has a discriminatory *result*. Procedures covered "include all action necessary to make a vote effective in any primary, special, or general election, including, but not limited to, registration." [20]

A number of cases in 1984–85 that emphasized the Voting Rights Act[21] argued that section 2 is clearly violated if restrictions in deputization, or on the times and places registration is available, mean that members of a protected class have less opportunity to register and vote than other citizens.

For instance, in Waterbury, Connecticut, plaintiffs argued that section 2 was violated by the registrar's refusal to deputize volunteers; by their refusal to provide bilingual registration materials or registrars; and by restrictions on the times and places that registrars were available. By introducing voter registration statistics into evidence, plaintiffs demonstrated that these registration procedures have a discriminatory effect on black and Hispanic citizens. Further, plaintiffs argued that had members of their organizations been deputized, many residents in minority and low-income neighborhoods could have had the opportunity to be registered to vote.

U.S. District Judge Warren Eginton upheld plaintiff's voting rights claim. He found that "a valid claim under this provision [of section 2, *supra*] need not allege that the registrars had invidious intent to deny plaintiffs their right to vote. In

---

[19] 42 U.S.C. Section 1973 (a) (1982).
[20] 42 U.S.C. Section 1973*i* (c) (1) (1982).
[21] Cases were brought in Arkansas, Connecticut, Georgia, Louisiana, and Mississippi emphasizing the Voting Rights Act. In Arkansas, the trial was put off, and a consent decree is being negotiated. The remaining cases are discussed below.

contrast, the court found that Congress's aim in amending section 2 was to eliminate the necessity of proving intent. Violations of the Voting Rights Act are determined by the "results" of the challenged practices, considered as part of the "totality of the circumstances."[22]

Judge Eginton went on to discuss some of the factors that are relevant in analyzing a section 2 claim. "The court [in *Marengo County*] noted that low minority elected representation is not, by itself, proof of dilution. Nor is unresponsiveness of government to minority needs." But "where a minority can demonstrate a lack of access to the process," then government unresponsiveness becomes significant. Unresponsiveness may be too mild a term to fairly describe the registrars' failure to provide bilingual registration forms available to them at no cost from the state. This unresponsiveness, coupled with the unregistered Hispanics' "lack of access" to the political process, adds up to the "totality of the circumstances" indicating a violation of the Voting Rights Act.[23] As a result of this successful motion for preliminary injunction, defendants were ordered to deputize sixty volunteers, to provide Spanish-language materials, to have a Spanish-speaking assistant at the registrar's office full-time, and to conduct mandatory outreach sessions and publicity.

Motions for preliminary injunctions based on a similar Voting Rights Act theory were not successful in Georgia and Louisiana. Both the Georgia and Louisiana lawsuits challenged the entire state's procedures as violative of the Voting Rights Act, rather than challenging a particular registrar's refusal to deputize volunteers, as in Connecticut. In addition, in Connecticut the state filed an *amicus* brief supporting the plaintiff's position, rather than being the defendant in an explicit attack. Perhaps most important, on a motion for preliminary injunction, one

---

[22] *Connecticut Citizens Action Group* vs. *Pugliese*, Civil Action No. 84-431, Ruling on Motion for Preliminary Injunction, U.S. District Court for the District of Connecticut. For purposes of these discussions, most internal citations have been omitted.

[23] Ibid. at 11.

judge presides without a jury, so a great deal depends on "luck of the judicial draw." Important consent decrees were eventually signed in both Georgia and Louisiana, despite denial of the preliminary injunctions.[24]

Constitutional Theories

Another major constitutional argument made in the voter registration litigation is that refusing to deputize volunteers is an abridgment of those volunteer's First and Fourteenth Amendment rights to protected political speech and association with others for political purposes.[25] This argument followed a line of precedent initiated in *NAACP* vs. *Alabama ex rel. Patterson*[26] and further developed in *Anderson* vs. *Celebrezze*,[27] a case that explicated the analysis used in evaluating restrictions on First and Fourteenth Amendment rights. The Supreme Court in *Anderson* made clear that state regulation of elections "whether it governs the registration and qualification of voters, the selection and eligibility of candidates, or the voting process itself" is subject to First Amendment scrutiny because it "inevitably affects the individual's right to vote and his (sic) right to associate with others for political ends."[28]

Another theory argued that since voting is a fundamental right, any restrictions on it resulting from registration procedures must be supported by a compelling state interest (the "strict scrutiny" standard). Once the compelling-state-interest standard

---

[24] The details of these consent decrees will be noted subsequently.

[25] For a discussion of constitutional theories addressing restrictions on voter registration, see Note, "Voter Registration: A Restriction on the Fundamental Right to Vote," 96 *Yale Law Journal* 1615 (1987).

[26] 357 U.S. 449, 460 (1958): "It is beyond debate that freedom to engage in association for the advancement of beliefs and ideas is an inseparable aspect of the 'liberty' assured by the Due Process Clause of the Fourteenth Amendment, which embraces freedom of speech."

[27] 460 U.S. 780 (1983).

[28] Ibid. at 788.

is triggered, the state must show that restrictions on the exercise of the fundamental right are precisely tailored and employ the least restrictive means possible to protect the state's interest.

The equal protection theory (Fourteenth Amendment) held that any restrictive registration practice within a county discriminates between potential voters who become registered and those who don't; while differences between county registration practices within the same state discriminate against residents in counties with the more restrictive procedure.

Another constitutional theory claimed that since voting practices and procedures were enacted for a discriminatory purpose historically, and since they continue to have a discriminatory effect, they are violative of the equal protection clause (Fourteenth Amendment) and the Fifteenth Amendment. This theory demands that a reasonable claim of racial discrimination be made in order to be successful.[29]

One example of the constitutional theories being argued is provided by the brief filed in 1984 in the U.S. District Court for the Eastern District of Michigan asking for injunctive relief. This brief was written by Ron Reosti and Richard Sobel, cooperating attorneys for the Michigan Civil Liberties Union.

---

[29] In 1984, cases emphasizing constitutional theories were brought in Michigan, Missouri, New Hampshire, Rhode Island, and Iowa. The Michigan case was brought against the state on a motion for preliminary injunction; although it was unsuccessful, a consent decree was negotiated that defines nondiscriminatory standards for the deputization of volunteers. The Missouri case was brought against the board of elections of St. Louis asking for declaratory and injunctive relief (permanent injunction). It was unsuccessful both in the district court and in the 8th Circuit Court of Appeals. The New Hampshire case was brought against the board of registrars of the city of Manchester on a motion for preliminary injunction. It was unsuccessful, but the case is still pending, and negotiations with the board of registrars continue. The Rhode Island case was brought against the state board of elections. There, a motion for preliminary injunction was successful. Rhode Island had explicitly used membership in the Rhode Island League of Women Voters, the Rhode Island Minority Caucus, or the Rhode Island Governor's Committee on Employment of the Handicapped as the controlling factor in the selection of nonpartisan voter registrars, and this procedure was attacked on equal protection grounds. A similar case brought by the Iowa Socialist Caucus was successful in 1985 in that state, where deputization was limited to members of the Democratic and Republican parties.

A. The right to vote necessarily encompasses the right to register.

It is apparent that voter registration statutes burden the right to vote. They are in a very real sense a licensing of the right to vote. Because voter registration laws burden the right to vote, the restrictions such laws impose may withstand constitutional scrutiny only if warranted by a compelling state interest. If the state chooses to require registration, it must do so in a manner which is "precise," it must choose the "least drastic means," and it may impose only the "imperatively needed restrictions" on the right to vote.[30]

B. The right to engage in voter registration activities is protected against abridgement under the first amendment.

In addition to the right to vote, registration laws in Michigan also burden the right of speech and assembly. . . . [F]undamentally, "freedom to associate with others for the common advancement of political beliefs and ideas is a form of 'orderly group activity' protected by the First and Fourteenth amendments."[31] Similarly, voter registration conducted in the belief that all citizens eligible to vote *should* vote is political expression.

C. Michigan's voter registration system, permitting local officials to burden, as they may see fit, the rights to vote and to engage in political activity violates the first, fourteenth, and fifteenth amendments, and the Voting Rights Act. . . .

[T]he state can advance no compelling state interest in permitting some localities to refuse to deputize anyone as a registrar, while other localities impose various arbitrary numerical limits on their deputization programs, and

---

[30] *C.A.P.* vs. *Austin,* 387 MI 506, 198 N.W.2d 385, 388 (1972).
[31] *Kusper* vs. *Pantikes,* 414 U.S. 51, 56–57 (1973).

still others refuse to deputize particular individuals or members of particular groups; in permitting various localities to limit the time and place of deputy registration, with widely varying results; in permitting localities to limit the number of voters who may be registered by deputy registrars, or who may be registered by deputy registrars during a given period; in permitting some localities to require deputy registrars to reside in the same community as the voters they register, and other localities to refuse to permit deputy registrars to register voters in more than one community. . . . Quite simply, the state can have no compelling interest in regulating a subject when it leaves such regulation entirely to the discretion of about 1500 local officials. States have broad power under the Equal Protection Clause to determine the conditions under which the right to vote may be exercised. Nevertheless, they cannot do so in a manner which is inconsistent with the Equal Protection Clause. In determining access to the right to vote, states cannot distinguish between long term and short term residents;[32] or between rich and poor;[33] nor can the right to vote vary from one locality to another.[34]

Judge Stewart Newblatt, U.S. district judge for the Eastern District, ruled against the plaintiffs' motion for a preliminary injunction. In denying injunctive relief,[35] Judge Newblatt con-

[32] *Dunn* vs. *Blumstein,* 405 U.S. 330 (1972).

[33] *Harper* vs. *Virginia Board of Elections,* 383 U.S. 663 (1966); *Arlee* vs. *Lucas,* 55 Mich. Appl. 340 (1974).

[34] *Reynolds* vs. *Sims,* 377 U.S. 533 (1964).

[35] The legal standard for granting injunctive relief requires plaintiffs to show a *substantial likelihood* of success on the merits; a showing of *irreparable harm* to the plaintiffs if an injunction is not granted; a showing that the injury suffered by the plaintiffs will be greater than that suffered by the defendants if relief is granted; and a showing that it is in the *public interest* for an injunction to be granted.

centrated on what he determined to be the improbability of success on the merits. "In a nutshell, plaintiffs argue that since a greater number of deputy registrars will result in an increased number of registered voters, the failure to appoint deputy registrars unduly burdens the right to vote. Such an argument misses the point. By refusing to appoint deputy registrars absent a showing of need, the local clerks are doing nothing more than refusing to enhance voter turnout. The refusal to *enhance* voter turnout cannot be equated with a *violation* of the right to vote." [36]

Judge Newblatt next analyzes the plaintiffs' equal protection claims:

First, plaintiffs argue that citizens who reside in a community with a restrictive registrar deputization policy have less of a voice in elections than communities with liberal registrar deputization policies. . . . In order to accept plaintiffs' proposition, one must accept as an underlying premise that every member in a given community will vote the same way. Otherwise, there is an equal chance that increased registration may diminish the effectiveness of an individual's vote since those additional voters may vote contrary to the desires of that individual. Something else is strange and troublesome with plaintiffs' argument. Since the boundaries of election districts . . . were based on the population residing within the district rather than on the number of persons who vote, restrictions on registration would enhance rather than diminish the impact of those who do register and vote. While this point is truly nonsensical, it does point out how equating the right to vote with easier registration can produce inconsistencies in both reasoning and result. [37]

[36] *Edwards* vs. *Austin*, Memorandum opinion, No. 84-CV-8347-FL, U.S. District Court for the Eastern District of Michigan, September 26, 1984, at page 6.
[37] Ibid. at 7.

In rejecting the plaintiffs' First and Fourteenth Amendment claim regarding unlicensed discretion granted to registrars to restrict deputization, Judge Newblatt held that

> by refusing to appoint as deputy registrars the members of the organizational plaintiffs, the local officials have not prevented plaintiffs from doing anything in the way of campaigning, organizing, or encouraging others to register to vote. . . . Furthermore, in the abstract, the First Amendment does not include the right "to be appointed to a public office such as that of voter registrar" . . . nor is the denial of a request to be so named actionable under the Voter's [*sic*] Rights Act.[38]

Judge Newblatt also notes that

> the due process clause may be invoked to strike down a state statute in which a broad grant of discretion creates "a substantial risk of arbitrary action where important rights are involved." For reasons already noted, there is no constitutional right to be a deputy registrar. Therefore the grant of discretion contained in [Michigan's deputization law] is not subject to due process consideration.[39]

This overall logic is not worth refuting. However, Judge Newblatt's particularly egregious opinion does typify some of the problems encountered during the litigation campaign initiated in 1984.

[38] Ibid. at 8–9.
[39] Ibid. at 10.

Future Prospects

Despite some negative decisions resulting from the suits taken in the 1984 period, there is cause for optimism. First, in all but three instances (Arkansas, Missouri, and Mississippi), lawsuits were brought seeking preliminary injunctions. The standard for granting a preliminary injunction, in general, is that the plaintiffs are strongly or substantially likely to succeed on the merits. This standard is more difficult to meet than it is to win on the merits, where plaintiffs need only show that a preponderance of the evidence supports their position. Since this was essentially a new legal issue, the courts did not have precedent to refer to in deciding that the plaintiffs were substantially likely to succeed on the merits. Given novel legal theories and no precedent, the safest course is to deny injunctive relief and put the plaintiffs to their proof. Since only decisions on the merits create judicial precedents, little bad case law has been created as a result of these losses.

Second, both litigants and judges were somewhat unfamiliar with the intricacies of this issue in 1984. Litigants did not have time, given the impending election, to develop the factual record in the detail they would have liked. The Missouri case, for instance, was probably lost because the defendants were able to portray their voter registration procedures as accessible, thorough, and nondiscriminatory, and the plaintiffs did not have a sophisticated analysis of the actual availability of voter registration, its precise impact on minority citizens, or how aware people were of voter registration opportunities. The same dynamic was at work in the Michigan case, where Judge Newblatt (interpreting the facts in a light most favorable to his opinion) found that wholly adequate means were available for registering citizens, and that the plaintiffs' contentions thus did not address a "real" problem.

In addition, plaintiffs lacked adequate data with which to counter registration claims by state officials who use numbers supplied by local boards of elections. These numbers, however, are inflated over time by the names of people who have died or moved. Since 16 percent of the American population move every year, this source of error can be quite considerable. Michigan officials claimed, for example, that "85.6%, 98.9% and 87.9% [of eligible voters were] registered in Dearborn, West Bloomfield, and North Muskegon," respectively.[40] These statistics are clearly inflated, but litigants had no better data to use at the time. In addition, as a general matter, voter registration litigation is hobbled by the paucity of comprehensive and up-to-date studies of the effects of voter registration laws on voting.

However, the litigation had positive effects despite unfavorable decisions. In Michigan, for instance, plaintiffs and defendants agreed to a consent decree requiring the secretary of state to develop uniform, nondiscriminatory regulations for the appointment of deputy registrars to go into effect in all fifteen hundred election districts. In Georgia, a consent decree was signed in January 1987 that requires the secretary of state and the state board of elections to report quarterly to plaintiffs on outreach methods and numbers of new registrants in each county, as well as to describe any complaints they have received from around the state. In addition, during the two years of discovery, plaintiffs found that every time they started to study a particularly recalcitrant county's practices, the county would find itself interested in reform. In Louisiana, a consent decree required the state to do an extensive survey of voter registration practices by registration district, as well as to develop ideas for more effective outreach into the black community. Both the Georgia and Louisiana cases were dismissed without prejudice, which means litigants can go back into court if problems continue. In Arkansas, community activists claim that the lawsuit opened up deputiza-

---

[40] Ibid. at 7. The inflation of voter registration statistics is discussed in appendix C.

tion in many of the larger counties that did not want to risk legal challenges.

Moreover, it is only in the Missouri case that the constitutional theories have been heard on the merits, so it is too soon to say that these theories have been definitively discredited. Both the District Court for the Eastern District of Missouri and the U.S. Court of Appeals for the Eighth Circuit decided in favor of the defendants, the Missouri board of elections. However, the court of appeals did not challenge the logic of the district court's initial decision that "officials did not infringe [plaintiff's] constitutional right to vote because the Board had afforded her reasonable opportunities to register to vote."[41] Further, the court of appeals found that

> the claim that the Board's refusal to appoint qualified volunteers as deputy registrars restricts the accessibility of voter registration facilities and thus indirectly constitutes an unconstitutional infringement of the right to vote is more troublesome. We believe that the limited accessibility of voter registration facilities cannot be analyzed only in terms of relative inconvenience. . . . It is apparent that disproportionate numbers of unregistered voters are poor. We cannot overlook the fact that many persons are deterred from registering to vote during normal business hours at the Board's office in the downtown business district by factors that are essentially financial. . . . Sensitivity to these considerations supports increasing the availability of voter registration facilities. Yet there is no evidence in the record establishing that the Board has limited accessibility of voter registration facilities even indirectly on the basis of impermissible or suspect classifications such as race, language, or wealth.[42]

---

[41] Coalition for Sensible and Humane Solutions, 771 F.2d 395, 398 (8th Cir. 1985).
[42] Ibid. at 400.

From this language we conclude that the Missouri decision was a statement concerning the factual record which had been developed, not a repudiation of the constitutional "right to register" theories.

CONCLUSION

The Voting Rights Act, as amended, is clearly a principal statute to use in litigation challenging the discriminatory effects of voter registration provisions. The Supreme Court recently upheld the 1982 amendments in *Thornburg* vs. *Gingles*,[43] making it clear that a violation of section 2 could be proved by showing the discriminatory results of contested electoral practice, rather than having to show a discriminatory purpose in the enactment of that practice.[44] A case challenging Mississippi's voter registration practices on a section 2 theory was tried on the merits in July of 1987 and the court held in November 1987 that restrictions on voter registration contained in the challenged statutes were enacted for discriminatory purposes, constitute administrative barriers to voter registration, and "have a discriminatory result and deny black voters equal access to the political process." The court also found that "difficulty in registration is the main reason for not voting." This case resulted in part from an action by the Mississippi Legislature in 1955, shortly after the *Brown* vs. *Board of Education* decision, prohibiting county voter registrars from removing the voter registration books from their offices to register voters, except with the permission of the county board of supervisors. The effect of this statute generally has been to restrict voter registration to the county courthouse and to limit it to regular office hours during weekdays only. The court accepted evidence from a survey of eighty-one Mississippi circuit clerks

[43] *Thornburg* vs. *Gingles*, 106 S. Ct. 2752 (1986).
[44] Ibid. at 2763.

(that is, county registrars) showing that the clerks had conducted satellite registration, or held evening or Saturday registration, only on a limited basis if at all. The court also found that although state law permits the appointment of volunteer deputy registrars, "few deputy registrars have been appointed." Taken as a whole, the court held that these restrictions on times and places of registration, including restrictions on deputization, depressed voting by blacks and by poor whites. The court also struck down Mississippi's "dual registration" law requiring that people register with municipal clerks in order to vote in municipal elections, and again with county voter registrars to vote in county, state, and federal elections. The court ordered that state officials enact a program of remedies within 120 days. With this precedent, similar suits can now be undertaken in states throughout the country with restrictions on times and places of registration, and on deputization.

Further First and Fourteenth Amendment cases could also be productive. Supreme Court decisions in the early 1960s made it clear that legislation which limits voting must be subjected to the strictest constitutional scrutiny. However, litigators in 1984, in the context of cases that had to be filed quickly, had difficulty convincing courts that structural restrictions on *registration* still exist, and should be evaluated by the same standards as restrictions on *voting*.

In fact, the Supreme Court has implicitly recognized that restrictions on registration are the logical equivalent of restrictions on voting. *Harper* vs. *Virginia Board of Elections*,[45] which struck down Virginia's poll tax as violative of the Fourteenth Amendment, indicates that not paying the poll tax led to denial of registration.[46] Yet the opinion discusses the problem solely in terms of an impermissible burden on the right to vote.

In *Louisiana* vs. *United States*, the Supreme Court struck

[45] 383 U.S. 663 (1966).
[46] Ibid. at 664, fn. 1: "Section 20 provides that a person must 'personally' pay all state poll taxes for the three years preceding the year in which he applies for registration."

down Louisiana's literacy test for conferring on voting *registrars* "virtually uncontrolled discretion as to who should vote and who should not."[47] In *Louisiana,* provisions that denied voter registration status were clearly analyzed in terms of their burden on voting.

Implicitly the Court has thus recognized that state voter registration procedures may constitute restrictions on voting.[48] One can argue that binding Supreme Court precedent exists applying identical constitutional standards in analyzing voter registration procedures as are used in analyzing restrictions on voting. In the present context, that could mean applying a compelling state interest standard, which current voter registration procedures could not meet, and rejecting administrative convenience as a convincing rationale for upholding procedures that fundamentally restrict voter registration. Thus, as a matter of legal theory, there is no reason to assume that litigation challenging restrictive voter registration procedures could not be successful in the near future.

---

[47] 380 U.S. 150 (1965).

[48] These cases, striking down poll taxes and literacy tests, were concerned with an absolute bar to registration. Contemporary structural barriers, in some sense, constitute a relative bar to registration. yet this distinction goes more to differing problems of proof than to a different logical relationship between registration practices and impermissible burdens on voting.

Cited References

ABRAMSON, PAUL R., and JOHN H. ALDRICH. 1982. "The Decline of Electoral Participation in America." *American Political Science Review* 76, 3 (September).

ABRAMSON, PAUL R., JOHN H. ALDRICH, and DAVID W. ROHDE. 1983. *Change and Continuity in the 1980 Elections.* Washington, D.C.: Congressional Quarterly Press.

———. 1986. *Change and Continuity in the 1984 Elections.* Washington, D.C.: Congressional Quarterly Press.

ALDRICH, JOHN H., and DENNIS M. SIMON. 1986. "Turnout in American National Elections." In *Research in Micropolitics*, vol. 1. Greenwich, Conn.: JAI Press.

ALFORD, ROBERT R. 1963. *Party and Society: The Anglo-American Democracies.* Chicago: Rand McNally & Co.

ALFORD, ROBERT R., and EUGENE C. LEE. 1968. "Voting Turnout in American Cities." *American Political Science Review* 62, 3 (September).

ALFORD, ROBERT R., and HARRY SCOBLE. 1968. "Sources of Local Political Involvement." *American Political Science Review* 62, 4 (December).

ALLEN, HOWARD W., and KAY WARREN ALLEN. 1981. "Voter Fraud and Data Validity." In Jerome Clubb, William H. Flanigan, and Nancy Zingale, eds. *Analyzing Electoral History.* Beverly Hills, Calif.: Sage Publications.

ALMOND, GABRIEL, and SIDNEY VERBA. 1963. *The Civic Culture: Political Attitudes and Democracy in Five Nations.* Boston: Little, Brown.

ANDERSEN, KRISTI. 1982. *The Creation of a Democratic Majority, 1928–1936.* Chicago: University of Chicago Press.

ARGERSINGER, PETER H. 1980. "A Place on the Ballot: Fusion Politics and Antifusion Law." *American Historical Review* 85 (April).

———. 1985–86. "New Perspectives on Election Fraud in the Gilded Age." *Political Science Quarterly* 100, 4 (Winter).

ASBURY, HERBERT. 1928. *The Gangs of New York.* New York: Alfred A. Knopf.

BANFIELD, EDWARD, and JAMES Q. WILSON. 1963. *City Politics.* Cambridge, Mass.: Harvard University Press.

BARTLEY, NEUMAN V. 1969. *The Rise of Massive Resistance.* Baton Rouge: Louisiana State University Press.

BEAN, WALTER. 1952. *Boss Ruef's San Francisco.* Berkeley: University of California Press.

BECK, LEWIS. 1985. "Pocket Book Voting in U.S. Election Studies: Fact or Artifact." *American Journal of Political Science* 29, 2 (May).

BECKER, CARL LOTUS. 1968. *The History of Political Parties in the Province of New York.* Madison: University of Wisconsin Press.

BELL, DANIEL. 1978. *Cultural Contradictions of Capitalism.* New York: Basic Books/Harper Colophon Books.

BENDIX, REINHARD. 1964. *Nation Building and Citizenship.* New York: John Wiley.

BENSEL, RICHARD FRANKLIN. 1984. *Sectionalism and American Political Development, 1880–1980.* Madison: University of Wisconsin Press.

BENSON, LEE. 1961. *The Concept of Jacksonian Democracy: New York as Test Case.* Princeton, N.J.: Princeton University Press.

BERELSON, BERNARD, PAUL F. LAZARSFELD, and WILLIAM MC-PHEE. 1954. *Voting.* Chicago: University of Chicago Press.

BERMAN, WILLIAM. 1970. *The Politics of Civil Rights in the Truman Administration.* Columbus: Ohio State University Press.

BERNSTEIN, IRVING. 1970. *The Lean Years: A History of the American Worker, 1930–1933.* Baltimore: Penguin Books.

BLOCK, FRED. 1987. "Rethinking the Political Economy of the Welfare State." In Fred Block, Richard A. Cloward, Barbara Ehrenreich, and Frances Fox Piven, *The Mean Season: The Attack on the Welfare State.* New York: Pantheon Books.

BLUESTONE, BARRY, and BENNETT HARRISON. December 1986. *The Great American Job Machine: The Proliferation of Low Wage Employment in the US Economy.* Report Prepared for the Joint Economic Committee of Congress. Washington, D.C.

BOWLES, SAMUEL, and HERBERT GINTIS. 1982. "The Crisis of Liberal Democratic Capitalism: The Case of the United States." *Politics and Society* 11, 1.

BOWLES, SAMUEL, DAVID M. GORDON, and THOMAS E. WEISS-KOPF. 1984. *Beyond the Wasteland: A Democratic Alternative to Economic Decline*. Garden City, N.Y.: Doubleday/Anchor Books.

BOYD, RICHARD W. 1981. "Decline of U.S. Voter Turnout: Structural Explanations." *American Politics Quarterly* 9 (April).

BRECHER, JEREMY. 1974. *Strike!* Greenwich, Conn.: Fawcett Publications.

BRIDGES, AMY. 1984. *A City in the Republic: Ante-Bellum New York and the Origins of Machine Politics*. New York: Cambridge University Press.

————. 1987. "Rethinking the Origins of the Political Machine." In John Mollenkopf, ed., *Power, Culture, and Place*. New York: Russell Sage Foundation.

BRITTAN, SAMUEL. 1975. "The Economic Contradictions of Democracy." *British Journal of Political Science* 5, 22 (April).

BROWN, COURTNEY. 1987. "Voter Mobilization and Party Competition in a Volatile Electorate." *American Sociological Review* 52, 1 (February).

BRYCE, JAMES. 1924. *The American Commonweal*. New York: Macmillan Co.

BUCKLEY, PETER G. 1987. "Culture, Class and Place in Antebellum New York." In John Mollenkopf, ed., *Power, Culture, and Place*. New York: Russell Sage Foundation.

BURNHAM, WALTER DEAN. 1965. "The Changing Shape of the American Political Universe." *American Political Science Review* 65, 1 (March).

————. 1970. *Critical Elections and the Mainsprings of American Politics*. New York: W. W. Norton.

————. 1974a. "The United States: The politics of Heterogeneity." In Richard Rose, ed., *Electoral Behavior: A Comparative Handbook*. New York: Free Press.

————. 1974b. "Theory and Voting Research: Some Comments on Converse' 'Change in the American Electorate.'" *American Political Science Review*. 68, 3 (September).

————. 1974c. "Rejoinder to Comments by Philip Converse and Jerrold Rusk." *American Political Science Review* 68, 3 (September).

————. 1979. "The Appearance and Disappearance of the American Voter." In *The Disappearance of the American Voter*. Washington, D.C.: American Bar Association.

————. 1981a. "The 1980 Earthquake: Realignment, Reaction, or What?" In Thomas Ferguson and Joel Rogers, eds., *The Hidden Election: Politics and Economics in the 1980 Presidential Campaign*. New York: Pantheon Books.

————. 1981b. "Toward Confrontation." In Seymour Martin Lipset, ed., *Party Coalitions in the 1980s*. San Francisco: Institute for Contemporary Studies.

————. 1981c. "The System of 1896: An Analysis." In Paul Kleppner et al., eds., *The Evolution of American Electoral Systems*. Westport, Conn.: Greenwood Press.

————. 1982a. *The Current Crisis in American Politics*. New York: Oxford University Press.

————. 1982b. "The Eclipse of the Democratic Party." *Democracy: A Journal of Political Renewal and Radical Change* 2, 3 (July).

————. 1985. "The 1984 Election and the Future of American Politics." In Ellis Sandoz and Cecil V. Crabb, Jr., eds., *Election 1984: Landslide Without a Mandate?* New York: New American Library/Mentor Books.

BURNS, JAMES MACGREGOR. 1982. *The Vineyard of Liberty*. New York: Alfred A. Knopf.

————. 1985. *The Workshop of Democracy*. New York: Vintage Books.

CAIN, BRUCE E., and KEN MCCUE. June 1984. "The Efficacy of Voter Registration Drives." Social Science Working Paper 531, Division of the Humanities and Social Sciences, California Institute of Technology, Pasadena.

————. 1985. "Do Registration Drives Matter? The Realities of Partisan Dreams." Paper delivered at the Annual Meeting of the American Political Science Association, New Orleans, August 29–September 1.

CAMPBELL, ANGUS, PHILIP E. CONVERSE, WARREN MILLER, and DONALD STOKES. 1960. *The American Voter*. New York: John Wiley.

————. 1965. *Elections and the Political Order*. New York: John Wiley.

CAMPBELL, ANGUS, and WARREN MILLER. 1957. "The Motivational Basis of Straight and Split Ticket Voting." *American Political Science Review* 51 (June).

CAMPBELL, BRUCE A. 1979. *The American Electorate: Attitudes and Action*. New York: Holt, Rinehart & Winston.

CARLSON, RICHARD JOHN. 1976. *The Effect of Voter Registration*

Systems on Presidential Election Turnout in Non-Southern States: 1912–1924. Ann Arbor, Mich.: University Microfilms International.

CAVANAUGH, THOMAS. 1981. "Changes in American Voter Turnout, 1964–76." *Political Science Quarterly* 96, 1 (Spring).

CENTER ON BUDGET AND POLICY PRIORITIES. Undated. *Economic Recovery Fails to Reduce Poverty Rate to Pre-recession Levels: Gaps Widen Further Between Rich and Poor.* Report no. 71:18. Washington, D.C.

CHAMBERS, WILLIAM N. 1967. "Party Development and the American Mainstream." In William Nisbet Chambers and Walter Dean Burnham, eds., *The American Party System: Stages of Political Development.* New York: Oxford University Press.

CHAMBERS, WILLIAM N., and PHILIP C. DAVIS. 1978. "Party Competition and Mass Participation: The Case of the Democratizing Party System, 1824–1852." In Joel Silbey, Allen G. Bogue, and William H. Flanigan, eds., *The History of American Electoral Behavior.* Princeton, N.J.: Princeton University Press.

CLAUSON, AAGE. 1968. "Response Validity: Vote Report." *Public Opinion Quarterly* 32, 4 (Winter).

CLUBB, JEROME M., WILLIAM H. FLANIGAN, and NANCY H. ZINGALE. 1980. *Partisan Realignment: Voters, Parties, and Government in American History.* Beverly Hills, Calif.: Sage Publications.

COHEN, JOSHUA, and JOEL ROGERS. 1983. *On Democracy: Toward a Transformation of American Society.* New York: Penguin Books.

———. Forthcoming. " 'Reaganism' After Reagan." *Socialist Register.*

COMMISSION ON NATIONAL ELECTIONS. April 1986. *Final Report of the Commission on National Elections.* Center for Strategic and International Studies, Georgetown University, Washington, D.C.

COMMITTEE FOR THE STUDY OF THE AMERICAN ELECTORATE. Press release dated November 1, 1984. Washington, D.C.

———. Press release dated November 9, 1984. Washington, D.C.

———. Undated. *Voter Registration 1984: A Report and Evaluation.* Washington, D.C.

CONGRESSIONAL QUARTERLY. July 23, 1983. Editorial article entitled "Reagan's Legacy: 'Have-Not' Surge to Polls: Major Force in 1984 Election." Washington, D.C.

———. August 1, 1987. Editorial article entitled "Changing South Perils Conservative Coalition." Washington, D.C.

CONVERSE, PHILIP E. 1972. "Change in the American Electorate." In Angus Campbell and Philip E. Converse, eds., *The Human Meaning of Social Change.* New York: Russell Sage Foundation.

————. 1974. "Comment on Burnham's 'Theory and Voting Research.' " *American Political Science Review* 68, 3 (September).

————. 1976. *The Dynamics of Party Support.* Beverly Hills, Calif.: Sage Publications.

CROTTY, WILLIAM J. 1977. *Political Reform and the American Experiment.* New York: Thomas Y. Crowell.

CROZIER, MICHAEL, SAMUEL P. HUNTINGTON, and JOJI WATANUKI. 1975. *The Crisis of Democracy: Report on the Ungovernability of Democracies to the Trilateral Commission.* New York: New York University Press.

CUNNINGHAM, N. 1957. *The Jeffersonian Republicans: The Formation of Party Organization, 1789–1801.* Chapel Hill: University of North Carolina Press.

DAHL, ROBERT. 1961. *Who Governs?* New Haven, Conn.: Yale University Press.

DALTON, RUSSELL J., SCOTT C. FLANAGAN, and PAUL ALLEN BECK, eds. 1984. *Electoral Change in Advanced Industrial Democracies: Realignment or Dealignment?* Princeton, N.J.: Princeton University Press.

DAVIDSON, CHANDLER, ed. 1984. *Minority Vote Dilution.* Washington, D.C.: Joint Center for Political Studies.

DAVIS, MIKE. 1980. "Why the U.S. Working Class Is Different." *New Left Review* 123 (September/October).

————. 1986. *Prisoners of the American Dream: Politics and Economy in the History of the United States Working Class.* New York: New Left Books.

DAWLEY, ALAN. 1976. *Class and Community: The Industrial Revolution in Lynn.* Cambridge, Mass.: Harvard University Press.

DiGAETANO, ALAN. 1985. "Urban Political Machines: A Structural Approach." Doctoral dissertation, Boston University.

DOLBEARE, KENNETH M. 1984. *Democracy at Risk: The Politics of Economic Renewal.* Chatham, N.J.: Chatham House Publishers.

DORSETT, LYLE W. 1977. *Franklin D. Roosevelt and the City Bosses.* Port Washington, N.Y.: Kennikat Press.

DOWNS, ANTHONY. 1957. *An Economic Theory of Democracy.* New York: Harper & Brothers.

DREISER, THEODORE. 1956. *An American Tragedy.* New York: Modern Library.

————. 1981 [1917]. *Sister Carrie.* Philadelphia: University of Pennsylvania Press.

DUNNING, W. A. 1901. "The Undoing of Reconstruction." *Atlantic Monthly* 88.

ECKSTEIN, HARRY. 1966. *Division and Cohesion in Democracy: A Study of Norway.* Princeton, N.J.: Princeton University Press.

EDELMAN, MURRAY. 1971. *Politics as Symbolic Action.* New Haven, Conn.: Yale University Press.

EDSALL, THOMAS B. 1984. *The New Politics of Inequality.* New York: W. W. Norton.

EDSALL, THOMAS B., and HAYNES JOHNSON. April 22, 1984. "High-Tech Impersonal Computer Net Is Snaring Prospective Republicans." *Washington Post*, A8.

―――. July 7, 1984. "In Mississippi District, Race and Class Likely to Govern Turnout." *Washington Post.*

EISENSTADT. S. N., and LUIS RONIGER. 1981. "The Study of Patron-Client Relations and Recent Development in Sociological Theory." In S. N. Eisenstadt and René Lemarchand, eds., *Political Clientelism, Patronage and Development.* Beverly Hills, Calif.: Sage Publications.

ENELOW, JAMES M., and MELVIN J. HINICH. 1982. "Ideology, Issues, and the Spatial Theory of Elections." *American Political Science Review* 76, 3 (September).

EPSTEIN, GERALD. 1981. "Domestic Stagflation and Monetary Policy: The Federal Reserve and the Hidden Election." In Thomas Ferguson and Joel Rogers, eds., *The Hidden Election: Politics and Economics in the 1980 Presidential Campaign.* New York: Pantheon Books.

ERIKSON, ROBERT S. 1981. "Why Do People Vote? Because They Are Registered." *American Political Science Review* 75, 2 (July).

ERIKSON, ROBERT S., and KENT L. TEDIN. 1981. "The 1928–1936 Partisan Realignment: The Case for the Conversion Hypothesis." *American Political Science Review* 75, 4 (December).

EULAU, HANS. 1956. "The Politics of Happiness." *Antioch Review* 16.

EVANS, ROWLAND, and ROBERT NOVAK. 1966. *Lyndon B. Johnson: The Exercise of Power.* New York: New American Library.

FALER, PAUL. 1981. *Mechanics and Manufacturers in the Early Industrial Revolution: Lynn, Massachusetts. 1780–1860.* Albany: State University of New York Press.

FERGUSON, THOMAS. 1983. "Party Realignment and American Industrial Structure: The Investment Theory of Political Parties in Historical Perspective." *Research in Political Economy*, vol. 6. Greenwich, Conn.: JAI Press.

————. 1984. "From Normalcy to New Deal: Industrial Structure, Party Competition, and American Public Policy in the Great Depression." *International Organization* 38, 1 (Winter).

FERGUSON, THOMAS, and JOEL ROGERS. 1986. *Right Turn.* New York: Hill & Wang.

FIORINA, MORRIS. 1981. *Retrospective Voting in American Presidential Elections.* New Haven, Conn.: Yale University Press.

FLANIGAN, WILLIAM H., and NANCY H. ZINGALE. 1979. *Political Behavior of the American Electorate.* Boston: Allyn & Bacon.

FORMISANO, RONALD. 1969. "Political Character, Antipartyism and the Second Party System." *American Quarterly* 21, 4 (Winter).

————. 1974. *Political Order in Changing Societies.* New Haven, Conn.: Yale University Press.

FRANKLIN, JOHN HOPE. 1969. *From Slavery to Freedom: A History of Negro Americans.* 3rd ed. New York: Vintage Books.

FREEMAN, RICHARD B. 1986. *Why Are Unions Faring Badly in NLRB Representation Elections?* Cambridge, Mass.: National Bureau of Economic Research.

FRIEDLAND, ROGER. 1983. *Power and Crisis in the City: Corporations, Unions and Urban Policy.* New York: Schocken Books.

FULLER, HELEN. 1962. *Year of Trial.* New York: Harcourt, Brace.

GALAMBOS, LOUIS. 1975. *The Public Image of Big Business in America, 1880–1940.* Baltimore: Johns Hopkins University Press.

GALSTON, WILLIAM. 1985. "The Future of the Democratic Party." *Brookings Review* (Winter).

GIENAPP, WILLIAM E. 1982. " 'Politics Seem to Enter into Everything': Political Culture in the North, 1840–1860." In Stephen E. Maizlish and John J. Kushman, eds. *Essays on Antebellum Politics, 1840–1860.* Arlington: Texas A&M University Press.

GINSBERG, BENJAMIN, and MARTIN SHEFTER. 1985. "Critical Realignment? The New Politics, the Reconstituted Right, and the 1984 Election." In Michael Nelson, ed., *The Elections of 1984.* Washington, D.C.: Congressional Quarterly Press.

GLASS, DAVID, PEVERILL SQUIRE, and RAYMOND WOLFINGER. 1984. "Voter Turnout: An International Comparison." *Public Opinion* 6, 6 (December/January).

GOLD, DAVID. 1977. "The Rise and Decline of the Keynesian Coalition." *Kapitalistate* 6 (Fall).

GOLDFIELD, MICHAEL. 1985. "Labor's Subordination to the New Deal. Part One: The Influence of Labor on New Deal Labor Legislation."

Paper delivered at 1985 meeting of the American Political Science Association, New Orleans.

GOLDSTEIN, ROBERT JUSTIN. 1978. *Political Repression in Modern America from 1870 to the Present.* Boston: G. K. Hall.

GOODMAN, PAUL. 1967. "The First American Party System." In William Nisbet Chambers and Walter Dean Burnham, eds., *The American Party System: Stages of Political Development.* New York: Oxford University Press.

GOODWYN, LAWRENCE. 1976. *Democratic Promise: The Populist Movement in America.* New York: Oxford University Press.

———. 1978. *The Populist Moment: A Short History of the Agrarian Revolt in America.* New York: Oxford University Press.

GOSNELL, HAROLD G. 1927. *Getting Out the Vote.* Chicago: University of Chicago Press.

———. 1930. *Why Europe Votes.* Chicago: University of Chicago Press.

———. 1937. *Machine Politics: Chicago Model.* Chicago: University of Chicago Press.

GREEN, JAMES. 1975. "Fighting on Two Fronts: Working Class Militancy in the 1940s." *Radical America* 9, 4–5.

GREENSTONE, J. DAVID. 1969. *Labor in American Politics.* New York: Vintage Books.

GROB, GERALD N., and GEORGE ATHAN BILLIAS, eds. 1987. *Interpretations of American History.* Vol. 2: *Since 1877.* 5th ed. New York: Free Press.

GURR, TED ROBERT. 1968. "A Causal Model of Civil Strife: A Comparative Analysis Using New Indices." *American Political Science Review* 62 (December).

GUTH, JAMES L. 1983. "Southern Baptist Clergy: Vanguard of the Christian Right?" In Robert C. Liebman and Robert Wuthnow, eds., *The New Christian Right: Mobilization and Legitimation.* New York: Aldine Publishing.

GUTMAN, HERBERT G. 1976. *Work, Culture, and Society in Industrializing America.* New York: Alfred A. Knopf.

HABER, SAMUEL. 1964. *Efficiency and Uplift: Scientific Management in the Progressive Era, 1890–1920.* Chicago: University of Chicago Press.

HAMMOND, PHILLIP E. 1983. "Another Great Awakening." In Robert C. Liebman and Robert Wuthnow, eds., *The New Christian Right: Mobilization and Legitimation.* New York: Aldine Publishing.

HARRIS, JOSEPH P. 1929. *Registration of Voters in the United States.* Washington, D.C.: Brookings Institution.

HARTMANN, SUSMAN. 1971. *Truman and the 80th Congress.* Columbia: University of Missouri Press.

HARTZ, LOUIS. 1955. *The Liberal Tradition in America.* New York: Harcourt, Brace.

HARVARD/ABC NEWS SYMPOSIUM. 1984. *Voting for Democracy.* New York: American Broadcasting Companies, Inc.

HAYDUK, RON. 1986. "Electoral Politics." Political Science Program, Graduate School and University Center of the City University of New York. Mimeo.

HAYS, SAMUEL P. 1958. *Conservation and the Gospel of Efficiency.* Cambridge, Mass.: Harvard University Press.

————. 1964. "The Politics of Reform in Municipal Government in the Progressive Era." *Pacific Northwest Quarterly* 55, 4 (October).

————. 1967. "Political Parties and the Community-Society Continuum." In William Nisbet Chambers and Walter Dean Burnham, eds., *The American Party System: Stages of Political Development.* New York: Oxford University Press.

————. 1981. "Politics and Society: Beyond the Political Party." In Paul Kleppner et al., eds., *The Evolution of American Electoral Systems.* Westport, Conn.: Greenwood Press.

HERBES, JOHN. October 26, 1984. "Drive to Sign Up New Voters Brings Surge to the Polls." *New York Times*, A20.

HIBBS, DOUGLAS A. 1977. "Political Parties and Macroeconomic Policy." *American Political Science Review* 71, 4 (December).

————. 1982. "Economic Outcomes and Political Support for British Governments Among Occupational Classes: A Dynamic Analysis." *American Political Science Review* 76, 2 (June).

HIMMELSTEIN, JEROME L. 1983. "The New Right." In Robert C. Liebman and Robert Wuthnow, eds., *The New Christian Right: Mobilization and Legitimation.* New York: Aldine Publishing.

HOFSTADTER, RICHARD. 1948. *The American Political Tradition.* New York: Random House.

————. 1955. *The Age of Reform: From Bryan to F.D.R.* New York: Alfred A. Knopf.

HUNTINGTON, SAMUEL. 1968. *Political Order in Changing Societies.* New Haven, Conn.: Yale University Press.

————. 1974. "Postindustrial Politics: How Benign Will It Be?" *Comparative Politics* 6, 2 (January).

————. 1975. "Chapter 3—The United States." In Michael Crozier, Samuel P. Huntington, and Joji Watanuki, eds., *The Crisis of Democracy: Report on the Ungovernability of Democracies to the Trilateral Commission.* New York: New York University Press.

―――. 1985. "A New Role for the Democrats: The Visions of the Democratic Party." *Public Interest* 79 (Spring).

JACKMAN, ROBERT W. 1987. "Political Institutions and Voter Turnout in the Industrial Democracies." *American Political Science Review* 81, 2 (June).

JENSEN, RICHARD. 1971. *The Winning of the Midwest: Social and Political Conflict, 1888–1896.* Chicago: University of Chicago Press.

―――. 1981. "The Last Party System: Decay of Consensus, 1932–1980." In Paul Kleppner et al., eds., *The Evolution of American Electoral Systems.* Westport, Conn.: Greenwood Press.

JOHNSON, HAYNES, and THOMAS B. EDSALL. September 30, 1984. "North Carolina Sparks Registration War." *Washington Post*, A16.

JOHNSON, PAUL. 1978. *A Shopkeeper's Millennium.* New York: Hill & Wang.

KARP, WALTER. July 1984. "Playing Politics: Why the Democratic Bosses Conspired with Reagan, and Do Not Care If They Lose in November." *Harper's.*

KATOSH, JOHN P., and MICHAEL W. TRAUGOTT. 1979. "Response Validity in Surveys of Voting Behavior." *Public Opinion Quarterly* 43, 3 (Fall).

―――. 1981. "The Consequences of Validated and Self-Reported Voting Measures." *Public Opinion Quarterly* 45, 4 (Winter).

KATZNELSON, IRA. 1981. *City Trenches: Urban Politics and the Patterning of Class in the United States.* New York: Pantheon Books.

KELLER, MORTON. 1977. *Affairs of State: Public Life in Late Nineteenth Century America.* Cambridge, Mass.: Harvard University Press.

KELLEY, STANLEY, JR., RICHARD AYRES, and WILLIAM C. BOWEN. 1967. "Registration and Voting: Putting First Things First." *American Political Science Review* 61, 2 (June).

KEY, V. O., JR. 1955. "A Theory of Critical Elections," *Journal of Politics* 17, 1 (February).

―――. 1956. *American State Politics: An Introduction.* New York: Alfred A. Knopf.

―――. 1966. *The Responsible Electorate.* Cambridge, Mass.: Harvard University Press.

―――. 1984 [1949]. *Southern Politics in State and Nation.* New ed. New York: Alfred A. Knopf.

KIM, JAE-ON, JOHN R. PETROCIK, and STEPHEN N. ENOKSON.

1975. "Voter Turnout Among the American States: Systemic and Individual Components." *American Political Science Review* 69, 1 (March).

KIRBO, HAROLD R., and RICHARD SHAFFER. 1986. "Elite Recognition of Unemployment as a Working Class Issue, 1890–1940." *Sociology and Social Research* 70, 4 (July).

KLEPPNER, PAUL. 1970. *The Cross of Culture: A Social Analysis of Midwestern Politics, 1850–1900.* New York: Free Press.

———. 1979. *The Third Electoral System. 1853–1892: Parties, Voters, and Political Cultures.* Chapel Hill: University of North Carolina Press.

———. 1981a. "Critical Realignments and Electoral Systems." In Paul Kleppner et al., eds., *The Evolution of American Electoral Systems.* Westport, Conn.: Greenwood Press.

———. 1981b. "Partisanship and Ethnoreligious Conflict: The Third Electoral System, 1853–1892." In Paul Kleppner et al., eds., *The Evolution of American Electoral Systems.* Westport, Conn.: Greenwood Press.

———. 1982. *Who Voted? The Dynamics of Electoral Turnout.* New York: Praeger.

KLEPPNER, PAUL, and STEPHEN C. BAKER. 1980. "The Impact of Voter Registration Requirements on Electoral Turnout, 1900–1916." *Journal of Political and Military Sociology* 8, 2 (Fall).

KOLKO, GABRIEL. 1977. *The Triumph of Conservatism.* New York: Free Press.

KOUSSER, J. MORGAN. 1974. *The Shaping of Southern Politics: Suffrage Restrictions and the Establishment of the One-Party South.* New Haven, Conn.: Yale University Press.

KRIEGER, JOEL. 1986. *Reagan, Thatcher, and the Politics of Decline.* New York: Oxford University Press.

LADD, EVERETT CARLL. 1985. "As the Realignment Turns: A Drama in Many Acts." *Public Opinion* 7, 6 (December/January).

LAZARSFELD, PAUL F., BERNARD BERELSON, and HELEN GAUDET. 1948. *The People's Choice.* New York: Columbia University Press.

LEE, EUGENE C. 1960. *The Politics of Nonpartisanship.* Berkeley: University of California Press.

LEMARCHAND, RENÉ. 1981. "Comparative Political Clientelism: Structure, Process and Optic." In S. N. Eisenstadt and René Lemarchand, eds., *Political Clientelism, Patronage, and Development.* Beverly Hills, Calif.: Sage Publications.

LENS, SIDNEY. 1959. *Crisis in American Labor.* New York: Sagamore Press.

LEUCHTENBERG, WILLIAM E. 1963. *Franklin D. Roosevelt and the New Deal, 1932–1940.* New York: Harper & Row.

LEVIN, MURRAY. 1971. *Political Hysteria in America.* New York: Basic Books.

LICHTMAN, ALLAN J. 1979. *Prejudice and the Old Politics: The Presidential Election of 1982.* Chapel Hill: University of North Carolina Press.

————. 1987. *Analysis of Racial Distinctions in Voter Registration Rates: State of Mississippi.* Report prepared for the Lawyers Committee for Civil Rights Under Law, in the matter of *Mississippi State Chapter Operation Push et al.* vs. *William Allain, Governor of Mississippi, et al.*, Washington, D.C.

LIEBMAN, ROBERT C. 1983a. "Mobilizing the Moral Majority," In Robert C. Liebman and Robert Wuthnow, eds., *The New Christian Right: Mobilization and Legitimation.* New York: Aldine Publishing.

————. 1983b. "The Making of the New Christian Right." In Robert C. Liebman and Robert Wuthnow, eds., *The New Christian Right: Mobilization and Legitimation.* New York: Aldine Publishing.

LINEBERRY, ROBERT L., and EDMUND P. FOWLER. 1967. "Reformism and Public Policies in America." *American Political Science Review* 61, 3 (September).

LIPSET, SEYMOUR MARTIN. 1960. *Political Man: The Social Bases of Politics.* Garden City, N.Y.: Doubleday & Co.

————. 1985. "The Elections, the Economy, and Public Opinion: 1984." *PS: The Journal of the American Political Science Association* 18, 1 (Winter).

————. 1986. "Beyond 1984: The Anomalies of American Politics." *PS: The Journal of the American Political Science Association* 19, 2 (Spring).

LIPSET, SEYMOUR MARTIN, and EARL RAAB. 1981. "The Election and the Evangelicals." *Commentary* 71 (March).

LIVINGSTON, DEBRA. April 1985. "Survey of 1984 Registrants." Churches' Committee for Voter Registration/Education, Washington, D.C.

LOWI, THEODORE. 1968. "Foreword." In Harold Gosnell, *Machine Politics: Chicago Model.* Chicago: University of Chicago Press.

MANN, ARTHUR F. 1965. *LaGuardia Comes to Power, 1933.* Philadelphia: Lippincott.

MARABLE, MANNING. 1986. *Black American Politics: From the March on Washington to Jesse Jackson.* New York: Verso/Schocken.

MARKUS, GREGORY B. 1982. "Political Attitudes During an Election Year: A Report on the 1980 NES Study." *American Political Science Review* 76, 3 (September).

MARTIN, JOHN B. 1976. *Adlai Stevenson of Illinois*. Garden City, N.Y.: Doubleday & Co.

MCCORMICK, RICHARD P. 1953. *The History of Voting in New Jersey: A Study of the Development of Election Machinery, 1664–1911*. New Brunswick, N.J.: Rutgers University Press.

———. 1960. "New Perspectives on Jacksonian Politics." *American Historical Review* 65, 2 (January).

———. 1967. "Political Development and the Second Party System." In William Nisbet Chambers and Walter Dean Burnham, eds., *The American Party System: Stages of Political Development*. New York: Oxford University Press.

———. 1979. "The Party Period and Public Policy: An Exploratory Hypothesis." *Journal of American History* 66, 2 (September).

———. 1981. *From Realignment to Reform: Political Change in New York State, 1893–1910*. Ithaca, N.Y.: Cornell University Press.

MCDONALD, ARCHIE P. Undated. *The Texas Experience*. Published for the Texas Committee for the Humanities. College Station: Texas A&M University Press.

MCGERR, MICHAEL E. 1986. *The Decline of Popular Politics: The American North, 1965–1928*. New York: Oxford University Press.

MCLOUGHLIN, WILLIAM G. 1978. *Revivals. Awakenings and Reform*. Chicago: University of Chicago Press.

MENENDEZ, ALBERT J. 1977. *Religion at the Polls*. Philadelphia: Westminster.

MERRIAM, CHARLES E., and HAROLD G. GOSNELL. 1924. *Non-Voting: Causes and Methods of Control*. Chicago: University of Chicago Press.

MILLER, ARTHUR H., and WARREN E. MILLER. 1977. "Partisanship and Performance: 'Rational' Choice in the 1976 Presidential Elections." Paper presented at the APSA meeting in Washington, D.C.

MILLER, ARTHUR H., and MARTIN P. WATTENBERG. 1985. "Throwing the Rascals Out and Performance Evaluations of Presidential Candidates, 1952–1980." *American Political Science Review* 79 (June).

MILLER, WARREN E. August 1963. "Assessment of the Significance of State Laws Governing Citizen Participation in Elections." Survey Research Center, University of Michigan, Ann Arbor.

———. March 1987. "Party Identification Re-Examined: The Reagan Era." In *Where's the Party? An Assessment of Changes in Party Loyalty and Party Coalitions in the 1980s.* Report no. 21. Washington, D.C.: Center for National Policy.

MILLER, ZANE L. 1968. *Boss Cox's Cincinnati.* New York: Oxford University Press.

MILLIS, HARRY A., and E. C. BROWN. 1950. *From the Wagner Act to Taft-Hartley.* Chicago: University of Chicago Press.

MOLLENKOPF, JOHN. 1975. "The Post-War Politics of Urban Development." *Politics and Society* 5, 3.

———. 1983. *Contested Cities.* Princeton, N.J.: Princeton University Press.

MONTGOMERY, DAVID. 1979. *Workers' Control in America.* New York: Cambridge University Press.

———. 1980. "Strikes in Nineteenth Century America," *Social Science History* 4, 4 (Fall).

———. 1981. *Beyond Equality: Labor and the Radical Republicans, 1862–1872.* Urbana: University of Illinois Press.

MOON, HENRY LEE. 1957. "The Negro Vote in the Presidential Election of 1956." *Journal of Negro Education* 26 (Summer).

MOREHOUSE, WARD, and DAVID DEMBO. 1986. *The Underbelly of the U.S. Economy: Joblessness and Pauperization of Working America.* Special Report no. 6. New York: Council on International and Public Affairs.

MOSER, TED. 1980. April 16, 1980. "If Jesus Were a Congressman." *Christian Century* 97.

MOUZELIS, NICOS. 1985. "On the concept of Populism: Populist and Clientelist Modes of Incorporation in Semiperipheral Politics." *Politics and Society* 14, 3.

MYERS, GUSTAVUS. 1971. *The History of Tammany Hall.* New York: Dover Press.

NATIONAL ASSOCIATION OF SECRETARIES OF STATE. Undated. "The National Voter Education Project, 1984." Mimeo.

NAVARRO, VICENTE. 1985. "The 1980 and 1984 U.S. Elections and the New Deal: An Alternative Interpretation." *International Journal of Health Services* 15, 3 (Fall).

NEW YORK INTERFACE DEVELOPMENT PROJECT. July 10, 1985. *Expanding Voter Participation: An Assessment of the 1984 Non-Partisan Voter Registration Efforts.* New York.

NIE, NORMAN H., and KRISTI ANDERSEN. 1974. "Mass Belief Systems Revisited: Political Change and Attitude Structure." *Journal of Politics* 36, 3 (August).

NIE, NORMAN H., SIDNEY VERBA, and JOHN H. PETROCIK. 1976. *The Changing American Voter.* Cambridge: Harvard University Press.

NORPOTH, HELMUT, and JERROLD RUSK. 1982. "Partisan Dealignment in the American Electorate." *American Political Science Review* 76, 3 (September).

ORREN, GARY R. 1985. "Political Participation and Public Policy: The Case for Institutional Reform." Forthcoming in Alexander Heard and Michael Nelson, eds., *New Perspectives on Presidential Selection.*

OSBORNE, DAVID. February 25, 1985. "Registration Boomerang." *New Republic.*

OSTROGORSKI, M. 1964. *Democracy and the Organization of Political Parties.* 2 vols. Garden City, N.Y.: Doubleday/Anchor Books.

PALMER, JOHN L., and ISABEL V. SAWHILL, eds. 1982. *The Reagan Experiment.* Washington, D.C.: Urban Institute Press.

PELLING, HENRY. 1962. *American Labor.* Chicago: University of Chicago Press.

PENDLETON, WILLIAM C. 1927. *Political History of Appalachian Virginia.* Dayton, Va.: Shenandoah Press.

PETROCIK, JOHN R. 1987a. "Voter Turnout and Electoral Preference: The Anomalous Reagan Elections." In Kay Scholzman, ed., *Elections in America.* London: Allen & Unwin.

————. 1987b. "Realignment: The South, New Party Coalitions and the Elections of 1984 and 1986." In *Where's the Party? An Assessment of Changes in Party Loyalty and Party Coalitions in the 1980s.* Report no. 21. Washington, D.C.: Center for National Policy.

PHILLIPS, KEVIN P. 1969. *The Emerging Republican Majority.* New Rochelle, N.Y.: Arlington House.

————. 1983. *Post-Conservative America: People, Politics, and Ideology in a Time of Crisis.* New York: Random House.

PHILLIPS, KEVIN P., and PAUL H. BLACKMAN. 1975. *Electoral Reform and Voter Participation.* Stanford, Calif.: American Enterprise Institute and the Hoover Institution on War, Revolution, and Peace.

PIVEN, FRANCES FOX. 1974a. "The Urban Crisis: Who Got What, and Why?" In Richard A. Cloward and Frances Fox Piven. *The Politics of Turmoil: Essays on Poverty, Race, and the Urban Crisis.* New York: Pantheon Books.

————. 1974b. "The Great Society as Political Strategy." In Richard A. Cloward and Frances Fox Piven, *The Politics of Turmoil: Essays on Poverty, Race, and the Urban Crisis.* New York: Pantheon Books.

————. 1974c. "The New Urban Programs: The Strategy of Federal Intervention." In Richard A. Cloward and Frances Fox Piven, *The*

Politics of Turmoil: Essays on Poverty, Race, and the Urban Crisis. New York: Pantheon Books.

———. 1984. "Federal Policy and Urban Fiscal Strain." *Yale Law and Policy Review* 2, 2 (Spring).

PIVEN, FRANCES FOX, and RICHARD A. CLOWARD. 1977. *Poor People's Movements: Why They Succeed, How They Fail.* New York: Vintage Books.

———. 1985. *The New Class War: Reagan's Attack on the Welfare State and Its Consequences.* Rev. and exp. ed. New York: Vintage Books.

POLAKOFF, KEITH J. 1981. *Political Parties in American History.* New York: Alfred A. Knopf.

POMPER, GERALD. 1975. *Voter's Choice.* New York: Dodd, Mead.

———. 1977. "The Decline of the Party in American Elections." *Political Science Quarterly* 92, 1 (Spring).

POWELL, G. BINGHAM, JR. 1982. *Contemporary Democracies: Participation, Stability and Violence.* Cambridge: Harvard University Press.

———. 1986. "Voter Turnout in Comparative Perspective." *American Political Science Review* 80, 1 (March).

PROTHRO, JAMES W., and CHARLES M. GRIGG. 1960. "Fundamental Principles of Democracy: Bases of Agreement and Disagreement." *Journal of Politics* 22, 2 (May).

PRZEWORSKI, ADAM. 1975. "Institutionalization of Voting Patterns, or Is Mobilization the Source of Decay?" *American Political Science Review* 69, 1 (March).

———. 1977. "Proletariat into a Class: The Process of Class Formation from Karl Kautsky's *The Class Struggle* to Recent Controversies." *Politics and Society* 7, 4.

———. 1985. *Capitalism and Social Democracy.* New York: Cambridge University Press.

PRZEWORSKI, ADAM, and JOHN SPRAGUE. 1988. *Paper Stones: A History of Electoral Socialism.* Chicago: University of Chicago Press.

RANNEY, AUSTIN. 1983. "Nonvoting Is Not a Social Disease." *Public Opinion* 6, 5 (October/November).

RANNEY, AUSTIN, and W. KENDALL. 1956. *Democracy and the American Party System.* New York: Harcourt, Brace.

RAYBECK, JOSEPH G. 1966. *A History of American Labor.* New York: Free Press.

REYNOLDS, GEORGE M. 1936. *Machine Politics in New Orleans, 1897–1926.* New York: Columbia University Press.

RIKER, WILLIAM H. 1965. *Democracy in the United States.* 2nd ed. New York: Macmillan Co.

RIKER, WILLIAM H., and P. C. ORDESHOOK. 1968. "A Theory of the Calculus of Voting." *American Political Science Review* 62, 1 (March).

RIORDAN, WILLIAM L. 1963. *Plunkett of Tammany Hall.* New York: E. P. Dutton.

ROGIN, MICHAEL PAUL. 1967. *Intellectuals and McCarthy: The Radical Specter.* Cambridge: Massachusetts Institute of Technology Press.

ROSENSTONE, STEVEN J., ROY L. BEHR, and EDWARD H. LAZARUS. 1984. *Third Parties in America: Citizen Response to Major Party Failures.* Princeton, N.J.: Princeton University Press.

RUSK, JERROLD G. 1970. "Effect of the Australian Ballot Reform on Split-Ticket Voting, 1896–1908." *American Political Science Review* 64, 4 (December).

————. 1974. "Comment: The American Electoral Universe: Speculation and Evidence." *American Political Science Review* 68, 3 (September).

RUSK, JERROLD G., and JOHN J. STUCKER. 1978. "The Effect of the Southern System of Election Laws on Voter Participation: A Reply to V. O. Key." In Joel H. Silbey, Allan G. Bogue, and William H. Flanigan, eds., *The History of American Electoral Behavior.* Princeton, N.J.: Princeton University Press.

————. 1981. "Legal-Institutional Factors in American Voting." In Walter Dean Burnham, Jerome M. Clubb, and William Flanigan, eds., *A Behavioral Guide to the Study of American History.* Beverly Hills, Calif.: Sage Publications.

SALAMON, LESTER M., and MICHAEL S. LUND. 1984. *The Reagan Presidency and the Governing of America.* Washington, D.C.: Urban Institute Press.

SALMANS, SANDRA. July 6, 1984. "Democrats Press to Sign Up Women." *New York Times*, A49.

SALMORE, STEPHEN A., and BARBARA G. SALMORE. 1985. *Candidates, Parties, and Campaigns: Electoral Politics in America.* Washington, D.C.: Congressional Quarterly Press.

SAWYER, KATHY, and ROBERT KAISER. June 26, 1981. "Evangelicals Flock to GOP Standards." *Washington Post*, A1.

SCHAFFER, STEPHEN D. 1981. "A Multivariate Explanation of Decreasing Turnout in Presidential Elections, 1960–1976." *American Journal of Political Science* 25, 1 (February).

SCHATTSCHNEIDER, E. E. 1960. *The Semisovereign People.* New York: Holt, Rinehart & Winston.

SCHLESINGER, ARTHUR M., JR. 1957. *The Age of Roosevelt.* Vol. 1: *The Crisis of the Old Order, 1919–1933.* Boston: Houghton Mifflin Co.

————. 1960. *The Age of Roosevelt*. Vol 3: *The Politics of Upheaval, 1935–1936*. Boston: Houghton Mifflin Co.

SCHLESINGER, ARTHUR M., SR., and ERIK McKINLEY ERIKSSON. October 15, 1924. "The Vanishing Voter." *New Republic*.

SCHNEIDER, WILLIAM. January 1987. "The New Shape of American Politics." *Atlantic Monthly*.

SCOTT, JAMES C. 1969. "Corruption, Machine Politics and Political Change." *American Political Science Review* 63 (December).

SHEFTER, MARTIN. 1977. "New York City's Fiscal Crisis: The Politics of Inflation and Retrenchment." *Public Interest* 48 (Summer).

————. 1978a. "Party, Bureaucracy, and Political Change in the United States." In Louis Maisel and Joseph Cooper, eds., *Political Parties: Development and Decay*. Sage Electoral Studies Year Book, vol. 4. Beverly Hills, Calif.: Sage Publications.

————. 1978b. "The Electoral Foundations of the Political Machine: New York City, 1884–1897." In Joel H. Silbey et al., eds., *The History of American Electoral Behavior*. Princeton, N.J.: Princeton University Press.

————. 1983. "Regional Receptivity to Reform." *Political Science Quarterly* 98, 3 (Fall).

————. 1984. "Political Parties, Political Mobilization, and Political Demobilization." In Thomas Ferguson and Joel Rogers, eds., *The Political Economy*. Armonk, N.Y.: M. E. Sharpe.

————. 1986. "Trade Unions and Political Machines: The Organization and Disorganization of the American Working Class in the Late Nineteenth Century." In Ira Katznelson and Aristede Zolberg, eds., *Working Class Formation: Nineteenth Century Patterns in Western Europe and the United States*. Princeton, N.J.: Princeton University Press.

SHIENBAUM, KIM EZRA. 1984. *Beyond the Electoral Connection: A Reassessment of the Role of Voting in Contemporary American Politics*. Philadelphia: University of Pennsylvania Press.

SHINGLES, RICHARD D. 1981. "Black Consciousness and Political Participation: The Missing Link." *American Political Science Review* 75, 1 (March).

SHORTRIDGE, RAY M. 1981. "Estimating Voter Participation." In Jerome M. Clubb, William H. Flanigan, and Nancy H. Zingale, eds., *Analyzing Electoral History: A Guide to the Study of American Voter Behavior*. Beverly Hills, Calif.: Sage Publications.

SHUPE, ANSON, and WILLIAM STACEY. 1983. "The Moral Majority Constituency." In Robert C. Liebman and Robert Wuthnow, eds., *The*

New Christian Right: Mobilization and Legitimation. New York: Aldine Publishing.

SIMPSON, JOHN H. 1983. "Moral Issues and Status Politics." In Robert C. Liebman and Robert Wuthnow, eds., *The New Christian Right: Mobilization and Legitimation.* New York: Aldine Publishing.

SINCLAIR, UPTON. 1951 [1906]. *The Jungle.* New York: Harper & Row.

SITKOFF, HARVEY. 1974. "Years of the Locust." In Richard S. Kirkendall, ed., *The Truman Period as a Research Field: A Reappraisal, 1972.* Columbia: University of Missouri Press.

SKOWRONEK, STEPHEN. 1982. *Building a New American State: The Expansion of Administrative Capacities, 1877–1920.* New York: Cambridge University Press.

SMITH, DAVID MICHAEL. 1985. "Voter Registration on the Right: The Republican and Fundamentalist Christian Campaigns of 1984." Department of Political Science, Graduate School and University Center, City University of New York. Mimeo

SQUIRE, PEVERILL, DAVID P. GLASS, and RAYMOND E. WOLFINGER. 1984. "Residential Mobility and Voter Turnout." Paper presented at a conference, "Where Have All the Voters Gone?," University of Chicago, April 26–28.

SQUIRE, PEVERILL, RAYMOND E. WOLFINGER, and DAVID P. GLASS. 1987. "Residential Mobility and Voter Turnout." *American Political Science Review* 81, 1 (March).

STEFFEN, CHARLES. 1984. *The Mechanics of Baltimore: Workers and Politics in the Age of Revolution, 1703–1812.* Urbana: University of Illinois Press.

STEFFENS, LINCOLN. 1951 [1906]. *The Shame of the Cities.* New York: Harper & Row.

STONE, ALAN. 1981. "State and Market: Economic Regulation and the Great Productivity Debate." In Thomas Ferguson and Joel Rogers, eds., *The Hidden Election: Politics and Economics in the 1980 Presidential Campaign.* New York: Pantheon Books.

SUNDQUIST, JAMES L. 1973. *Dynamics of the Party System: Alignment and Realignment of Political Parties in the United States.* Washington, D.C.: Brookings Institution.

———. 1985. "The 1984 Election: How Much Realignment?" *Brookings Review* 3, 2 (Winter).

TAFT, PHILIP, and PHILIP ROSS. 1969. In Hugh Davis Graham and Ted Robert Gurr, eds., *The History of Violence in America: A Report to the National Commission on the Causes and Prevention of Violence.* New York: Praeger.

THOMPSON, E. P. 1963. *The Making of the English Working Class.* New York: Vintage Books.

TILLY, CHARLES, LOUISE TILLY, and RICHARD TILLY. 1977. *The Rebellious Century.* Cambridge, Mass.: Harvard University Press.

TINDALL, GEORGE BROWN. 1972. *The Disruption of the Solid South.* Athens: University of Georgia Press.

TOCQUEVILLE, ALEXIS DE 1969 [1831]. *Democracy in America.* New York: Macmillan Co.

TUFTE, EDWARD R. 1978. *Political Control of the Economy.* Princeton, N.J.: Princeton University Press.

U.S. BUREAU OF THE CENSUS. 1980. *Projections of Voting Age for States, November 1980.* Current Population Reports, Series P-25, no. 870.

VAUGHAN, PHILIP H. 1972. "President Truman's Committee on Civil Rights: The Urban Implications." *Missouri Historical Review* 66 (April).

VERBA, SIDNEY, and NORMAN H. NIE. 1972. *Participation in America.* New York: Harper & Row.

VERBA, SIDNEY, NORMAN H. NIE, and JAE-ON KIM. 1978. *Participation and Political Equality: A Seven-Nation Comparison.* New York: Cambridge University Press.

VOGEL, DAVID. 1983. "The Power of Business in America: A Reappraisal." *British Journal of Political Science* 13.

Voter Education Project News, vol. 3, no. 11, November 1969. Southern Regional Council, Atlanta, Georgia.

WALSH, J. RAYMOND. 1937. *CIO: Industrial Unionism in Action.* New York: W. W. Norton.

WEIBE, ROBERT H. 1967. *The Search for Order.* New York: Hill & Wang.

WEINSTEIN, JAMES. 1968. *The Corporate Ideal in the Liberal State: 1900–1918.* Boston: Beacon Press.

———. 1969. *The Decline of Socialism in America, 1912–1925.* New York: Vintage Books.

WHITE, CLAUDE R., and MARY K. WHITE. 1937. *Relief Policies in the Depression.* Social Science Research Council, Bulletin no. 38. New York.

WILENTZ, SEAN. 1982. "On Class and Politics in Jacksonian America." *Reviews in American History.* (December).

————. 1984. *Chants Democratic: New York City and the Rise of the Working Class, 1777–1850.* New York: Oxford University Press.

WILL, GEORGE F. October 10, 1983. "In Defense of Nonvoting." *Newsweek*, p. 96.

WILLIAMS, CYNTHIA A. June 1987. *Litigation Contesting Barriers to Minority and Low-Income Voter Registration.* A publication of the Human SERVE Campaign, 622 W. 113 Street, New York, New York 10025.

WILLIAMSON, CHILTON. 1960. *American Suffrage: From Property to Democracy, 1760–1860.* Princeton, N.J.: Princeton University Press.

WOLFE, ALAN. 1981. *America's Impasses: The Rise and Fall of the Politics of Growth.* New York: Pantheon Books.

WOLFINGER, RAYMOND E., and STEVEN J. ROSENSTONE. 1978. "The Effect of Registration Laws on Voter Turnout." *American Political Science Review* 72, 1 (March).

————. 1980. *Who Votes?* New Haven, Conn.: Yale University Press.

WOODWARD, C. VANN. 1951. *Origins of the New South: 1877–1913.* Baton Rouge: Louisiana State University Press.

————. 1968. *Burden of Southern History.* Enlarged ed. Baton Rouge: University of Louisiana Press.

WRIGHT, GAVIN. 1986. *Old South, New South: Revolutions in the Southern Economy Since the Civil War.* New York: Basic Books.

YARNELL, ELLEN. 1974. *Democrats and Progressives: The 1948 Election as a Test of Postwar Liberalism.* Berkeley: University of California Press.

ZINN, HOWARD. 1980. *A People's History of the United States.* New York: Harper & Row.

Index

Abramson, Paul R., 113*n*, 150*t*
ACORN, 187, 193
Adler, Norman, 227*n*
advertising, campaign, 52
AF of L, 60, 61
AF of L-CIO, 168
Aldrich, John H., 113, 150*t*
Alford, Robert R., 31*n*, 73*n*
aliens, deportation of, 61
alien-with-intent laws, 87
Allen, Howard W., 100*n*
Allen, Kay Warren, 100*n*
Almond, Gabriel, 13*n*, 113
Amalgamated Clothing Workers, 168
American Coalition for Traditional Values, 186, 191
American Enterprise Institute, 10–11
American Political Science Review, 99*n*
American Voter, The (Campbell, Converse, Miller, and Stokes), 98
Anaya, Toney, 227, 229
Andersen, Kristi, 135*n*, 151*n*
Anti-Monopoly party, 46
antipoverty programs, 174–77
apathy, 119
Argersinger, Peter H., 70*n*, 100
Asbury, Herbert, 32*n*

Australian ballots, 73–74
Austria, economic policy in, 249–50
Ayres, Richard, 98, 101

Badillo, Herman, 227*n*
Baker, Stephen C., 55, 101, 118*n*
ballots, 73–74, 81
Banfield, Edward, 38*n*, 73–74
Baptists, 184
Bartley, Neuman V., 142
Baxter, Elaine, 238
Bean, Walter, 38*n*
Beck, Lewis, 22*n*
Becker, Carl L., 29*n*
Bell, Daniel, 14*n*
Bellmon, Henry, 236–37
Bendix, Reinhard, xiii
Bensel, Richard Franklin, 33, 34*n*, 37*n*, 75*n*, 79–80, 137–38, 145
Benson, Lee, 32*n*, 39*n*
Berelson, Bernard, 113–14, 115
Berman, William, 141*n*
Bernstein, Irving, 126*n*, 129*n*, 133*n*, 141*n*
Blackman, Paul H., 16*n*, 82, 84, 88, 116*n*, 212
blacks: disenfranchisement of, 78–85; registration drives for, 181, 182, 193–94, 203; southern mobilization of, 144–48; turnout

blacks (*cont.*)
  levels of, 161–63; in urban
    North, 141, 152–53, 170,
    172–74
Block, Fred, 157n
Bluestone, Barry, 252
boards of elections, 195–200
Bourbons, 79–80
Bowen, William C., 98, 102
Bowles, Samuel, 156n
Boyd, Richard W., 161
Bradley, Tom, 240
Branstad, Terry, 239
Brecher, Jeremy, 43, 44
Bretton Woods agreement (1944),
  156n
Bridges, Amy, 32n, 33, 35n, 39,
  72n, 74
Brittan, Samuel, 4n, 14n
Brown, Courtney, 14n
Brown, E.C., 166n
Brown, Sherrod, 227n
Bryan, Richard H., 245n
Bryan, William Jennings, 47, 48–
  49, 51, 53, 82
Bryce, James, 38n
Buckley, Peter G., 32n
bureaucratic politics, urban, 170–71
Burnham, Walter Dean, 11n, 16n,
  22, 30t, 34, 35n, 40, 43n, 45,
  53, 54t, 55n, 66–69, 76–78, 85,
  93n, 94, 97, 99–100, 102–4,
  109, 112, 117–19, 125t, 135n,
  161t, 163, 173n, 270n
Burns, James MacGregor, 29n, 61n
business interests: both parties
  dominated by, 125–26; electoral
  reforms backed by, 71–72;
  machine politics and, 72–75; New
  Deal policies and, 166–67;
  political mobilization by, 10–11,
  158–59; popular hostility to, 51;
  Progressive era and, 58–60;
  registration reforms and, 213–14;
  Republican party allied with, 11,
  51–54, 62–63; social welfare
  programs and, 156, 159, 166
business-labor accord, postwar, 156–
  59

Cain, Bruce E., 189n, 203, 206,
  207n
California Election Code, 242–43
Cameron, Helen, 189
Campbell, Angus, 94n, 98, 113,
  115n, 140n
Campbell, Bruce, 29n
capitalism, industrial, 7–8, 9, 60,
  71–72, 75
Carlson, Richard John, 66n, 88,
  90n, 91, 92, 93, 94n–95n, 120n
Carter, Jimmy, 11–13, 21, 146
Carter Administration: business
  interests and, 158–59; registration
  bill of, 215
Cassatt, A. J., 59
Catholic candidates, 124–25
Cavanaugh, Thomas, 161
Celeste, Richard, 227, 231, 232–33
Census Bureau/Current Population
  Survey (CPS), 162t, 164t, 200–
  201, 204t, 205t, 218n, 220,
  257–59, 264, 268–69, 270n
Cermak, Anton, 132
Chamber of Commerce, U.S., 10
Chambers, William N., 29n, 30n,
  39, 107n, 116–17
Chicago, machine politics in, 110,
  132
Chicago Literary Bureau, 51n
Christian Democratic party, 35n–36n
Christian Right, 123; Republican
  voters mobilized by, 182–86,
  191–92, 206, 208; voter
  registration promoted by, 22, 25
Churches' Voter Registration
  Project, 187, 206, 207
CIO, 132–33, 167, 168
Cisneros, Henry, 240
cities: agency registration in, 239–
  41; federal service programs in,
  174–77; machine politics and,
  73–74; registration restrictions in,
  90–93; voter mobilization in,
  170–77
Citizen Action network, 186–87,
  193, 207
Civil Rights Acts (1957–1964), 211
civil rights movement, xv, xiii;

southern opposition to, 123, 141–
45; in urban North, 152–53;
voter registration in, 182
civil service, 73
Civil War (1861–1865): electoral
realignment and, 29; federal
patronage after, 37; sectional
loyalty and, 34, 53; third-party
system created by, 65
class interests: electoral reforms and,
100–106, 111; machine politics
and, 39–40; political parties and,
9, 254; sectional economic issues
vs., 34. *See also* elite class;
working class
Clayton Act (1914), 59
clergy, voter registration aided by,
182–86, 191
Cleveland, Grover, 80*n*, 125
clientelism, 35–41, 68, 73–74,
108, 109
Clifford, Clark, 141*n*
Cloward, Richard A., xi–xii, xv,
7*n*, 8*n*, 10*n*, 39*n*, 127*n*, 152*n*,
176*n*
Cohen, Joshua, 10*n*, 156*n*, 214
collective bargaining, xv, 7
Commission on Civil Rights, U.S.,
141
Committee for the Study of the
American Electorate, 201*n*, 203*n*,
206, 270–71
Committee on Political Education
(COPE), 168
Community Action Foundation, 226
Conference on Alternative State and
Local Policies, 223
conflict, partisanship reduced by,
152–55
Congress, U.S.: income tax cut by,
62; political parties and, 57;
proposed registration reform bill
in, 245–47; pro-union legislation
by, 59; veterans' pensions granted
by, 37*n*
Congressional Quarterly, 185–86,
190, 252*n*
conservative economic policy, 212–
13

conservative politics, 67–68
Constitution, U.S., 276, 279–84,
289
Converse, Philip E., 35*n*, 55*n*, 64*n*,
98–101, 103–4, 140*n*, 144,
150*n*, 151
Conyers, John, 245*n*
Coolidge, Calvin, 61, 62–63
corruption, 76–77, 100–101
Cranston, Alan, 245
Crotty, William J., 29*n*
Crozier, Michael, 14*n*
Cuomo, Mario, 227, 230, 232–33,
235

Dahl, Robert, 13*n*
D'Amato, Alfonse, 241
Davis, John W., 62
Davis, Mike, 10*n*, 166*n*, 168
Davis, Philip C., 30*n*, 107*n*, 116–
17
Dawley, Alan, 9*n*
"deadwood" registrants, 264–71
Debs, Eugene, 56, 61
Defner, Armand, 275*n*
Delaware, voter registration in, 93
Dembo, David, 157*n*
Democratic National Committee
(DNC), 188, 214, 247*n*
Democratic party: black vote and,
79–80, 141, 144–48; civil rights
movement and, xv, 141–46;
clientelist politics and, 38–39,
109; economic policies of, 75,
156–59; in elections of 1912, 58;
in elections of 1924, 62–63; in
elections of 1984, 21, 22–23, 69,
185–90; ethno-cultural rhetoric
of, 33; farmers' interests and, 45,
48; as minority, 57; Populist
alliance with, 47–49, 51, 52–53;
registration laws and, 104–5,
213–17; in the South, 54, 65–69,
123, 141–48; unions and, xiii,
124, 132–33, 164–70; urban
support for, 90–91, 170–77;
workers' defections from, 148–
60. *See also* parties, political;
partisanship; party competition

Depression, Great, 60, 126–27
depressions, 50, 52–53, 56*n*, 126–27
deputization practices, 193, 197–99, 229
Devine, Donald, 232–34
DiGaetano, Alan, 38*n*
direct primary elections, 75–76
disability agencies, 225
disenfranchisement, 70, 78; by boards of elections, 195–200; in the North, 85–94; of southern blacks, 78–85; of workers, 8–9, 70–71, 77
Dolbeare, Kenneth M., 10*n*
Dolan, Terry, 183*n*
Donnelly, Ignatius, 50
Dorr's Rebellion (1842), 85–86
Dorsett, Lyle W., 132*n*
Downs, Anthony, 111*n*, 114*n*
Dukakis, Michael, 198
Dunning, W. A., 81*n*

Eckstein, Harry, 13*n*
economic issues: conservative policy on, 212–13; Democratic party and, 75, 156–59; electoral volatility and, xiv; government intervention and, 7–8, 248, 249; party politics and, 126–27; presidential politics and, 11–12, 21–22; sectional identification and, 33–34; urban workers and, 52–53; of world markets, 249–50
Economic Opportunity Act (1964), 177
Edelman, Edmund, 243*n*
Edelman, Murray, xiii
Edsall, Thomas B., 10*n*, 11, 154, 158, 160*t*, 165*n*, 189, 190, 192
education levels, 114–15, 118, 119
Eginton, Warren, 277–78
eight-box law, 81
Eisenberg, Arthur, 230*n*
Eisenhower, Dwight D., 149
Eisenstadt, S. N., 36*n*
elections: federal intervention in, 80–81; gubernatorial vs. presidential, 29*n*; of 1896, 27,

47–54, 57, 64–65, 69, 111–12; of 1920, 62; of 1924, 62–63; of 1928, 122, 124–26; of 1930s, 126–27, 129–30, 132–37, 141–42; of 1952–1972, 149–55; of 1980, 11–13, 21; of 1984, 21–22, 69, 185–90, 203–6. *See also* turnout levels
electoral-representative system, expansion of, 28–29
electorates, British vs. U.S., 29
elite class, 27, 154–55; electoral reforms and, 65; political parties dominated by, 60, 63, 110–12, 119–20; Republican corporatism and, 68; southern Democratic mobilization in, 67, 79–80; suffrage limited by, 78, 254–55
Emergency Tariff (1921), 62*n*
employer associations, 43
Enelow, James M., 11*n*
enfranchisement: in France, 4*n*, 29*n*,; in U.S., 26
England: civil service reform in, 4*n*, 73*n*; economic policies of, 250; size of electorate in, 29*n*; unionism in, 169*n*
Enokson, Stephen N., 116*n*
Epstein, Gerald, 10*n*
Erikson, Robert S., 135*n*
Eriksson, Erik McKinley, 114*n*, 115*n*
ethnoreligious identifications, 31–33, 34–35, 77, 122, 124–25
Eulau, Hans, 13*n*
Europe: turnout levels in, 115; welfare states of, 9, 167; working class in, 8, 169*n*, 248–49
evangelicals, 184–85
Evans, John V., 236
Evans, Rowland, 143–44

Fahrenkopf, Frank K., Jr., 263*n*
Faler, Paul, 9*n*
Farmer-Labor party, 56–57
farmers: banking interests and, 42, 59; party alliances of, 42–43, 56, 126*n*; Republican indifference to, 62

Farmers' Alliances, 42–43, 46–47, 50, 67, 82
farmers' movements, 48, 49–50; antimonopoly candidates backed by, 44–45; black-white alliances and, 79; labor interests and, 49–50, 52; railroad expansion and, 41–42
Federal Reserve System, 58, 59
Ferguson, Thomas, 10n, 12n, 67n, 129n, 158n, 166n, 168–69
Fiorina, Morris, 12n
Flanigan, William, 29n
Flynn, Raymond, 198
Force Bill (1890), 80n, 145
Ford, Mike, 188
Fordney-McCumber Tariff (1922), 62n
Formisano, Ronald, 29n, 30n, 36–37
Fowler, Edmund P., 73n
France, enfranchisement in, 4n, 29n
Frank, Barney, 233
Franklin, John Hope, 79n
fraud, voter, 39, 71, 79, 99–100
Freedom Summer campaigns, 194
Friedland, Roger, 172n
Froude, J. A., 4n
Fuller, Helen, 173–74

Galambos, Louis, 51
Galston, William, 153, 165
Gans, Curtis, 270
Gardner, Booth, 237n
Gaudet, Helen, 113–14
General Agreement on Tariffs and Trade (1967), 156n
George, Henry, 46, 108
Georgia, poll taxes in, 80–81
Germany, 14
gerrymandering, 81n
ghettos, 174–77
Gienapp, William E., 28, 30n, 31n, 32, 37, 39n, 117n
Gilman, Ethel, 237n
Ginsberg, Benjamin, 154n, 166n
Ginsburg, Leon, 228n
Gintis, Herbert, 156n

Glass, David, 18n, 179n, 265, 266
Gold, David, 156n
Goldberg, Joseph, 227n
Golden Era of democracy, 28–35
Goldfield, Michael, 129n
gold standard, 48–49
Gold Standard Act (1900), 41
Goldstein, Robert J., 61n
Goldwater, Barry, 143
Gompers, Samuel, 61
Goodwyn, Lawrence, 34n, 37, 46, 48, 50, 52n, 53n
Gordon, David M., 156n
Gosnell, Harold G., 38n, 74, 90n, 132n
Gotbaum, Victor, 227n
governors, registration reform backed by, 227–34
Graeve, Sheryl, 238n
grandfather clauses, 83
Grange movement, 42
Great Society programs, 124, 153, 155, 174–77
Green, James, 167n
Greenback-Labor party, 45, 46, 49–50
Greenstone, J. David, 133n
Grigg, Charles M., 14n
Growe, Jean, 238
gubernatorial elections, 29n, 57
Guinier, Lani, 200
Gurr, Ted Robert, xiii
Guth, James L., 184n
Gutman, Herbert G., 43

Haber, Samuel, 72n
Halvorson, Rod, 238n
Hammond, Phillip E., 184n
Handlin, Oscar, 28
Hanna, Mark, 52, 59
Harding, Warren G., 62
Harris, Joseph, 81, 88–90, 91n, 92, 93, 105n, 106n, 109, 110
Harrison, Benjamin, 145
Harrison, Bennett, 252
Hart Research Associates, 202–3, 206, 207, 261
Hartmann, Susman, 167n
Hartz, Louis, 16n

Harvard/ABC News Symposium, 5*t*, 19*t*, 115*n*, 215, 246*n*, 263*n*
Hayduk, Ron, 88*n*
Haymarket bombing, 44
Hays, Samuel P., 28, 32*n*, 72*n*, 119*n*
Helms, Jesse, 191
Herbes, John, 191, 192
Heritage Foundation, 10–11
Hibbs, Douglas A., 12*n*
Hillquit, Morris, 57*n*
Himmelstein, Jerome L., 252*n*
Hinich, Melvin J., 11*n*
Hispanics: registration of, 181, 182, 187, 191, 203; urban politics and, 170, 172. *See also* minorities
Hofstadter, Richard, 46, 59
Home Owners' Loan Corporation, 130
Hoover, Herbert, 122, 124, 126, 127, 133–34
hospitals, voter registration in, 225
Human SERVE, 209–10, 220, 243, 245; executive orders sought by, 197, 227–29, 239; legislation efforts of, 238–39, 246; nonprofit agencies and, 222–27; reforms urged by, 193, 209–10; registration drives by, 187, 194; surveys by, 235
Hunt, James, 191
Huntington, Samuel, 13*n*, 14*n*, 36*n*, 154

immigrants: machine politics and, 39, 106, 108; suffrage reforms and, 78, 85, 86–87
income taxes, 62
"In Defense of Nonvoting" (Will), 14
Independent party, 44
individualism, 15–16
industrialization, 35–36, 43
Industrial Workers of the World (IWW), 56, 61
Intergovernmental Personnel Act (1970), 232, 233
Israel, machine politics in, 36*n*

issue politics, 110–11, 151–52
Italy, 35*n*–36*n*, 118, 169*n*

Jackman, Robert W., 5*t*, 13*n*, 15*n*, 21*n*
Jackson, Jesse, 230*n*
James, Hulbert, 200
Jarmin, Gary, 186
Jensen, Richard, 53*n*, 98*n*, 125*n*, 131–32, 134, 140, 149, 151
Johnson, Haynes, 33*n*, 189, 190, 192
Johnson, Lyndon B., 124, 143–44, 174
Juvenile Delinquency and Youth Control Act (1962), 176

Kaiser, Robert, 184
Karp, Walter, 155*n*
Katznelson, Ira, 38*n*
Keller, Morton, 37*n*
Kelley, Stanley, Jr., 11*n*, 69*n*, 90*n*, 98, 102, 159*n*
Kendall, W., 77*n*
Kennedy, John F., 124, 143, 173–74
Kest, Steve, 197
Key, V. O., Jr., 3, 12*n*, 36*n*, 76, 79*n*, 124*n*
Kilpatrick, James, 187–88
Kim, Jae-On, 116*n*, 118
Kleppner, Paul, 20*n*, 32*n*, 45*n*, 55–56, 66*n*, 68, 69, 77, 84*t*, 87, 92, 94, 95*n*, 98, 99, 100, 101–3, 107*n*, 111, 116*n*, 117, 118*n*, 120*n*, 125*n*, 126–27, 130, 133, 134*n*, 136, 144, 154*n*, 161, 217
Knights of Labor, 46, 50
Knox, Philander C., 59
Koch, Edward, 226–27, 240–41
Kolko, Gabriel, 60*n*
Kousser, J. Morgan, 48, 79, 80*n*, 81, 82, 84, 98
Krieger, Joel, 10*n*
Ku Klux Klan, 62
Kunin, Madeleine, 236

Labor, U.S. Department of, 231–32

Labor Management Relations (Taft-Hartley) Act (1947), 166–67, 168
labor movement: farmers and, 45, 46, 49–50, 52. *See also* unions; working class
Labor Reform party, 44
Labour party (England), 169*n*
Ladd, Carll Everett, 142, 146
La Follette, Robert, 63
LaGuardia, Fiorello, 132
Laird, Melvin R., 246*n*
laissez-faire doctrine, 7, 60, 63
Landon, Alf, 134
Lawyers' Committee for Civil Rights Under Law, 242
Laxalt, Paul, 191
Lazarsfeld, Paul F., 113–14, 115
Lee, Eugene C., 73*n*
Lens, Sidney, 168*n*
Leuchtenberg, William E., 130*n*
Levin, Murray, 62*n*
Levitan, Sar, 159*n*
Lichtman, Allan J., 125*n*, 148, 258, 268
Liebman, Robert C., 183*n*, 184
Lineberry, Robert L., 73*n*
Lipset, Seymour Martin, 12*n*, 14, 114*n*, 154*n*, 155*n*, 183*n*, 184, 252*n*
literacy tests, 81, 82, 83, 87–88, 93, 178
Livingstone, Debra, 206
Locke, John, 16*n*
Lowi, Theodore, 170*n*
Lund, Michael S., 10*n*
Luther, William, 238*n*

McAdoo, William Gibbs, 62
McAteer, E. E., 183*n*
McCall, Carl, 227
McCormick, Richard P., 29*n*, 30*n*, 31*n*, 32*n*, 72*n*, 76–77, 78, 91, 105–6
McCue, Ken, 189*n*, 203, 206, 207*n*
McDonald, Archie P., 83
McGerr, Michael E., 31*n*, 51–52, 72*n*, 75*n*, 91
McGovern, George, 154–55

machine politics, 35–40; business interests and, 72–75; New Deal revival of, 123–24, 131–32; registration procedures and, 106–10; urban population shifts and, 170
McKinley, William, 51, 53
McLoughlin, William, 184*n*
McPhee, William, 115
Mann, Arthur F., 131
Marable, Manning, 188
Markus, Gregory B., 11*n*
Marshall Plan, 156*n*
Martin, John B., 167*n*
Maryland, voter registration in, 93, 237–38
Massachusetts: Independent party in, 44; registration system in, 92
mayors, registration reform by, 239–41
Mellon, Andrew, 62
Messinger, Ruth, 227
Mexico, machine politics in, 36*n*
Michigan, agency registration blocked in, 228–29
Midwest Voter Education Project, 187
Miller, Arthur H., 11*n*, 150*n*
Miller, Warren E., 98, 150*n*
Miller, Zane L., 38*n*
Millis, Harry A., 166*n*
minimum wage, 159
Minnesota, agency registration in, 238
minorities: activists allied with, 154–55; Democratic party and, 104; in new working class, 148, 155, 165–66, 252–53; registration reform and, 218–19, 226–27; urban politics and, 171–77. *See also specific minority groups*
Mississippi, registration procedures in, 82, 241–42
Mollenkopf, John, 124*n*, 131*n*, 156*n*, 172*n*
Mondale, Walter F., 146, 188–89, 207
monetary policy, 41, 49, 52–53
Montgomery, David, 9*n*, 43, 56

Moon, Henry Lee, 172–73
Moral Majority, 183, 184–85, 186
Morehouse, Ward, 157*n*
Morgan, J. P., 51, 56*n*, 59
Morris, Horace, 226*n*
Moser, Ted, 184
motor voter programs, 220–22,
    237–39, 245
Mouzelis, Nicos, 38*n*
Moynihan, Daniel, 241
Mugwumps, 72*n*
Munro, Ralph, 237*n*
Myers, Gustavus, 40

NAACP, registration efforts by,
    193–94, 198, 241, 242
National Association of Community
    Health Centers, 226
National Association of Secretaries of
    State, 223, 247*n*
National Civic Federation, 61
National Coalition for Black Voter
    Participation, 182
National Council on Employment
    Policy, 159*n*
National Election Study (NES), 18*n*,
    256–57, 258, 264
National Elections Commission,
    195*n*
National Labor Relations Board,
    166, 167, 168
National Labor Union, 44, 45
National party, 45
National Puerto Rican/Hispanic
    Voter Participation Project, 187
National Youth Administration, 130
naturalization laws, 108
Navarro, Vicente, 12*n*, 154*n*
Newblatt, Stewart, 282–84, 285
New Class War, The (Piven and
    Cloward), 7*n*, 8*n*
New Deal: as big government, 11*n*;
    business interests and, 166–67;
    machine politics revived by, 123–
    24, 131–32; Progressive era and,
    60; protest movements and, 128–
    30, 133; southern labor system
    unchallenged by, 137–40; strike
    movement and, xv; turnout levels

and, 133–37; unions strengthened
    by, 132–33; working-class voters
    mobilized under, 24, 122–24,
    127–28, 135
New Jersey, registration procedures
    in, 91, 105–6, 241
Newman, Sanford, 192, 261*n*
New Politics, 123, 153–55, 182,
    207–8
New Right, 182
New York, N.Y.: agency-based
    registration in, 240–41; business-
    backed reforms in, 74; party
    organization in, 38–39, 132;
    Tammany Hall politics in, 76,
    86, 108, 109, 132
New York (state): franchise
    restrictions in, 87, 92–93;
    registration reform in, 230–31,
    235
Nie, Norman H., 11*n*, 113, 114*n*,
    116, 118, 150*n*, 151*n*
Nixon, Richard M., 151
nonprofit agencies, registration
    reform in, 209, 217–18, 222–27
nonvoting, 15–17, 24; democratic
    benefits of, 13–14; institutional
    vs. social-psychological analysis
    of, 96, 113–21; political-
    behavioral vs. legal-institutional
    views on, 97–112; as tacit
    consent, 13
Norpoth, Helmut, 149, 151
North, suffrage limitations in, 85–
    94
North Dakota Nonpartisan League,
    56–57
Novak, Robert, 143–44

October 4 National Day of Voter
    Registration, 194–95
Office of Personnel Management
    (OPM), 232–34
Ogren, Paul, 238*n*
Ohio, registration in, 231, 235–36
Oklahoma, registration in, 236–37
one-party politics, 67–68, 123, 140,
    148
Operation Dixie, 167

Ordeshook, P. C., 114*n*
Orren, Gary, 13*n*, 115*n*
Ostrogorski, M., 31*n*, 38*n*

Palmer, A. Mitchell, 61–62
Palmer, John L., 10*n*
Parker, Frank R., 242
Parkman, Francis, 91
participation, *see* turnout levels
parties, political: business
  domination of, 125–26; class
  interests and, 9, 254; clientelism
  and, 35–41; Congress and, 57;
  dealignment process and, 149–59;
  elite domination of, 60, 63, 110–
  12, 119–20; government
  decentralization and, 38–39; local
  organizations of, 27, 70;
  oligarchical character of, 67–68;
  procedural weakening of, 70–71;
  registration procedures and, 19–
  23, 104–12; rule changes and,
  101, 103–4, 109–11; in the
  South, 45–46, 54, 65–69. *See
  also specific parties*
partisanship, 77–78, 206–8
party competition: decline of, 65–
  68; procedural changes vs., 96–
  112; turnout levels and, 64–65,
  68–69. *See also specific parties*
patronage, 35–39, 73
Pelling, Henry, 133
Pendleton, William C., 83*n*–84*n*
Pennsylvania, voter registration in,
  89–90, 91, 109
People's Choice, The (Lazarsfeld,
  Berelson, and Gaudet), 113–14
People's party, 47, 50, 58
Perkins, George W., 59
Perpich, Rudy, 238
personal registration, 89–93
Petrocik, John R., 11*n*, 12–13,
  14*n*, 20*n*, 116*n*, 140*n*, 146, 147,
  150*n*, 151*n*, 251*n*
Philadelphia, franchise restrictions
  in, 89–90, 91, 109
Philippines, New Society movement
  in, 36*n*
Phillips, Howard, 183*n*

Phillips, Kevin P., 16*n*, 82, 84, 88,
  116*n*, 211, 212–13, 251–52
Pinkertons, 50
Piven, Frances Fox, xi–xii, xv, 7*n*,
  8*n*, 10*n*, 39*n*, 127*n*, 152*n*, 171*n*,
  175*n*, 176*n*
Polakoff, Keith J., 37, 41*n*, 45, 46,
  51, 57, 62*n*, 73*n*, 125
Political Action Committee (PAC) of
  CIO, 133, 167*n*, 168
poll taxes, 80–81, 82–83
Pomper, Gerald, 149, 150, 152*n*
Poor People's Movements (Piven and
  Cloward), xi–xii, xv
population shifts, urban, 170, 171
Populist movement: Democratic
  party united with, 47–49, 51,
  52–53; destruction of, xiii, 69;
  elite opposition to, 27, 67, 78;
  Farmers' Alliances and, 43, 46;
  T. Roosevelt and, 58
Post-Conservative America (Phillips),
  212–13
postindustrialism, 252
Powderly, Terence, 50
Powell, G. Bingham, Jr., 5*t*, 15*n*,
  21*n*, 118–19
primary elections, 75–76
Progressive era, 57–60, 72*n*
Project Vote, 187, 192–93
property requirements, 85–86
Prothro, James W., 14*n*
Przeworski, Adam, 9*n*, 254*n*
public agencies, registration in, 209,
  217–22
Public Interest Research Groups
  (PIRGs), 187, 195
Pullman strike, 44
purges of registration rolls, 264–68

Raab, Earl, 183*n*, 184, 252*n*
racism, 82, 250–52. *See also* blacks
radicalism, 61–62
railroads, 41–42, 45, 56*n*
Ranney, Austin, 20*n*, 77*n*
Raskin, A. H., 158*n*
Raskob, John J., 125
Raybeck, Joseph G., 43
"Readjusters," 45–46

Reagan, Ronald, 11–13, 21–22,
    182–83, 185–90, 204, 207
Reagan Administration, agency-
    based registration and, 226, 227,
    231–34
Reconstruction, 79
registration drives: clergy and, 182–
    86, 191; effectiveness of, 200–
    203; nonpartisan efforts in, 192–
    95, 206–7; organizations formed
    for, 186–87, 191, 194; strategies
    of, 189–95; for women, 187,
    203, 207
registration levels, 256–59;
    participation and, 260–63
registration procedures, 17–23; class
    interests and, 106; contemporary
    obstacles in, 178–80; "deadwood"
    registrants and, 264–71;
    deputization in, 193, 197–99,
    229; electoral constriction due to,
    96, 102; federal service programs
    and, 176–77; government
    responsibility in, 17, 242–44;
    increasing restrictions on, 92–94;
    legal challenges to, 241–44, 272–
    90; by mail, 178–79, 196;
    northern disenfranchisement
    efforts and, 88–94; obstructive
    board practices in, 195–200;
    partisan politics and, 19–23,
    104–12; personal appearance
    required for, 89–94; southern
    disenfranchisement and, 81–85;
    urban vs. rural, 104–5
registration reform, agency-based:
    bill drafted for, 245–47; current
    status of, 235–39; by executive
    order, 227–37, 239–41;
    government structure and, 210–
    11; lawsuits and, 241–44; in
    nonprofit sector, 209, 217–18,
    222–27; partisan opposition to,
    212–16; political reprisals risked
    by, 226–27; in public sector,
    209, 217–20; state legislatures
    and, 228–29, 230, 237–39;
    Voting Rights Act vs., 25, 211–
    12, 215–17

religious differences, 53, 124–25
religious revivalism, 32
Reosti, Ron, 280–82
Republican party: black voters and,
    79; business interests and, 11,
    51–54, 62–63, 68, 125;
    campaign tactics of, 51–52, 77;
    Civil War pensions distributed
    by, 37; conservative wing of, 53;
    Democratic-Populist challenge to,
    51–54; domination by, 53–54,
    57; industrial workers and, 34n;
    regional strength of, 65–67, 82;
    registration drive by, 22, 182–
    83, 187–91, 206, 208;
    registration reform and, 212–14;
    southern whites and, 250–52;
    voter registration laws and, 104–
    5; Voting Rights Act of 1957
    backed by, 211–12. *See also*
    parties, political; partisanship;
    party competition
residence, change of, 179–80
residency requirements, 86–88
Reston, James, 187
Reynolds, George M., 38n
rights, political vs. economic, 7
Riker, William H., 86n–87, 114n
Riordan, William L., 38n
Riviles, Steve, 237n
Rockefeller empire, 56n, 59
Rogers, Joel, 10n, 12n, 156n, 158n,
    166n, 168–69, 214
Rogin, Michael Paul, 14n
Rohde, David W., 150t
Roniger, Luis, 36n
Roosevelt, Eleanor, 141
Roosevelt, Franklin D., 126–34,
    137, 139, 165
Roosevelt, Theodore, 57, 58–59
Rosenstone, Steven J., 20n, 45, 47,
    113, 114–15, 161, 262
Ross, Philip, 43
Rusk, Jerrold G., 31n, 40n, 55n,
    73, 74n, 80n, 81, 83t, 87n, 98–
    100, 103, 149, 151, 152n

Salamon, Lester M., 10n
Salmans, Sandra, 190

Salmore, Barbara G., 190*n*
Salmore, Stephen A., 190*n*
Sawyer, Kathy, 184
Sawhill, Isabel V., 10*n*
Schaffer, Stephen D., 113
Schattschneider, E. E., 54, 65–69,
   97, 100–101, 105, 112, 133*n*
Schienbaum, Kim Ezra, 114*n*
Schlesinger, Arthur M., Sr., 114*n*,
   115*n*, 129*n*, 133*n*
Schneider, William, 11–12, 153–
   54
Scott, James C., 38*n*
sectional interests, 33–35, 53
Senate, U.S., 211–12, 233
service sector, 155, 165, 168, 252–
   54
Shame of the Cities, The (Steffens),
   74
Shefter, Martin, 34, 36*n*, 43, 45*n*,
   46, 50, 73*n*, 75*n*, 78, 108*n*,
   131*n*, 154*n*, 166*n*, 170*n*
Shortridge, Ray M., 55*n*
Simon, Dennis M., 113
Simpson, John H., 183*n*
Sitkoff, Harvey, 167*n*
Skowronek, Stephen, 35*n*
Smith, Al, 62, 122, 124–26, 132,
   137
Smith, David Michael, 186*n*, 191*n*
Smith-Connally Act (1943), 166–67
Sobel, Richard, 280–82
Socialist party, 56, 57
Social Security, 7
Social Security Act (1935), 130
social welfare programs: business
   interests and, 156, 159, 166;
   European vs. U.S., 9, 167; for
   inner cities, 174–77
South: black voters in, 144–48,
   172; Christian Right in, 191–92;
   civil rights movement opposed in,
   123, 141–45; Democratic party
   in, 54, 65–69, 123, 141–48;
   disenfranchisement in, 78–85;
   farmers in, 42, 48; labor system
   of, 9, 79; New Deal in, 137–41;
   one-party system fragmented in,
   123, 140, 148; political parties

of, 45–46, 54, 65–69; racism in,
   250–52
South Carolina, disenfranchisement
   efforts in, 81
Southwest Voter Education Project,
   182
Spellman, John, 237*n*
Squire, Peverill, 18*n*, 179*n*, 265, 266
state legislatures, registration reform
   and, 219–20, 237–39
Steffen, Charles, 9*n*
Steffens, Lincoln, 74
Stevenson, Adlai, 143, 172
Stillman, James, 59
Stone, Alan, 10*n*
Strauss, Robert S., 246*n*
strikes, 43–44, 56; government
   action against, 61, 167; New Deal
   politics and, xv
Stucker, John J., 80*n*, 81, 87*n*, 98
students, registration efforts by,
   194, 195, 224, 225
Sunbelt, increased employment in,
   165, 168
Sundquist, James L., 47*n*, 52*n*, 57*n*,
   58, 124, 126*n*, 134*n* and *t*, 135*n*,
   146
Supreme Court, U.S., 42, 59, 272–
   75, 279, 289–90
Sweden: economic policies in, 249–
   50; turnout levels in, 117–18
system of 1896, 54; electoral
   participation constricted in, 122–
   23, 135–37, 167; less party
   competition in, 65, 97; lower
   classes excluded by, 126; parties
   weakened in, 70–78, 95;
   persistence of, 112; procedural
   disenfranchisement of, 78–95;
   Republican-business alliance in,
   53–54, 68, 125; Southern
   Democracy entrenched by, 53–
   54, 68, 137–39

Taft, Philip, 43
Taft, William H., 57, 58, 62*n*
Taft-Hartley (Labor Management
   Relations) Act (1947), 166–67,
   168

Tammany Hall, 76, 86, 108, 109, 132
tariffs, 52, 62, 75
taxes, business-oriented policy for, 158
Tedin, Kent L., 135*n*
Terrance, Lance, 190
Texas, voter registration in, 82–83, 236, 240
third-party movements, 44–47, 56–57, 65, 70*n*
Third World, turnout levels in, 35*n*
Thompson, E. P., 16*n*
Tilden, Samuel J., 86
Tilly, Charles, 32
Tilly, Louise, 32
Tilly, Richard, 32
Tindall, George Brown, 142
Tocqueville, Alexis de, 28, 29*n*, 32, 184*n*
Travis County, Tex., voter registration in, 178–79, 180*n*
tribalism, 31–35, 40–41, 53
Truman, Harry S., 141–42, 167*n*
Tufte, Edward R., 12
turnout levels: behavioral interpretation of, 69; cross-national comparisons of, 35*n*, 117–18; decline in, 54–56, 60, 160–64; education and, 114–15; in election of 1984, 203–6; fraud reforms and, 99–101; in Golden Era, 29–31; Great Depression and, 126–27; New Deal politics and, 133–37; party competition and, 64–69; race vs. class factors in, 161–63; registration procedures and, 94–95; southern disenfranchisement effort and, 83–85. *See also* elections

unions: Congress and, 59; Democratic party and, xiii, 124, 132–33, 164–70; electoral politics and, 7; political party formed by, 44
United Automobile Workers, 168
United Hospital Fund, 225
United Labor party, 46

United Way of America, 226
Urban Coalition, 156
urban renewal, 171–72

Vaughan, Philip H., 141*n*
Verba, Sidney, 13*n*, 113, 114*n*, 115*n*, 116, 118, 150*n*, 151*n*
veterans' pensions, 37
Vietnam War, 11*n*, 157
Viguerie, Richard, 183*n*
Vogel, David, 158*n*
voter turnouts, *see* turnout levels
Voting Rights Act (1965): agency registration vs., 25, 211–12, 215–17; amendments to, 87*n*, 277, 288; litigation based on, 193, 276–79, 288; Republican support for, 211–12; southern black vote and, 144–46

Wagner Act (1935), 166
Wallace, George, 151
Wallace, Henry, 141*n*
Walsh, J. Raymond, 44
Washington, Harold, 239
Wattenberg, Martin P., 11*n*
Weaver, Edward, 228*n*
Weaver, James B., 45, 47
Weibe, Robert H., 72*n*
Weimar Republic, 14
Weinstein, James, 57*n*, 60*n*, 72*n*
Weisskopf, Thomas E., 156*n*
Wellstone, Paul, 238*n*
Weyrich, Paul, 183*n*
White, Claude R., 129
White, Mark, Jr., 227, 231, 232–33
White, Mary K., 129
Wilentz, Sean, 9*n*, 16*n*, 33
Will, George F., 13*n*, 14
Williams, Cynthia A., 272–90
Williamson, Chilton, 29*n*
Wilson, Harold, 12*n*
Wilson, James Q., 38*n*, 73–74
Wilson, Woodrow, 57, 58, 59*n*
Wolfe, Alan, 156*n*
Wolfinger, Raymond E., 18*n*, 20*n*, 113, 114–15, 179*n*, 161, 262, 265

women: agency registration and, 218–19, 225; registration drives for, 187, 203, 207; suffrage granted to, 55, 58; in work force, 124, 148, 155, 165–66, 252–53
Woodward, C. Vann, 47n, 48, 79n
Woolsey, Theodore Dwight, 91
working class, 122–24, 127–28, 135; Democratic economic policies and, 156–59; demographics of, 24, 124, 148, 165–66, 168; disenfranchisement of, 8–9, 70–71, 77; economic programs and, 52–53; in Europe, 8, 169n, 248–49; immigrant voters of, 39; machine politics and, 35–36, 108; partisanship weakened in, 148–60; party system severed from, 109–12; radicalism of, 61–62; registration procedures and, 18; Republican party and, 34n; in service sector, 252–54

World War I, radicalism repressed in, 61

World War II, unionism and, 166–67

Wright, Gavin, 140n

Yarnell, Ellen, 141n, 167n

Zingale, Nancy, 29n
Zinn, Howard, 56n, 59n, 61n, 62

About the Authors

Frances Fox Piven and Richard A. Cloward are co-authors
of *Regulating the Poor, The Politics of Turmoil, Poor
People's Movements, The New Class War*, and, with Fred
Block and Barbara Ehrenreich, *The Mean Season*. Piven
is Distinguished Professor of Political Science at the Graduate School and University Center of the City University
of New York. Cloward is a professor of social work at
Columbia University.